T0397805

The Ripple Effect

Advance Praise for *The Ripple Effect*

"Social scientists have grappled with the idea of influence for a long time. Enze Han continues this saga in this volume, seeking to capture China's rich historical relations with the countries in Southeast Asia and its complex contemporary interactions with these countries that appear to defy facile generalizations."
—Steve Chan, College Professor of Distinction,
University of Colorado, Boulder

"In this insightful book, Enze Han effectively rejects the notion that China's influence in Southeast Asia is simply directed by a monolithic state. Han masterfully reveals the 'complexity' of China's presence in the region, where unintended consequences and non-state actors are as much a part of the story as the intentions of Chinese leaders."
—Bruce Dickson, Professor of Political Science and
International Affairs, George Washington University

"Based on extensive fieldwork, Enze Han offers a major contribution to our understanding of Chinese influence in Southeast Asia by bringing into the picture quasi-official, unofficial, and even illicit Chinese actors, examining indirect and unintended consequences, and shedding light on local interactions and resistances. The result is a complex, nuanced account that is a must-read for anyone seeking to understand China's engagement with the region."
—Todd H. Hall, Professor of International Relations,
University of Oxford

"Enze Han's *The Ripple Effect* is an important contribution to our understanding of China as a great power and the nature of its influence in Southeast Asia. Elegantly written, Han reveals the complex nature of China's influence across a set of issues, both traditional and non-traditional. Social scientists and international relations specialists will find Han's spotlight on the role of Chinese non-state actors in spreading Chinese influence and his use of the notion of unintended consequences to assess China's 'policies' invaluable."
—Yuen Foong Khong, Li Ka Shing Professor of Political Science,
National University of Singapore

"Thematically imaginative and empirically illuminating, *The Ripple Effect* unpacks the complex nuances behind China's ubiquitous but ambivalent presence in Southeast Asia. Enze Han masterfully reminds us that while size does matter and historical memories are always complicated among neighbors, the effects of asymmetry and proximity are rarely straightforward, but ambiguous, multifaceted, and uncertain. Intended or not, China's action and interactions with smaller neighbors at state, sub-national, or societal levels are bound to affect their present and future ties. This book is a must-read for those interested in understanding China-Southeast Asia relations and the paradoxes of influence in international politics."
—Cheng-Chwee Kuik, Professor of International Relations and
Head of Asian Studies, Institute of Malaysian and
International Studies, National University of Malaysia

"In *The Ripple Effect*, Enze Han argues against the state-centric approach and focuses on the complexity of state-society relations to understand the increasingly globalized China and its influence on Southeast Asia. This book is a must-read for scholars and students of China and Southeast Asian studies."

—Yos Santasombat, Professor Emeritus,
Faculty of Social Sciences, Chiang Mai University

"Enze Han has written an outstanding book on the unintended consequences of actions by the Chinese state and non-state actors in Southeast Asia. An important contribution to a growing demand for assessments that center local actors and agency in shaping China's external footprint."

—Jessica Chen Weiss, Michael J. Zak Professor for China and
Asia-Pacific Studies, Cornell University

The Ripple Effect

China's Complex Presence in Southeast Asia

ENZE HAN

OXFORD
UNIVERSITY PRESS

OXFORD
UNIVERSITY PRESS

Oxford University Press is a department of the University of Oxford. It furthers
the University's objective of excellence in research, scholarship, and education
by publishing worldwide. Oxford is a registered trade mark of Oxford University
Press in the UK and certain other countries.

Published in the United States of America by Oxford University Press
198 Madison Avenue, New York, NY 10016, United States of America.

© Oxford University Press 2024

CIP data is on file at the Library of Congress

ISBN 978–0–19–769659–0 (pbk.)
ISBN 978–0–19–769658–3 (hbk.)

DOI: 10.1093/oso/9780197696583.001.0001

Contents

Acknowledgments

The writing of the book occurred during some of the most trying times in recent history, with the COVID-19 pandemic putting a halt to what is normal, including international travel. As the world grappled with the devastating effects of the virus, many countries imposed stringent measures to contain its spread, such as mandatory hotel quarantines for incoming travelers and periodic lockdowns. In my personal experience, I underwent a cumulative total of seven weeks of quarantines across three major cities—Singapore, Hong Kong, and Shanghai—in 2021 and 2022, where government measures to control the spread of the virus had been overly stringent.

I was fortunate enough to receive a Lee Kong Chian Fellowship on Contemporary Southeast Asia in 2020; however, the pandemic's onset forced me to postpone the fellowship for a year. In March 2021, I finally embarked on my journey from Hong Kong to Singapore, but I had to complete a two-week quarantine before beginning my visiting fellowship at the National University of Singapore. At that time, Singapore had effectively contained the virus due to stringent quarantine measures, and the government was actively promoting vaccinations among its citizens. Fortunately, I was able to spend three uninterrupted months in the city, working on this book. During my three-month stay at NUS, I would like to express my gratitude to Elaine Ho Lynn-Ee for facilitating my visit and Andrew Chang for making arrangements for my stay at Kent Vale and use of the office at the Faculty of Arts and Sciences. I would also like to thank Yang Yang and Shaun Lin for showing me around Singapore, and Yuen Foong Khong for welcoming me into his home.

At Kent Vale, I valued the consistent hospitality provided by my old friends Sayaka Chatani and Colm Fox, as well as the company of their two lovely children. Furthermore, I appreciated the insightful discussions with Andrew Ong about the political situation in Myanmar, often accompanied by pints of beer. I would also like to thank Alfred Wu for introducing me to a couple of Myanmar students at NUS, as our conversations greatly enhanced my understanding of the political situation in Myanmar following the February 2021 coup. Xiaojun Li also happened to be in Singapore at the time, and I enjoyed dining out together with him and Adam Liu. However, towards the end of my fellowship, a major wave of infections hit the city, resulting in a temporary lockdown of many establishments, including the university. As a consequence, I had to return to Hong Kong and undergo another two weeks of quarantine.

In November 2021, my father unexpectedly passed away. Unfortunately, traveling home presented a significant challenge due to the restrictions imposed by the Chinese government at that time. To be with my family in Hangzhou, I had to first endure a mandatory two-week quarantine in Shanghai, which delayed my arrival and prevented me from attending my father's funeral and cremation ceremony. This period of isolation proved to be particularly challenging, as I grappled with the reality of my loss and yearned to be with my loved ones during such a difficult time. Beyond the emotional struggle, I also found myself reflecting on the impact of these stringent government measures on individuals and families. The sense of powerlessness brought about by these restrictions took on a deeply personal significance.

In spring 2022, I had the opportunity to spend three months at Stanford as the other half of the Lee Kong Chian fellowship. I am deeply grateful for the hospitality of Don Emmerson, with whom I engaged in insightful conversations regarding China's relations with Southeast Asia. It was he who suggested the current book title, for which I am very grateful. Additionally, I would like to express my appreciation to the staff at the Shorenstein Asia-Pacific Research Center for their assistance in acclimating to both the office environment and life in Palo Alto. Furthermore, I am also indebted to Seinenu Thein Lemelson and Robert Lemelson for letting me stay at their apartment in San Francisco for two weeks, and for welcoming me to their home in Los Angeles.

At the University of Hong Kong, I am grateful to my outstanding colleagues who have offered invaluable emotional support to one another over the past few years. I would especially like to acknowledge John Burns, Haohan Chen, Wilfred Chow, Courtney Fung, Ian Holliday, Hui Li, Zhengyan Li, Daniel Marwecki, Kai Quek, Austin Strange, Xiaojun Yan, and Jiangnan Zhu. Trevor Won's exceptional research assistance greatly facilitated the writing of this book. Sirada Khemanitthathai has also always been there whenever I have questions about Thailand. I would also like to extend my appreciation to all the students who have participated in the POLI4092 capstone projects with me in recent years. Their research contributions have been integral to the foundation of this book. My two PhD students at HKU, Ric Neo and Siyang Liu, have been quite remarkable. Lastly, my heartfelt thanks go to Bruce Dickson, Rhacel Parreñas, and Cameron Thies, who have been there for me whenever I needed career guidance or recommendation letters.

Angela Chnapko at Oxford University Press has been an exceptional editor, providing me with steadfast support over the years when it comes to publication ideas. Portions of this book were presented at City University of Hong Kong, Oxford University, National University of Singapore, and Stanford University. Additionally, the book was inspired by a workshop I organized alongside my colleagues Courtney Fung, Kai Quek, and Austin Strange at the University of Hong Kong, which focused on diverse conceptualizations of China's global influence. I am truly grateful for all the comments and feedback I have received throughout this journey.

Over the years, I have been fortunate to have the companionship of many friends. I would like to express my gratitude to Jean Hong, Xiaojun Li, Joseph O'Mahoney, and Christopher Paik for our engaging conversations about life, despite the vast distances that separate us. Additionally, I am thankful for the numerous friends in Hong Kong who have offered their company during the most challenging times of COVID restrictions. Without their support, I might have struggled to maintain my sanity. It is through these friendships that I have been able to focus on my writing.

In the midst of writing this book, my son was born. Embracing parenthood has brought both a whirlwind of activity and a profound sense of purpose and responsibility to my life. Remarkably, even with the chaos of childcare, I managed to complete this book. My mother, sister, brother-in-law, niece, and nephew have consistently been there for me. I dedicate this book to my son, Yihao Han, and to my late father, Denghan Tang, who, sadly, did not have the opportunity to meet his grandson. I have no doubt that he would have been filled with delight and pride with this little bundle of joy.

Abbreviations

ASE	AN Association of Southeast Asian Nations
BGF	Border Guard Force
BRI	Belt and Road Initiative
CCP	Chinese Communist Party
CI	Confucius Institute
CNRP	Cambodia National Rescue Party
CNTA	China National Tourism Administration
CPP	Cambodian People's Party
CPV	Communist Party of Vietnam
CRPH	Committee Representing Pyidaungsu Hluttaw
DPP	Democratic Progressive Party
EAG	ethnic armed group
EEC	Eastern Economic Corridor
EU	European Union
EV	electric vehicle
FPC	Five Point Consensus
FUNCINPEC	National United Front for an Independent, Neutral, Peaceful and Cooperative Cambodia
HSR	high-speed rail
KMT	Chinese Nationalist Party (Kuomintang)
LPRP	Lao People's Revolutionary Party
NCPO	National Council for Peace and Order
NLD	National League for Democracy
NUG	National Unity Government
OCAO	Overseas Chinese Affairs Office
ODA	Official Development Assistance
OTM	online tourism market
PAGCOR	Philippine Amusement and Gaming Corporation
PDF	People's Defense Forces
PLA	People's Liberation Army
POGO	Philippine Offshore Gambling Operations
PRC	People's Republic of China
RCEP	Regional Comprehensive Economic Partnership
RIP	Rayong Industrial Park
ROC	Republic of China

SAC	State Administration Council
SEZ	special economic zone
SLORC	State Law and Order Restoration Council
SOE	state-owned enterprise
SPDC	State Peace and Development Council
SSEZ	Sihanoukville Special Economic Zone
UFWD	United Front Work Department
UN	United Nations
UNSC	United Nations Security Council

1

China's Complex Presence

Introduction

The COVID-19 pandemic, first identified in China, has ravaged the world since the beginning of 2020. The politicization of the virus as the "China Virus" has not only intensified divisions within Western societies along racial lines, but also fueled widespread blame games, impacting China's foreign relations with the United States and other countries globally. It is evident that the heightened tension between the United States and China has persisted during President Biden's administration. For instance, in his first speech to Congress on April 28, 2021, President Biden asserted that the United States is "now in competition with China and other countries to win the 21st century."[1] During President Biden's administration, the overall hawkish approach towards China continues, similar to that taken by the Trump administration, which keeps the competitive atmosphere between the two countries alive.

Even before the COVID-19 pandemic, the divide between China and the United States had been expanding. Geostrategic confrontations, such as President Trump's trade war with China, heightened tensions across the Taiwan Strait, and territorial disputes in the South China Sea involving China and other Southeast Asian countries set the stage for a potential showdown. Indeed, U.S. concern over China's growing global influence has become increasingly evident. Particularly in Southeast Asia—a region at the forefront of U.S.-China strategic competition—there has been significant speculation about the extent of Beijing's influence. As Southeast Asia, situated at the doorstep of the continental giant, China, finds itself either living in the "dragon's shadow" or "where great powers meet," the area has attracted renewed interest.[2]

At least rhetorically, a consensus is emerging within Western media, academic scholarship, and policy circles that Chinese influence in the region has become predominant, suggesting that the United States has some catching

The Ripple Effect. Enze Han, Oxford University Press. © Oxford University Press 2024.
DOI: 10.1093/oso/9780197696583.003.0001

up to do. For instance, in a study analyzing China's influence in Southeast Asia conducted by the Center for Strategic and International Studies, a prominent think tank in Washington D.C., the researchers note that "China is seen as holding slightly more political power and influence than the United States in Southeast Asia today, and considerably more power relative to the United States in 10 years . . . In terms of economic power and influence, the region views China as much more influential than the United States today, and this gap is expected to grow in the next 10 years."[3] However, the same report also highlights the complexities of opinions in the region regarding China, stating that "there is no consensus on whether China's role is beneficial or detrimental to the region."[4]

This lack of consensus reflects in some ways the considerable uncertainty in Southeast Asia regarding China. Over the past four decades, the once impoverished communist country has emerged as the world's second-largest economy, transforming the image of Chinese people from famine-stricken to major consumers and investors. Due to the immense size of the Chinese economy, its vast population, and its enigmatic authoritarian government, China's intentions towards the region remain a significant question mark looming in the north for these Southeast Asian countries. Many people in the region are uncertain about the Chinese state and society's intentions, as well as the potential outcomes that might stem from this massive neighbor.

Debates abound within Southeast Asia regarding the implications of this "re-emergence" of a historical hegemon for the region, primarily due to the deep, historical interconnectedness between China and Southeast Asia, established through tribute, trade, and migration. In one way or another, such uncertainty stems from a lack of consensus on the nature of the great power China represents and may become. Is China the celestial kingdom of the past, seeking to reassert its former tributary relations with Southeast Asia? Will China resemble the colonial powers of the imperial West, which seized control of the region, plundered resources, and enslaved people? Will the Chinese government and its Communist Party repeat its revolutionary past by exporting communist ideologies and an authoritarian system to impose on the region? Alternatively, is Beijing primarily interested in economic development and fostering further regional economic interdependence? Will contemporary China embody something entirely different? How should Southeast Asia as a region address the challenges posed by a neighbor that is both enormous and complex?

This book is an attempt to explain the complexities of China as a great power and the inherent difficulties in understanding the murky nature of its influence in Southeast Asia. This situation arose for two prominent sets of reasons. First, the contemporary People's Republic of China is a complex great power in the sense that despite its overall colossal economic and military power, the country is populous, diverse, still in the developing stage, and full of contradictions. Additionally, China has complex historical relations with Southeast Asia through centuries of economic and political interactions, with a long history of Chinese migration to the region. Thus, reception towards China's presence has varied in the region, conditioned by historical relations as well as countries' contemporary encounters with a variety of actors from China. Second, we have to differentiate between the intended versus unintended consequences of China's presence in Southeast Asia, particularly when we want to understand what kind of "influence" China wields in the region. The Chinese state intends for some of its policies or actions to cause deep repercussions in Southeast Asia. But we must also consider the unintended consequences of a variety of Chinese actors to fully comprehend the nature of interactions between China and Southeast Asia.

This introductory chapter outlines the two main ideas that the book will explore. Moving away from conventional international relations approaches that predominantly focus on the influence exerted by the Chinese state or state-related actors, this book not only examines the Chinese state and its policies but also delves into the substantial impact of Chinese non-state actors on state-society relations in Southeast Asia, which in turn, affects state-to-state relations. This focus on non-state actors complements the extensive body of literature that has already studied China-Southeast Asia relations from a state perspective,[5] while importantly shifting gears to investigate the complex nature of diverse non-state actors from China, which hold significant implications for Southeast Asia.[6] Furthermore, the book closely engages with sociological theories of "unintended consequences of purposive social action,"[7] demonstrating how intentionality, or the absence thereof, is crucial to understanding the intricate nature of China's presence in the region. Consequently, this work conceptually differentiates between what conventional studies assume as the Chinese state's intended goal of influence and those instances where such intentionality is difficult to establish. Following this, the chapter outlines the structure of the book.

Varieties of Actors and Complexity of China's Presence in Southeast Asia

There is considerable complexity and debate within the political science and international relations literature regarding the nature of China as a great power. The PRC, after four decades of rapid and consistent economic growth, has emerged as the world's second-largest economy and is increasingly striving to reassert its historically dominant position in regional affairs, particularly in East and Southeast Asia.[8] Nonetheless, doubts regarding the extent to which China is a great power and debates about the nature of its great power status have never subsided. For instance, Susan Shirk once described China as a "fragile superpower" and warned that the West should not be concerned with China's economic or military strength, but rather concentrate on its internal fragility.[9] According to Shirk, even though China is economically stronger and enjoys greater international security today, its domestic politics are fraught with insecurity and a variety of looming crises.[10] Similarly, Yukon Huang recently dubbed China an "abnormal" great power, in the sense that "it is the first great power that is a developing rather than a developed country, the first to get old before it gets rich. China's weak institutions and historical legacies mean that it has more insecurity than would otherwise be expected of a great power."[11] Indeed, for Huang, China is too populous, too large, and too regionally diverse to draw accurate conclusions about the country's overall economy and the implications of China as a great power for international relations.

However, few scholars in international relations have taken seriously the complex nature of China as a great power. The literature on the rise of China and its challenges to the existing U.S.-led international order tends to present China as a monolithic authoritarian state with enormous military and economic power at its disposal.[12] Many realist scholars, for example, have primarily looked at China's growing power, measured by its exponential growth in economic and military capabilities, and pondered the implications for the stability of the international order.[13] Many others are concerned about the nature of China's political regime and question what the rise of an authoritarian state under the leadership of a communist party will mean for the existing international order of free trade, human rights, democracy, and the institutions that promote these liberal values.[14] Meanwhile, some scholars pay special attention to the historical and cultural context of China's rise in the East and Southeast Asian region.[15] Some, like Kang, discuss the legacies of the tributary system and the historical legacies of the Chinese empire for a contemporary meaning of the rise of China for the rest of East Asia;[16] they contemplate how much political authority China can wield in the region because the United States established an institutionalized alliance structure in place since the end of World War II.[17] Indeed, how China will establish its legitimacy in international leadership or exert authority over other regional states becomes an open question. Relatedly, scholars have also discussed China's lack of cultural appeal or soft power to grant it the same kind of international leadership that the United States has enjoyed.[18]

Similar narratives reveal China's relations with Southeast Asia. Many assume that China is a monolith that enjoys an asymmetrical power balance towards its southern neighbors.[19] A considerable amount of the research tends to focus on the security dimension,[20] with much of it concentrating on China's bullying behavior in the South China Sea.[21] With respect to foreign policy, many scholars are concerned about interstate diplomacy, especially in terms of alliance choices between the United States and China.[22]

Yet most accounts of China as a great power remain at the abstract level. As Hameiri and Jones point out, the literature on China as a great power often ignores the situation of the contemporary Chinese state as fragmented, decentralized, and internationalized. China today, despite its overall economic growth, has deep intra-regional disparities between its coastal and inland provinces, as well as between cosmopolitan urban centers and left-behind rural areas.[23] Such domestic inequality also means a variety of actors with different institutional capacity and monetary means are seeking international presence for either profit or prestige. Therefore, globalized China in this context means that we face the reality in which "disaggregated state apparatuses and quasi-independent, market-facing actors are increasingly acting overseas in ways not effectively coordinated in Beijing."[24]

For example, much of China's financing and investment in developing countries is not uniformly coordinated from a central authority, but rather driven and implemented by regional and local interests, such as state-owned, private and hybrid companies linked predominantly to subnational governments that seek business opportunities by lobbying the Chinese state in pursuit of their interests.[25] Such diverse actors possess distinct interests that are not always in alignment. Ching Kwan Lee demonstrates this using Chinese investment in Zambia, where Chinese state-owned enterprises

(SOEs) operate differently from global private capital in their approach to capital accumulation.[26] As Lee points out, "Global China is taking myriad forms, ranging from foreign direct investment, labor export, and multilateral financial institutions for building cross-regional infrastructure to the globalization of Chinese civil society organizations, creation of global media networks, and global joint ventures in higher education, to name just a few examples."[27] Thus, for the purpose of understanding China's influence, we should analyze the objectives and actions of, at least, SOEs,[28] large and small private businesses,[29] and even ordinary Chinese citizens who seek opportunities abroad.[30] These actors have their own agency and interests that may not closely align nor be in direct response to the Chinese state; as such, their actions can create influence externalities. It is crucial to understand the presence and impact of these diverse actors within host societies, which may vary according to their size, the sectors they are in, as well as the interactive dynamics they have with local population. Therefore, we need conceptual flexibility to understand an increasingly globalized China and its variegated local impact—as well as how the behavior of different intermediaries results in different implications for China's overall influence.[31]

Again, an illustrative example from the domain of foreign economy policy demonstrates the value of differentiating between intermediaries. Chinese SOEs have been some of the most high-profile overseas actors since the onset of China's "Going Out" strategy. They can serve as the "right arm" to the Chinese government, implementing resource deals or infrastructure construction projects as contractors that support China's political objectives. However, despite the fact that they are state-backed, SOEs are by no means state-dictated, and there is often a principle-agent problem in coordination between firms and the state.[32] In particular, large SOEs often have considerable autonomy from other ministerial interests, such as the Ministry of Foreign Affairs.[33] In many cases, the Chinese state's strategic interests do not necessarily align with the SOEs' commercial interests,[34] leading to SOEs behaving in ways that contradict the Chinese government's foreign policy interests. In addition, SOEs themselves are complex and operate under fragmented and competing domestic bureaucratic politics.[35] There is often intense competition among different SOEs in securing domestic and international contracts from the central or provincial governments. Finally, SOEs operating in different sectors abroad, such as resource extraction and construction, typically have distinct economic, labor, social, and environmental impacts on local communities. Thus, the "fragmented authoritarianism" framework as applied to the Chinese state can illuminate the complexities of Chinese SOEs and their global presence and impacts.[36]

In addition to SOEs, Chinese private capital has also gone global. Driven mostly by "market opportunities, competition within China and the presence of a strong entrepreneurial spirit,"[37] these companies tend to have their own modus operandi distinct from the state's foreign policy goals. Of course, outgoing Chinese private capital also varies significantly in terms of scale and sectoral focus, from multinational corporations to petty businesses that sell made-in-China products at the local markets in developing countries. As Lee's research demonstrates, their intense focus on profit makes private Chinese construction companies in Zambia operate differently from Chinese SOEs in the same country, such as their approaches towards labor management.[38] In Southeast Asia, many private Chinese investments have entered agricultural planation sectors, such as rubber, banana, and sugar cane. Because of their relatively short investment and profit horizon, their modes of intensive plantations often lead to negative consequences for the local environment.[39] Moreover, some of these private business operations may engage in illicit activities, such as illegal mining, logging, trafficking of goods, and gambling. As a result, dealing with Chinese private capital can pose even more complex challenges for host societies.[40]

Finally, we also need to take into consideration China's influence through the actions of ordinary Chinese individuals living or migrating abroad. Domestically, Chinese society has transformed itself from the image of a "global sweatshop," with workers at the bottom of global capitalist value chain to now consumers with growing purchasing power. Yet even amid improved domestic economic conditions, a combination of demographic pressure, a competitive market environment, and China's evolving political situation have prompted many people to emigrate. This fits within a broad pattern of the "new wave" of Chinese migration (*xin yimin*) to many parts of the world.[41] More and more Chinese moving abroad for study, travel, and work have created an unprecedented level of encounters between these individuals and local host societies.[42]

Some statistics of such encounters between Chinese migrants and Southeast Asia are warranted. One prominent area is tourism. For example, in 2019, 11 million tourists from China visited Thailand, accounting for 28 percent of all Thailand's total foreign tourists. For Vietnam, the total number of Chinese tourists visiting the country in 2019 was 5.8 million, or 32 percent of all Vietnam's foreign tourists. For Cambodia, the numbers were

Table 1.1 Mainland Chinese tourism to Southeast Asia in 2019

Country	Total Tourist Visits	Share of Total Tourist Visits
Thailand	11 million	28%
Vietnam	5.8 million	32%
Singapore	3.4 million	19%
Malaysia	2.9 million	12%
Cambodia	2.4 million	36%
Indonesia	2.1 million	14%
Philippines	1.3 million	18%
Laos	0.8 million	19%
Myanmar	0.7 million	17%

Note: *Economist Intelligence*, February 10, 2020, accessible at http://country.eiu. com/article.aspx?articleid=1429060926&Country=China&topic=Economy_1#.

2.4 million and 36 percent. As we can see from Table 1.1, Chinese tourism comprises a substantial share of tourism to all of Southeast Asian countries, and such a magnitude indicates the intensity of such encounters.

These interactions can play into larger processes of influence. For example, studies of Chinese tourism abroad illustrate how the arrivals of millions of Chinese tourists have led to heightened prejudice against them despite their economic contribution to local societies.[43] This prejudice, in addition to worsening negative popular opinion towards China, mixes with geopolitical fears of China's efforts at territorialization, particularly in the East and Southeast Asian regions.[44] Similarly, problems of racial discrimination that Chinese people abroad experience interact with perceived threats of Chinese migration and the Chinese state's "influence operations" in host societies.[45]

This re/encountering with the Chinese is particularly relevant for Southeast Asia due to the long history of Chinese migration to the region because of China's internal turmoil and poverty in the past. Centuries of tributary and trading relations between China and Southeast Asia brought large numbers of Chinese migrants to the region. Traders as well as refugees from the Chinese coastal provinces of Fujian and Guangdong traveled to Southeast Asia and settled there. As a result, the overseas Chinese population accounts for a sizable percentage in several Southeast Asian nations.[46] Yet their reception in host countries in Southeast Asia varies,[47] which has led to different modes of institutionalized ethnic boundary making and the subsequent politicization of, or its lack of, the ethnic Chinese identity.[48] This historical legacy of Chinese migration to the region needs to be taken seriously in our understanding of contemporary encounters between China and Southeast Asia.

This book thus takes the initiative and presents China as a complex great power, examining the variety of influences in its neighboring states in Southeast Asia. Characterizing China in this way concurs with Yukon Huang's analysis: although overall China enjoys asymmetrical power over the smaller states to its south, China's influence is far more complex because of the presence of numerous state and non-state actors in Southeast Asia.

Of course, some scholars have emphasized the difference between China and other leading great powers, suggesting that China is not truly a global power but only a partial one, meaning that China has no genuine interest in becoming a global power in the image of the United States.[49] Yet, intentions aside, the country's complex nature as populous, diverse, and still in the developing stage, plus its complex historical relations, mean that its influence in Southeast Asia will differ from the United States of the present or a European power of the past. Finally, the intensive encounters between Chinese state and non-state actors and their Southeast Asian counterparts are also due to geographical reasons. Geography is certainly a crucial factor since mainland Southeast Asia is within easy reach of China, facilitated by the relatively easy visa regimes and frequent and convenient travel modes, at least before COVID-19 temporarily shut down national borders. These encounters are happening on an everyday basis and on a large scale.

Intended Versus Unintended Influences

To study the varieties of China's influence in Southeast Asia, this book builds on the conceptual definition of "influence" from Evelyn Goh's work to differentiate power from influence.[50] Goh makes a distinction between the two concepts, arguing that the former should be understood as encompassing resources and latent capability, while the latter constitutes the actual effective exercise of power. Specifically, she defines influence as "the act of modifying or otherwise having an impact upon another actor's preferences or behavior in favor of one's own aims."[51] Thus, her theoretical framework examines how China coerces, induces, and persuades others to behave in a particular way. Yet Goh strongly emphasizes the intentionality of China's influence, which somehow limits the scope of her study. Such an emphasis would lead researchers to look at China's influence only at the state level and ignore the diverse actors coming out of China and their intended and unintended influence on the global stage.

In addition to the variety of actors, the issue of intentionaltiy in China's influences abroad must be taken seriously. As we discussed earlier, there is a tendency to focus on the intention of the Chinese state to foment changes in target countries. Thus, to understand China's influence in Southeast Asia, Goh discusses how to "find evidence of China converting its power resources into influence over these neighbors' strategic decisions to bring about outcomes favorable to China."[52] Yet this issue of intentionality on the part of the Chinese state is sometimes difficult to prove. Indeed, many transformations in Southeast Asia that are often associated with China's influence are not even closely related to the design and intention of the Chinese state.

Here I borrow the concept of "unintended consequences of purposive social action" that has a long history in behavioral sociology. American sociologist Robert Merton, who coined the term in his 1936 article, argues that "with the complex interaction which constitutes society, action ramifies, its consequences are not restricted to the specific area in which they were initially intended to center, they occur in interrelated fields explicitly ignored at the time of action. Yet it is because these fields are in fact interrelated that the further consequences in adjacent areas tend to react."[53] That means, there are many such unexplored reactions that constitute an important part of social actions, from daily activities to government policies. Today, a dictionary definition suggests that "unintended consequences" includes outcomes that are unintended and unanticipated, in the sense that these consequences result from behaviors initiated for other purposes. Although the literature also further differentiates outcomes that can be anticipated yet still undesirable in policymaking, in this book the focus is specifically on unforeseen consequences that were not outcomes by design.[54]

In the disciplines of political science and international relations, often the purpose of research inquirey is to figure out a linear and rational causalities. However, the social reality is messy and we can cast doubt on the linear relationship in causal political/social actions in different ways. For example, Portes provides five categories of possibile incongruence between intended goal and outcomes: "(1) The announced goal is not what it seems—that is, it is not what the actor or those in authority in a collectivity actually intend;

(2) the announced goal is intended by the actors, but their actions have other significant consequences of which they are unaware; (3) the goal is what it seems—but the intervention of outside forces transforms it mid-course into a qualitatively different one; (4) the goal is what it seems—but the intervention of outside forces produces unexpected consequnces different and sometimes contrary to those intended; (5) the goal is what it seems—but its achievements depends on fortuitous events, foreign to the original plans."[55]

Following Portes' intervention, we can see different implications to understanding the relationship between intention and outcome. First, in many situations, inferring an actor's real goal is impossible. In international relations, discerning the true intention of a state's foreign policymaking is extremely difficult.[56] Thus, we should no more infer intention from action than we should take at face value what statesmen say to the public.[57] Therefore, when we talk about influences in international relations, we have to be careful about the differences beween the state's professed goal and its true intention. Indeed, a state's foreign policy often involves hidden agendas that few people from the outside would know ex ante. We need to note that in many such situations, a state has the desire to conceal its real intention in dealing with other countries.[58]

Still, in the other four categories Portes discussed, the incongruence between intended goal and outcomes occurs, albeit for different reasons. Sometimes actions lead to byproduct outcomes not previously envisioned. Sometimes, through the force of outside intervention, the achieved outcome is either different or the total opposite of what was originally intended. And finally, situations also arise when outcomes are achieved simply by natural coincidence and not through one's own action. Therefore, to summarize Portes' descriptions of these five categories, different end-states from those assumed by a purposive logic will result: "(1) the real goal is not the apparent one; (2) the real goal is not what the actors actually achieve; (3) the real goal emerges from the situation itself; (4) the original goal is real, but the end-state is contrary to its intent; (5) the original goal is real, but it is achieved by an unexpected combination of events."[59]

Thus, since this book is about how to understand Chinese influence and unintended consequences in Southeast Asia, the first category—whether the real goal is the apparent one—is the most difficult to empirically demonstrate because of the difficulty in knowing precisely the real intention of the Chinese state, or any state for that matter. Thus, in reality we often look at the statements and policy guidelines coming out from China at face value. Although we do need to be aware of this discrepancy between true intention and stated goals, this category of investigation is not the goal here. Instead, this book is primarily interesed in situations when actions taken by the Chinese state as well as non-state actors have led to political and socio-economic changes in Southeast Asia, but were unintended originally, or occurred through interventions by outside forces or even fortuitous events. The empirical chapters on unintended consequences all fall into these cateogries of events where it is difficult to draw a direct link between the stated goals of the Chinese state and non-state actors and the outcomes in host societies in Southeast Asia.

Agencies of Local Actors in Southeast Asia

An additional critique of the conventional literature on China's influence abroad is the unidirectional treatment of such relations, where China is presented as the only meaningful actor, whether "state' or "non-state," in creating such influences. However, there is a lack of focus on the "agency" of actors in Southeast Asia, state or otherwise, in engaging, manipulating, acting in consonance with, or acting against, the Chinese actors. Thus, to explain infrastructure cooperation for example, Cheng-Chwee Kuik focused on the "capacity of a sovereign actor hosting a foreign-backed venture in making its own decisions, shaping the circumstances, and pursuing its desired outcomes during the micro-processes, despite power asymmetry, rivalry, and uncertainty."[60] Thus, there is a spectrum of such state agency we have to take into consideration that is specific to the domestic political contexts in individual Southeast Asian states.[61] Even though China's relations with the smaller Southeast Asian states have often been portrayed as asymetrical,[62] China's influences often depend upon these states' own movivations and calculations because "weaker actors may conform to the will of the strong not only because the latter wield greater incentives, sanctions, or legitimacy but also to further the former's political or strategic agendas."[63] Therefore, we have to take into account the agencies of actors located in Southeast Asia in terms of how their own intentions and actions can affect the China's influence outcomes on the ground. In fact, many of the empirical cases presented in the book on these unintended consequences of China's influence involve such dialogic and mutually shaping processes between local and Chinese actors.

Methodology

This book is the culmination of my extensive fieldwork conducted in several Southeast Asian countries, including Cambodia, Laos, Myanmar, Singapore, and Thailand, prior to the COVID-19 pandemic. These countries were selected as my research sites because of Southeast Asia's geographical proximity to China, placing it at the forefront of outbound Chinese investment and migration. Consequently, the region has gained significant attention within the Chinese government's Belt and Road Initiative (BRI). Additionally, Southeast Asia has emerged as the focal point of great power competition between the United States and China. The United States' policy of "rebalancing" towards Asia has brought renewed focus on the ways in which China's "influence" is shaping the region. As a result, Southeast Asia offers a valuable lens through which to examine China's multi-layered influence, supported by rich, empirical data.

Over the years, I have conducted hundreds of interviews exploring various aspects of Chinese influence in these countries, speaking with policymakers, scholars, Chinese businesspeople, tourists, restaurant owners, and numerous other individuals. Many of these were informal, loosely structured conversations, typically lasting around thirty minutes and conducted in English, Thai, Burmese, and Mandarin Chinese. Local research assistants occasionally provided translation assistance when needed. Additionally, I collected newspaper articles from both international and local sources and reviewed writings by various scholars. All of these materials have been integrated into a narrative that encompasses numerous daily encounters, making the text engaging, relatable, and accessible to a wide audience.

Outline of Chapters

After the present introduction, the next three chapters are dedicated to explaining how the Chinese state has been more explicitly involved in trying to influence Southeast Asia, with a specific focus on authoritarian regime durability in the region, economic relations between the two, and China's promotion of the Chinese langauge and culture. Here, the focus is on the Chinese state, but I still pay attention to the differences between the intended versus unintended consequences of the Chinese state's actions. Then, the next three chapters look at how non-state actors from China impact Southeast Asia;

namely, how Chinese consumption demand has generated an agricultural transformation in the region, the Chinese illicit economy in Southeast Asia, and the influence of outbound migration from China and the socioeconomic impact on host societies in Southeast Asia. Additionally, I include another chapter to explore how China's diaspora governance policies have affected its historial and contemporary relations with Southeast Asia. Summaries of these chapters and the conclusion are discussed in turn below.

Chapter 2: Authoritarian Resilience

This chapter presents China's most commonly assumed negative influence, namely meddling in the internal politics of Southeast Asian governments and contributing to the revival and endurance of authoritarian governments in the region.[64] It provides an overview of three modes of Chinese influence on authoritarian governments in Southeast Asia. The first is China's explicit support to sustain authoritarian governments such as the military junta in Myanmar.[65] The second mode is that through economic engagement China unintentionally provides performance legitimacy for the authoritarian government in power. By offering aid and investment, China's injection of capital into Cambodia's domestic economy, for example, has helped the Cambodian government to improve its domestic rule. The third mode is that China can also indirectly empower authoritarian governments by setting up an example for how authoritarian governments can make things work, with its stress on economic development and social order. This is the case in Thailand, where the right-wing military government often cites China as the role model, while the government's supporters encourage further Chinese influence in the country.

Chapter 3: Trade, Investment, and Economic Influence

This chapter provides a general overview of China's economic influence in Southeast Asia, with a focus on the overall trade patterns between the two as well as the ongoing trend for Chinese investment in Southeast Asia, particularly in infrastructure development and a few key industries. It looks at a few prominent infrastructure projects that China has pushed in the region, such as the HSR in both Laos, Thailand, and Indonesia. It also examines how

Chinese investments in Southeast Asia take advantage of special economic zones SEZ that some regional governments have set up with a detailed discussion of the Rayong Industrial Park (RIP) in Thailand.[66] Although much Chinese investment might be the relocation of manufacturing from China to Southeast Asia, as a result of its upgrade of the industrial value chain and to bypass the ongoing trade war between Beijing and Washington, there are also certain key industries that we can see clearly that Chinese capital envisions expanding to Southeast Asia, such as electric vehicles (EVs). What we are witnessing, despite the slump during COVID-19, is an increasingly influential China in its economic relations with Southeast Asia.

Chapter 4: Contesting "Re-Sinicization"

This chapter focuses on the promotion of Chinese language education in Southeast Asia, using Thailand as an example to examine how the Chinese government has pushed for an export of China's soft power. It demonstrates how, through the promotion of its language and culture, the Chinese government aims to propagate its own versions of political history, particularly on issues that relate to the "One China Principle," and others that affect China's perceived national interests. The chapter discusses how Beijing competes with Taipei in education outreach to the Yunnanese Kuomintang (KMT) community in Northern Thailand, and contextualizes the phenomenon of "re-Sinicization," as well as pointing out some of the contestations against the Chinese government's re-territorialization of the overseas Chinese community in Southeast Asia.

Chapter 5: Chinese Consumption

The size of the Chinese population and its growing middle class means increasing food consumption. This increase in demand has led to a variety of contract farming practices in the Mekong region, where, depending on the type of agricultural products, different non-state Chinese actors engage with local farmers to satisfy Chinese consumers' demands. This chapter provides a few snapshots of China's domestic consumption's ripple effects in mainland Southeast Asia. First, it analyzes the effects of the maize boom in northern Myanmar on its ecological system by showing how rising demand for maize in China has led to an accelerated rate of deforestation. The chapter then presents the story of how China's demand for beef has led to a transnational network of live cattle smuggling. It then looks at the case of Chinese demand for durian and watermelon and its implications for business networks in Thailand and Myanmar. Finally, the chapter examines Chinese businesses' commercial banana plantation in Laos and their environmental externalities. The chapter will conclude with some preliminary thinking about the effect on borderland economies of the closure of the Chinese border due to COVID-19.

Chapter 6: Illicit Political Economy

Legitimate investment in Southeast Asia has been accompanied by a parallel flow of illegal "black money" from China.[67] This chapter looks at the illicit dimension of China's regional economy in Southeast Asia, and it looks at how the growth of the online casino economy has been deeply tied with Chinese capital looking for investment opportunities in Southeast Asia. Closely associated with these opportunities are the online scammers that specifically target ethnic Chinese communities across national boundaries. The chapter then tentatively discusses the relationship between the illicit economies and the existing Special Economic Zones in Southeast Asia,[68] and how the lack of state regulation and capacity and rampant corruption have facilitated the growth of these illicit activities.

Chapter 7: Migration Encounters

This chapter addresses the issue of how the mass movement of people from China in recent years has left unintended consequences on host countries and their local communities. Using Thailand as the focus, the chapter situates this mass movement of people within the context of the long history of migration from China to Southeast Asia, while emphasizing the similarities and differences between these different waves of Chinese migration to the region. The chapter specifically discuss three categories of such population movement: tourists, businesses, and students. It then considers the changing perception towards the Chinese in Thailand and explores how to explain such changing perceptions with a view of the Chinese migration history to Southeast Asia.

Chapter 8: Diaspora Engagement

This chapter reflects on what factors condition different Southeast Asian states' responses to China's influence in the region. It introduces a conceptualization on diaspora politics and how it affects Southeast Asian states' relations with China. The chapter details the history of Chinese migration to the region and the different patterns of treatment that migrants have received in Southeast Asia, using Indonesia, Myanmar, and Thailand as examples. The chapter then analyzes China's changing diaspora governance practices in the context of its miraculous rise in recent decades, by pointing out how such changing power dynamic matters for Beijing's relations with its diaspora and the three countries in Southeast Asia. The chapter concludes with some reflections on how the dynamics of diaspora politics is one important aspect that will continue to define China is perceived by regional states in Southeast Asia and their future relations.

Chapter 9: Conclusion

The concluding chapter provides a summary of the intricate landscape of China's impact on mainland Southeast Asia. It reviews how China has become the primary and diversified partner for Southeast Asia across various fields. The relationship between China and Southeast Asian countries encompasses political, economic, and cultural dimensions, and the influence of China in the region has been profoundly experienced by regional governments and the populace. Additionally, the chapter reflects on the effects of COVID-19 and how the post-pandemic era might shape China's ties with Southeast Asia.

2

Authoritarian Resilience

Introduction

I arrived in Bangkok on the evening of May 25, 2014, three days after the military coup that established the National Council for Peace and Order (NCPO). I was staying at a hotel in the Ratchaprasong area; the hotel had agreed to send a car to pick me up at the airport because no public services were available. The journey from the Suvarnabhumi airport to the hotel was eerie because the otherwise neon-lit Bangkok city skyline was pitch black because of the curfew. But military coups in fact are not an unusual political phenomenon in Thailand because of the long history of military intervention in Thai politics. Only in 2006 did another military coup remove Thaksin Shinawatra from office. At that time, the military junta did not stay in office very long. Yet at this time, General Prayuth Chan-ocha, who came to power in the 2014 coup, remained in office until 2023. Despite the king's passing and periodic anti-government protest movements, the military seems to be as entrenched as ever in Thai politics. At the same time, Thailand seems to have improved its relations with China, and pundits have called out Beijing's backing for Bangkok's authoritarian turn.[1]

A military coup also occurred in Myanmar. On February 1, 2021, tanks rolled into Naypyidaw to announce the National League for Democracy (NLD) government's removal. The military, under the leadership of Min Aung Hlaing, took over the government and put Aung San Suu Kyi and several other prominent NLD leaders under house arrest. While the military was cracking down on popular resistance and the civil disobedience movement, wide-ranging rumors spread online about Beijing's support of the military takeover. For example, rumors included how a Myanmar Air international flight arriving at Yangon airport from Kunming was in fact carrying Chinese military equipment. And pictures were circulating about white-skinned slant-eyed soldiers, presumably more Chinese looking, who were patrolling the streets in Yangon. Both were used as evidence of Chinese military support for the junta. Moreover, an online story about a group of

The Ripple Effect. Enze Han, Oxford University Press. © Oxford University Press 2024.
DOI: 10.1093/oso/9780197696583.003.0002

Chinese nationals checking into the Pan Pacific Hotel in Yangon immediately portrayed them as spies.[2] In the coup's early days, the international media seemed to be fixated on China and its role in the military takeover in Myanmar.

Indeed, China has been featured prominently in recent literature on authoritarian resilience around the world, where democracy seems to be in retreat while authoritarian governments have expanded their influence. When people are trying to figure out why this trend is happening, many have pointed the finger at the Chinese government under the CCP's leadership. Specifically, in Southeast Asia, as the region most economically intertwined with China and geographically proximate, a long list of allegations has emerged on how China has influenced the persistence of authoritarianism in the region.

Significant evidence supports such allegations. In Myanmar, China has provided diplomatic shelter to the military government from international censure. Particularly sensitive to the West's use of "human rights violations" to push for "regime changes," Beijing has consistently emphasized non-interference in domestic politics to protect the military junta in various international forums, but particularly the United Nations. Beijing has also been generously providing aid and investment to countries without any strings attached to the receiving countries' domestic governance. One example is Cambodia, in which Hun Sen's authoritarian government has boosted its ruling legitimacy through many of China's development projects.

However, Beijing's explicit support for authoritarian governments in the region should also be contextualized. In addition to supporting Myanmar's military junta, Beijing also shielded Myanmar's democratically elected government under Aung San Suu Kyi when it was under international pressure during the Rohingya crisis since 2015.[3] In Thailand, China seems to have equally good relations with both the military government under Prayuth and the democratically elected Shinawatras.[4] However, it is an exaggeration to claim that China aims to prop up authoritarian governments and defeat democracies whenever it can.[5] In terms of aid and investment, China is not simply investing in authoritarian states alone, but also in democracies in the region, such as the Philippines and Indonesia. It seems that Beijing does not specifically seek out authoritarian governments in the region to sustain its rule, so perhaps its influence over authoritarian resilience in the region might be much more nuanced than is often claimed.

This chapter provides an overview of three modes of Chinese influence on authoritarian governments in Southeast Asia. The first is China's explicit support to sustain authoritarian governments such as the military junta in Myanmar. For the regime, which is battered both by domestic resistance and international condemnation, China's support is crucial for the military to salvage any of the remaining legitimacy it has enjoyed. One qualification is that China has intended its support for the incumbent government rather than the military government per se.

The remaining two modes are rather unintended consequences by China's existing policies. The second mode is that through economic engagement China unintentionally provides performance legitimacy for the authoritarian government in power. By offering aid and investment, China's injection of capital into Cambodia's domestic economy, for example, has helped the Cambodian government to improve its domestic rule. The third mode, on the other hand, is that China can also indirectly empower authoritarian governments by setting up an example for how authoritarian governments can make things work, with its stress on economic development and social order. This is the case in Thailand, where the right-wing military government often cites China as the role model, while the government's supporters encourage further Chinese influence in the country.

This chapter is organized as follows. First, it reviews the literature on China and authoritarian resilience around the world, paying specific attention to the different modes of Chinese influence. It then presents three examples of Chinese influence in authoritarian resilience in the cases of Myanmar, Cambodia, and Thailand. The chapter concludes with some cautionary tales about how Chinese support for authoritarian governments in the region can or has already backfired against Chinese interests.

Authoritarian Resilience and China's Influence

Thomas Ambrosio once discussed factors that affect the global balance between democracy and authoritarianism. The first factor has to do with the global normative power of democracy itself, which rests upon the health of democratic institutions and changing values in many Western societies. Decay of domestic political order, in the case of rising right-wing populism in many European countries, and degradation of democratic institutions in the United States during Trump era, for example, bode ill for the promotion of democracy globally. The second factor hinges on whether authoritarian states can present convincing alternatives that decrease democracy's appeal.[6] Here, scholars and practitioners have all pointed the finger at China.

Indeed, China's economic success and growing authoritarian rule under President Xi Jinping has rung a worrying alarm in many Western capitals. Particularly in Washington, consensus has emerged in recent years about how China represents a threat to the U.S.-led international order and the survival of democracy, despite that many scholars disagree on whether China intends to export its model elsewhere.[7] While concern remains over whether the CCP is going all out to undermine the global democracy movement by exporting its way of government. However, empirically, how China is related with authoritarian resilience around the world is not uniform. In general, we can think of three modes of such influence.

First, the direct influence mode is when the Chinese government makes explicit efforts to support other authoritarian states. Certainly, the Chinese government's dislike of foreign intervention in the name of regime change or human rights has led to its sheltering of certain authoritarian regimes, particularly at the UN.[8] The Chinese government seems to be increasingly more willing to veto UN Security Council (UNSC) resolutions on issues relating to "regime change" instigated by foreign powers, that is, the United States in the case of Myanmar but also Syria and Venezuela. Furthermore, China has also provided training and knowledge exchange for authoritarian regimes in recent years. Particularly, China has been exporting technologies for authoritarian control, such as face recognition, internet firewalls, and information censorship software.[9] This export of digital authoritarianism has directly increased many authoritarian states' capacity in surveillance and repression.

On the other hand, in certain circumstances Chinese economic engagement, such as aid, trade, and investment has had a stabilizing effect on authoritarian rule, irrespective of Chinese intentions.[10] Such effects might be due to China's selective engagement of domestic political forces through its so-called non-interventionist foreign policy, which might benefit the incumbent and its associated economic interests and help prolong preexisting patronage networks. Although some studies have found China's aid has a negative effect on democratization,[11] the long-term effect of China's engagement on authoritarian resilience is inconclusive,[12] to say the least, and in some cases can even undermine autocratic political structure.[13]

Finally, Chinese influence on authoritarian resilience can occur through unintentional diffusion.[14] That is, there might be active learning on the part of some authoritarian regimes to emulate the Chinese experience without Beijing's active support. Here, China's economic development success under the CCP, as has often been claimed, provided a "China model" as a potential alternative to the democratic governance model that the West has long championed. The duality of economic freedom and absolute political control thus offered a blueprint for other authoritarian states to copy because it betrayed conventional wisdom of requiring democratic institutions for economic development.[15] Furthermore, the "China model" success can be used discursively by other authoritarian states to secure more political control and domestic order in contrast to the "messy" democratic counterparts in the West.

Three Modes of Chinese Influence in Authoritarian Southeast Asia

The Southeast Asian region is characterized by its regime diversity. Even with the region's few authoritarian regimes, variations arise from the single party communist state such as Vietnam and Laos, to military or military-dominated governments in Myanmar and Thailand, and autocratic rule in places such as Cambodia. In general, these mainland countries tend to be more authoritarian than those in maritime Southeast Asia.[16] Geographically close to China, the region is economically deeply intertwined with China and is at the forefront of many Chinese attempts to create regional infrastructural integration, as I will discuss in more detail in the next chapter.[17] Therefore, from Beijing's point of view, this is the region where political stability is fundamental, and China wants to maintain friendly and cooperative neighborly relations.[18]

Ironically, Vietnam is where one might argue that the Chinese influence over the Communist Party of Vietnam's (CPV) regime resilience is more limited. Because of the nationalistic legitimacy that the CPV enjoys, which is based on a long tradition of anti-China sentiments within the country, its regime resilience is quite distinct from Chinese influence.[19] On the other hand, for the remaining mainland Southeast Asian countries, China lacks direct conflicts of interest such as territorial disputes, and China does not stand out necessarily as the national foe for the domestic public. Here, we can argue that China's influence in authoritarian regime resilience is more perceptible. Indeed, China's warm political relations with these governments has drawn criticisms that Beijing's support has led to the authoritarian resilience in the region. Thus, we can see the three different modes of Chinese influence in the cases of Myanmar, Cambodia, and Thailand.

Political Crisis and the Military Junta in Myanmar

Myanmar's military has dominated the country's politics since the late 1950s, when General Ne Win instigated the first military coup.[20] Thereafter, the military generals became entrenched in politics and ruled the country as one of the most reclusive yet least-developed countries in Southeast Asia.[21] Particularly since the end of the Cold War, global waves of democratization ushered in a new international order no longer defined by the ideological divisions between communism and anti-communism. Thus, the military's crackdown on the democracy movement in 1988 and the nullification of the 1990 election that Aung San Suu Kyi's NLD party won, made the country's military government one of the most notorious rogue regimes. The State Law and Order Restoration Council (SLORC), which later changed its name to State Peace and Development Council (SPDC), became a target of the West's economic sanctions and popular boycott, while Aung San Suu Kyi became an idol for democracy and human rights throughout the world.

Facing international isolation and in desperate need of economic development and trading opportunities, the SPDC re-oriented its existing trade relations with Europe and America to its neighboring states in East and Southeast Asia. More importantly, the SPDC came to see the value of depending on China for diplomatic protection in international forums against any censure towards its domestic repression of the democracy movement. At the same time, Beijing was sympathetic to the SPDC's fate because it was also the target of international condemnation after the Tiananmen Incident in 1989. The post-Cold War changing international order that emphasized democratization, human rights, and regime change pushed Beijing and Yangon closer in their common opposition towards the West. Indeed, during this period, Beijing kept emphasizing the Five Principles of Peaceful Coexistence as its foreign policy guidelines and its objection to foreign interference in other countries' internal affairs. When the SPDC government was facing international isolation, Chinese leaders and dignitaries made frequent visits to Myanmar, including President Jiang Zemin's visit in December 2001.[22]

Beijing provided explicit support for Myanmar's military junta by sheltering the generals from international censure. The most significant event was in 2007, when China vetoed a UN draft resolution on Myanmar. This resolution was prepared by the United States and was put on the UNSC. U.S. ambassador to the UN John Bolton argued that Myanmar's domestic situation posed a threat to regional and international peace and security. In the end, China together with Russia vetoed the resolution. This veto was the only time that China used its UNSC veto for Myanmar.[23] Also in the same year, a "saffron revolution" emerged in Myanmar when monks led anti-government protests across the country. While both the United States and the United Kingdom wanted to push for a UN resolution in the revolution's wake, fearing Beijing's possible veto, only a lukewarm UNSC presidential statement was issued that stressed the need for political dialogue.[24] Beijing also facilitated the UN Special Adviser Ibrahim Gambari's visit to Myanmar during this period, which eventually helped dampen the international pressure the military generals faced. Indeed, one might argue that Chinese support for the SPDC was instrumental to its survival.

Then, Myanmar went through a decade of political transformation. From a position of strength, the military junta pushed for a transition to a civilian government while holding veto power.[25] Later, the Thein Sein government unleashed genuine political reforms that led the NLD to win the national election in 2015, and Aung San Suu Kyi became the de facto leader of a much more democratic Myanmar. Despite some initial setbacks during Thein Sein's period (2010–2015), China's relations with Myanmar remained unscathed after Aung San Suu Kyi came to power.

However, even during Suu Kyi's period, China continued to offer protection for Myanmar when her government was facing international pressure on charges of "ethnic cleansing" or "genocide" towards the Rohingya minority in the Rakhine State.[26] For example, in March 2017, China and Russia together blocked a UNSC statement on the Rohingya situation.[27] Instead of condemning the Myanmar government and its military, Beijing supported "Myanmar's efforts to safeguard the peace and stability of the Rakhine State and sincerely hopes that the Rakhine State can restore stability as soon as possible and the local people can live a normal life again."[28]

Just as in the previous decade, China did not support international sanctions on Myanmar and used its veto power at the UNSC to shelter the Myanmar government from such censure. In November 2017, given the clear intention from China as well as Russia that they would not support a UN resolution, the Security Council instead adopted a statement that condemned the violence in the Rakhine State, but excluded the phrase "ethnic cleansing." Again in March 2018, China resisted British efforts at forcing a UNSC statement calling on Myanmar to try those responsible for attacks on the Rohingya, by offering a watered down amendment that dropped all mention of investigations or accountability. Thus, even Myanmar during this period was no longer as authoritarian as before, China's support was critical for Suu Kyi's government to fend off the mounting criticism the country faced.

However, Myanmar's political fate took another disastrous turn. After the NLD won a landslide election in November 2020, the domestic power balance versus the military broke down. Fearing that its veto power in politics was under threat, General Min Aung Hlaing announced a military takeover in February 2021. This time, popular resistance to the coup was fierce. In the early days of the coup, widespread demonstrations and civil disobedience called for the return of the democratically elected government. The military junta, the State Administrative Council (SAC), cracked down hard on popular resistance with the indiscriminate use of violence towards civilians.

Myanmar, indeed, has entered a downward spiral into domestic political chaos. The SAC seems to lack the capacity to fully subdue popular resistance. On the other hand, a Committee Representing Pyidaungsu Hluttaw (CRPH) was formed by a group of legislators in exile, and through them a National Unity Government (NUG) was created as the legitimate government of Myanmar. Ordinary people have also taken up arms by forming People's Defense Forces (PDF) across the country to fight against the military government. Myanmar of course is no stranger to civil war,[29] but this time much of the fighting was in urban and in the central plain Bamar areas, instead of the peripheral borderland areas with ethnic armed groups (EAGs). The country is now in a critical stage, and the international community is expected to do more to help the country in crisis.

The international community has acted quickly to condemn the situation in Myanmar. Many Western governments have called on the military to return power to the NLD, and the generals were once again put on the sanctions list. This time around, even ASEAN started to put more pressure on the SAC. In April 2021, the ASEAN's Leaders' Meeting issued a Five Point Consensus (FPC) on the situation in Myanmar and used relatively strong language to demand changes from the SAC.[30] Although ASEAN was criticized for its lack of enforcement measures towards the FPC, it has since shunned the SAC representatives from attending its meetings. Yet such measures fall short of exerting genuine pressure on the SAC, and thus China's role in Myanmar's domestic political crisis is even more important.

Beijing's position on the coup has been in stark contrast with coups in other countries. On February 2, China blocked the UNSC from issuing a joint statement to condemn the coup.[31] And instead of calling it a coup, China used the words "a major cabinet reshuffle" and some Chinese scholars opined that it was in the military's right to do so according to the 2008 constitution. China also dislikes sanctions and considers them counterproductive to fostering political dialogue within Myanmar. China's refusal to condemn the coup sparked speculation that Beijing had been backing the generals. For instance, China was accused of providing technical assistance to the military junta in developing a cyber firewall in Myanmar, which would block protestors' access to social media and internet access.[32] As we mentioned earlier, many online rumors pointed to China's involvement and even outright support for the coup.

Although the Chinese government denied the allegations, its actions nonetheless qualify as tacit support. Beijing continues to deal with the SAC as if it is the legitimate government, for example, by sending its military attaché to SAC's military parade, together with Russia and most of Myanmar's neighboring states.[33] China has received an official visit from the SAC foreign minister, U Wunna Maung Lwin, while the then Chinese foreign minister, Wang Yi, also visited Myanmar in return. In Beijing's words, Myanmar needs to find "a development path in line with its national conditions,"[34] that is, Myanmar's internal politics and needs should be sorted out by the Myanmar people alone. Through formal diplomacy, China is seen as granting the military junta *de facto* recognition and legitimizing its forceful power takeover.

But it is also clear that Beijing does not see the continuation of the military junta would best serve its interests in the region, which is why Beijing fully supported ASEAN's FPC proposal. In August 2021, after Sun Guoxiang's week-long visit to Myanmar, China's senior special envoy for Asian Affairs, Chinese Foreign Ministry spokesperson Wang Wenbin stated, "China actively supports Myanmar's cooperation with the Association of Southeast Asian Nations (ASEAN) in implementing the five-point consensus on Myanmar reached by ASEAN and opposes undue external intervention."[35] To make the FPC a success would not only satisfy Beijing's interests in Myanmar but also consolidate ASEAN-centrality for regional cooperation instead. This outcome is crucial given how many Indo-Pacific related grand schemes the United States has proposed with the aim to encircle China.

Thus, emphasizing ASEAN's centrality in regional cooperation is an effective mechanism Beijing can rely on to push back against the United States and its Indo-Pacific designs. On the other hand, ASEAN also understands the crucial role China can play in realizing the FPC. ASEAN believes China possesses access to the Myanmar military junta, and Beijing can use certain leverage for pressure. Thus, ASEAN requires China's assistance to bring the various parties to the negotiation table and considers China's resources valuable in delivering humanitarian assistances to the country as well.

For these reasons, international diplomacy towards the Myanmar crisis is now stuck. Beijing seems to have the capacity to put pressure on the SAC, but was unlikely to openly condemn the military junta, and it didn't. China's official foreign policy principle is non-interference in other countries' domestic politics, no matter how others might accuse Beijing as being hypocritical. Beijing simply will not call for outright regime change in Myanmar and would only treat the political crisis in Myanmar as a domestic matter that should be dealt with through political dialogue. Beijing seems to have come to terms with working with the SAC, even though this is not the ideal situation it wants to see in Myanmar. What Beijing has done is talk with the SAC and hope that through diplomacy some type of comprise might occur. For example, when Sun Guoxiang visited Myanmar in August 2021, he reportedly requested to meet with Aung San Suu Kyi, but the military declined the request. The denial did not stop Sun from visiting Myanmar again three months later, while emphasizing "China will work together with the international community to play a constructive role in Myanmar's efforts to restore social stability and resume democratic transformation at an early date."[36] At the end of the day, international diplomacy has failed Myanmar, and China's tacit support for the SAC is certainly to blame for the lack of progress in reversing Myanmar's worsening political crisis.

The Strongmen Regime in Cambodia

Cambodia is arguably the country in mainland Southeast Asia with the longest spell of stable post-independence relations with China. Ever since the establishment of bilateral relations in 1958, Cambodia has regarded China as its closest strategic ally to push back against two of its bigger neighbors, Vietnam and Thailand.[37] Depending on whether China's foreign policy priority was against U.S. or Soviet hegemony in Southeast Asia, Beijing supported various regimes in Cambodia during the Cold War, from King Norodom Sihanouk to the Khmer Rouge. After the country's civil war and UN peace-building occupation, Cambodia initially went through a power sharing arrangement between the National United Front for an Independent, Neutral, Peaceful and Cooperative Cambodia (FUNCINPEC), led by Prince Norodom Ranariddh, and the Cambodian People's Party (CPP), led by Hun Sen, until the latter carried out a coup by removing the former in 1997.[38]

Cambodia's domestic regime type has gradually deteriorated to resemble a personalistic dictatorship since Hun Sen consolidated his domination in domestic politics and the CPP monopolized all seats in the national assembly after the 2018 election, which was widely disputed as unfree.[39] During these two decades, international observers have witnessed the breakup of opposition parties, the violent suppression of dissidents, and the concentration of power in Hun Sen and his network of stooges. According to Morgenbesser, Cambodia today should be classified as a party-personalistic dictatorship, where Hun Sen maintains unconstrained and discretionary authority in various domains.[40] For Cambodia's regime regression, China's role can be seen in separate dimensions.

First, and just as in the Myanmar case discussed above, is Beijing's explicit support towards Hun Sen and the CPP as the incumbent government. For example, before the Hun Sen coup, China's then president, Jiang Zemin, invited him as a representative of the CPP to Beijing for political meetings in 1996, while leaders of FUNCINPEC were precluded. After Hun Sen expelled FUNCINPEC from the government, many Western governments suspended aid to Cambodia, which led Hun Sen to condemn foreign interference in Cambodia's internal affairs.[41] On the other hand, China became the first country to recognize the coup and Hun Sen's rightful leadership, while berating Western interference in Cambodia's domestic politics.[42] Moreover, China provided financial and material assistance to fill the vacancy left by the retreat of Western countries.[43] In the next few years, China injected more than US$600 million of grants, aid, and investment into Cambodia, and boosted bilateral trades. And in 2000, President Jiang Zemin became the first Chinese head of state to visit Cambodia.[44]

A similar pattern occurred after the opposition party, the Cambodia National Rescue Party (CNRP), was banned in 2017. Chinese Premier Li Keqiang visited Phnom Penh in January 2018, when a joint communiqué used similar language to the ones used in the Myanmar case, whereby China "reiterated its respect for the independence, sovereignty and territorial integrity of Cambodia, and reaffirmed its support to the Cambodian people in selecting a development path which suits their national conditions."[45] After Hun Sen's CPP won all the seats in the national assembly, both the Chinese president and premier sent congratulatory messages, in stark contrast to many Western governments that refused to recognize the election results.[46] Thus, Chinese explicit support is one reason for Hun Sen and the CPP's political longevity in Cambodia.

Additionally, China's pervasive economic presence in Cambodia has contributed to the Cambodian state's economic performance, which indirectly boosted Hun Sen's ruling legitimacy. As Cambodia's largest foreign investor, China accounted for almost a quarter of all foreign investment in Cambodia between 2012 and 2018.[47] China is also the largest donor to Cambodia, and by 2019 provided 48 percent of the country's official development assistance (ODA) came from Beijing.[48] Given China's dominant share of its investment and aid to Cambodia, it is not an exaggeration to claim that China has contributed substantially to Cambodia's economic growth for the past decades. Indeed, before the COVID-19 pandemic, Cambodia's annual economic growth rate from 1998 to 2019 was 7.7 percent, which has contributed significantly to the reduction of poverty and inequality in the country as well.[49]

The Cambodian government considers infrastructure improvement as a key to its economic growth, and Beijing has offered a helping hand. A significant share of China's investment went to infrastructure construction. Under the BRI, many such projects have gone ahead in Cambodia for desperately needed infrastructure in this formerly war-torn country. For example, in 2017, China financed almost 70 percent of Cambodia's roads and bridges. China has also built a major expressway linking the capital city Phnom Penh and Sihanoukville that became operational in 2023.[50] Additionally, China is building hospitals, powerplants, a new port in Kampot, and a new airport for Phnom Penh, over and above several other updates of Cambodia's national road system.[51] Such infrastructure projects have been presented as indicators for the CPP's performance legitimacy and are in fact well recognized by ordinary Cambodians.[52]

During the COVID-19 pandemic, China has greatly assisted Hun Sen's regime's vaccination campaigns in the country. Until early November in 2021, China had sent more than 35 million vaccines to Cambodia, which accounted for over 90 percent of its total vaccines received from other countries, and a considerable percentage of them were donated for free.[53]

In addition, China delivered material supplies and medical professionals to assist Cambodia during this period. With China's help, Cambodia achieved impressive outcomes during the pandemic. In Southeast Asia, a country's vaccination level is usually positively related to its economic level. For example, Singapore has the highest rate of vaccination in the region. But Cambodia, despite having the second lowest per capita GDP in the region, achieved remarkable success in vaccinating its population and had the highest vaccination rate in Southeast Asia outside of wealthy Singapore.[54]

Moreover, having efficiently controlled the spread of COVID-19, Hun Sen managed to also limit the damage to the national economy. Overall, Cambodian people give positive evaluations of the government's efforts during the pandemic. In a report published by ISEAS, more than 80 percent of participants acclaimed Cambodia's government for its efficient response to COVID-19, and over one-quarter expressed strong approval. They particularly appreciate that the government implemented powerful public health measures to control the spread of the virus. Additionally, half the respondents viewed China as having delivered the most support to Cambodia during the pandemic.[55] Thus, China's support for Hun Sen's regime during the COVID-19 crisis arguably improved its ruling effectiveness and regime legitimacy in the eyes of the general public.

At the same time, the country's governing elites reap benefits through patronage networks that tap into Chinese capital coming into Cambodia. Because of Hun Sen's and other high-ranking CPP officials' domination, getting contracts and other money-making opportunities from the Chinese investments in Cambodia requires their blessing. Thus, Cambodia's crony-capitalist networks have developed this symbiotic relationship with their support for the CPP.[56] Meanwhile, Cambodia's security forces also received Chinese financial aid, and they are part of the CPP's patronage networks and provide repressive support for the regime in time of need.[57]

Thus, although Western governments tried to use their trade preferences to pressure the Hun Sen government to improve Cambodia's domestic human rights records and restore democratic practices, China's economic engagement with Cambodia essentially makes such threats futile. Hun Sen clearly realized how important China is for his rule. For example, at a Nikkei's Future of Asia conference, he specifically defended the dependence of Cambodia on China on development assistance, by saying "If I don't rely on China, who will I rely on? If I don't ask China, who am I to ask?"[58]

Most recently, Chinese Premier Li Keqiang visited Cambodia in November 2022 to attend the ASEAN Summit, during which he pledged that China "will continue to advance major projects in Cambodia and support its effort to accelerate industrialization. China will . . . effectively implement China-aided projects on roads, medical care, water supply, among others, and do its best to assist Cambodia in improving its people's livelihood."[59] Thus, it seems Hun Sen and his CPP government will continue to benefit from the Chinese largess and the economic dividend generated through bilateral cooperation. As long as the country's economic performance continued, popular grievances could not translate into large scale anti-regime resistance. Cambodia's authoritarian rule would be most likely to persist even after Hun Sen, who has groomed his eldest son, Hun Manet, to be his successor as the next CPP leader.[60]

Persistence of Military Rule in Thailand

Thailand has witnessed domestic instability since the start of the twenty-first century, with rounds of mass protests with competing rallies and counter-rallies between political forces loosely defined as "yellow shirts" and "red shirts."[61] Such grassroots confrontations reflected the political polarization within the country as well as the power struggles between the ousted prime minister, Thaksin Shinawatra, and supporters of the royalist order, which prompted the military to take over the government twice, in 2006 and again in 2014. In particular, General Prayuth's most recent coup has created a domestic political environment of deteriorating civil liberties and human rights violations, not only because of the continual rule by the military but also in the draconian application on political dissidents of Article 112 of the Thai Constitution that punishes *lèse-majesté* offenses.[62]

Rounds of anti-government protest spread across the country from the start of 2020, particularly among university students and urban youth.[63] Into fall 2020, this protest movement transformed into one of the most anti-establishment protest movements the country has witnessed in the recent past. In conjunction with the economic and social hardships that Thai society experienced during the COVID-19 lockdowns, there were explicit calls for fundamental reforms to the monarchy and its royalist political establishments, on top of demands for constitutional changes and the resignation of Prime Minister Prayuth.[64] This target on the monarchy, an extremely controversial move, ultimately drew harsh state repression with the arrests of protest leaders using the *lèse-majesté* clause.

However, despite the protest movements, the Thai political establishment has not budged, which indicates the deep entrenchment of authoritarian rule in the country with the royalist military government firmly in control. When facing demands for his resignation, Prayuth replied, "I will not run away from problems. I will not leave my duty by resigning at a time when the country has problems," while calling the protests illegal assemblies.[65] With such an uncompromising stance, the political turmoil within the country is sure to continue.

If Myanmar and Cambodia represent two small states where the Chinese government has propped up their authoritarian governments, the case of China's role in Thailand's authoritarian regression is not as straightforward. As a middle power with a long history of military coups, Thailand's regime changes during the past decade have clear domestic political logics.[66] As a long-term ally of the United States, Thailand has sophisticated weapon systems the military can use for domestic suppression. Bangkok also benefited from Washington's diplomatic protection throughout the Cold War and after and does not face the same type of international pressure as either Myanmar or Cambodia. For this reason, Thailand does not need China's diplomatic support as much as the others. Furthermore, Thailand's economy is also much better developed than its poorer neighbors, and for decades Thailand has been a popular FDI destination for many Western states. For example, in 2021, the top two countries investing in Thailand were Japan and the United States; China was only ranked fifth.[67] Certainly, China is Thailand's top trading partner, but Chinese economic engagement with Thailand is by no means as hegemonic as in either Myanmar or Cambodia. How, then, can we make sense of the alleged Chinese influence in authoritarian regression in Thailand?

Here, I argue that the "China factor" works through existing domestic political divisions within Thailand. The country's domestic institutions and political contestations are in fact conduits of Chinese influence. As Fung and colleagues point out, "countries are receptive or resistant to China's attempts at international influence because their domestic institutions create particular payoff matrices and empower particular political players, in ways that encourage or discourage receptivity."[68] In Thailand's case, China's influence is filtered through domestic political divisions between those who support the current government/authoritarianism and those who support the opposition/democracy. For those who support authoritarian rule, they overall praise the Chinese model of development, welcome Chinese investments in Thailand, and would like to see more Chinese influence at the expense of the United States in Thailand. Particularly, many royal nationalists in Thailand tend to view the United States with hostility, accusing it of hypocrisy and political interference in Thailand's domestic politics.[69] Thus, the heated great power competition between the United States and China has also been filtered through domestic political polarization in Thailand; the pro-government forces tend to praise China to put down the United States. On the flipside, people who have more democratic values would have the opposite preferences. Indeed, often Thailand's foreign policy support for China or the United States can be interpreted as a form of domestic political contestation between those who support the military government and those who do not.

Such polarization can be seen through competing discourses about China. A few months after the coup in 2014, for example, Prayuth praised China as a good example of economic development and noted that Thailand should learn from Beijing.[70] For many Thai people who are right-wing nationalists and who have supported the military takeover, they somehow consider the Chinese political model a better alternative to the American-style electoral democracy.[71] Right-wing media in Thailand also tend to recycle news that shows the positive side of China, either in its domestic governance or foreign policy, while denigrating the United States for its imperial behavior around the world. For example, the Thai Move Institute, which is right-wing pro-government media, generally broadcasts pro-China and anti-U.S. news. It considers China to be a "close, congenial, power and sympathetic regional ally" and thinks Thailand should orient to Beijing instead of Washington.[72]

For the opposition, one of Thailand's opposition politicians, Thanathorn Juangroongruangkit, the former leader of the now dissolved Future Forward Party, has increasingly become an avid critic of China. For example, in 2019, he met with Hong Kong activist Joshua Wong at an Open Future Festival, who later tweeted "Under the hard-line authoritarian suppression, we stand in solidarity" with their picture.[73] This tweet occurred during the anti-China protest movement in Hong Kong, which prompted the Chinese Embassy in Bangkok to issue a statement to condemn the meeting by saying "the action is extremely wrong and irresponsible. China hopes the relevant individuals can recognize the facts about the Hong Kong issue, be cautious, and do what is beneficial for the friendship between China and Thailand."[74] Three years later at the Olso Freedom Forum in Taiwan, Thanathorn once again criticized Thai

PM Prayuth's embrace of China. He even drew a parallel between Thailand and Myanmar by hinting that the reason for Myanmar's domestic political crisis was because of China's influence in that country. He stated: "Our submarines are from China. We are the first country to buy a submarine from China. Our high-speed trains are from China. We are opening up our economy for China . . . It's China's footprint everywhere . . . It's the same with Myanmar. Look at what's happening in Myanmar right now."[75]

To see whether any empirical support for such political polarization exists in Thailand and the contrasting views towards China versus the United States, I conducted a survey in Thailand with colleagues at the University of Hong Kong and Chiang Mai University in November 2021.[76] In an online survey of 1,800 Thai correspondents through an international survey company Dynata, we try to gauge how the Thai public perceives China and its influence in the country. As Figure 2.1 shows, Thailand's overall stance on China is more neutral. Figure 2.1(a) shows that 39 percent consider Thailand should stay neutral between China-U.S. competition. In terms of perceptions of China's political, economic, and cultural influence, the mode of distribution seems again to be in the middle ground, although people tend to view China's economic influence more positively overall. In Figure 2.2, on a list of issue topics related to China, we can see that the Thai public is cautiously more positive about Thailand's relations with China. People seem to agree

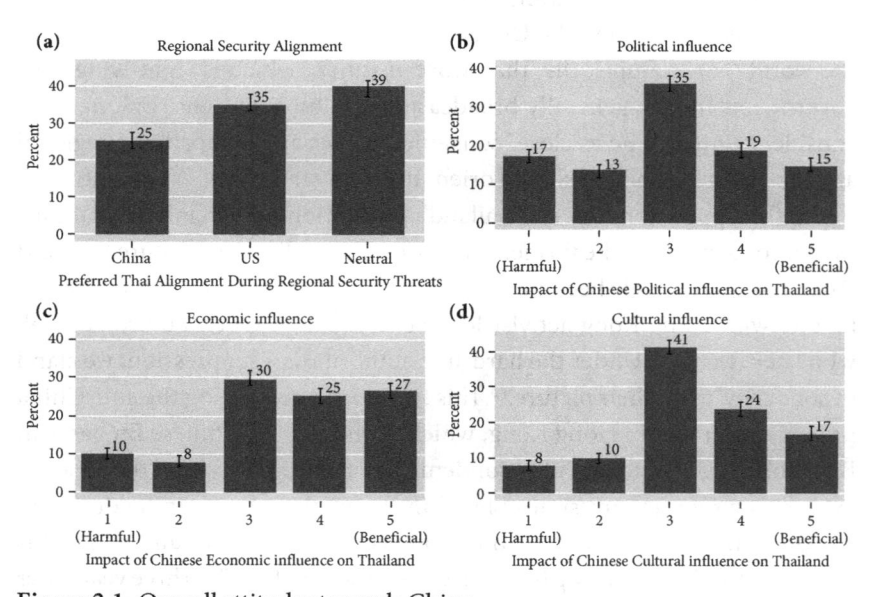

Figure 2.1 Overall attitudes towards China

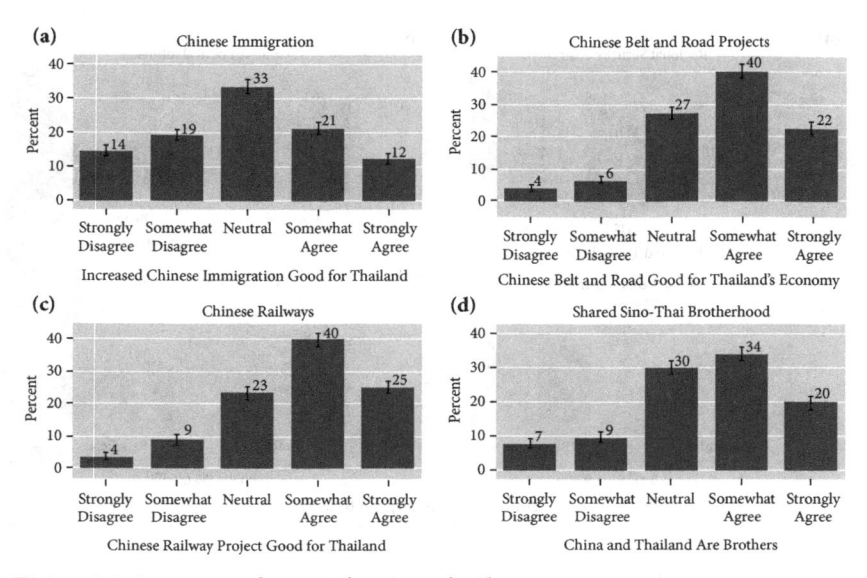

Figure 2.2 Issue-specific attitudes towards China

with China's BRI projects in the country and positively perceive the railway project and China-Thailand relations as friendly. On the other hand, people are more neutral on the issue of Chinese migration to Thailand, which perhaps indicate the complicated history of Chinese migration to the country, which will be the focus in Chapter 7.[77]

However, if we dig deeper to see what the perception of China and its influence on Thailand are conditioned upon, we can see that people's political orientation between autocracy and democracy is a powerful mediating mechanism. Specifically, we try to estimate people's preferences between autocracy and democracy through one question: "Do you think having a democratic political system is a good way of governing this country?" We then created a binary variable between those who prefer a more democratic political system versus those who are leaning more towards authoritarianism.[78] As we can see from Figure 2.3, people who are more pro-authoritarianism are more likely to support an alliance with China instead of the United States. They are also more likely to see China's positive influence in political, economic, and cultural domains than those who are more pro-democracy. Similarly, on the list of issue topics of China-Thailand relations, respondents' views are also bifurcated along the line of political orientation. From Figure 2.4, we can tell that people who are pro-democracy are much more unlikely to agree China

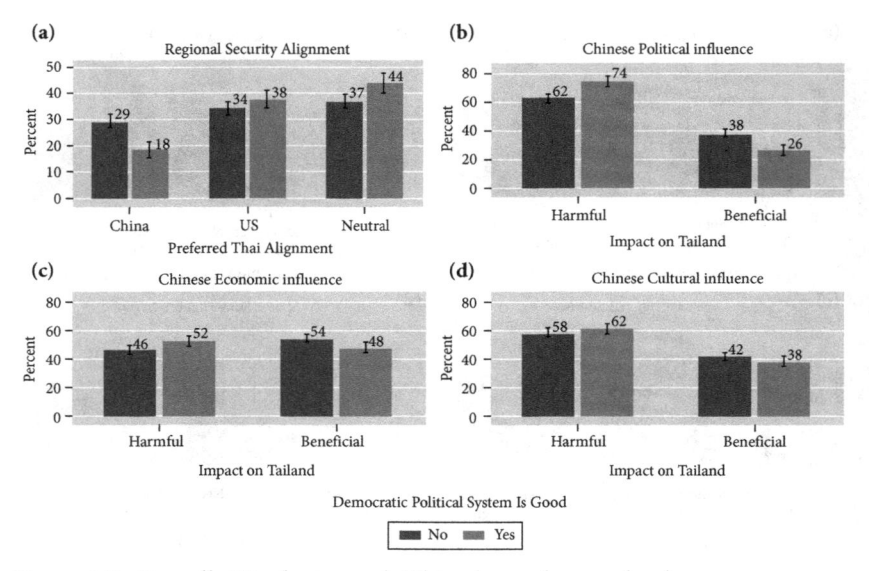

Figure 2.3 Overall attitudes towards China by preference for democracy

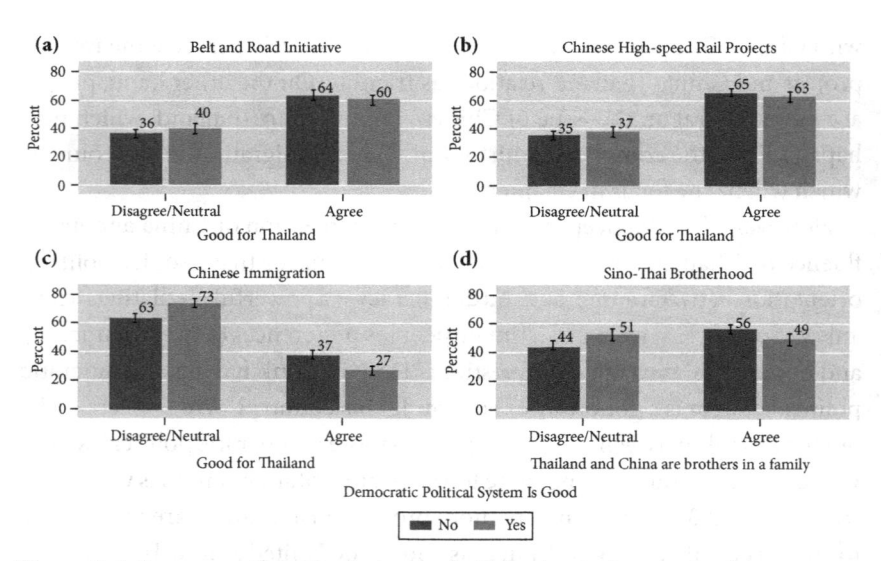

Figure 2.4 Issue-specific attitudes towards China by preference for democracy

and Thailand have brotherly relations, and they are also much less likely to see good value in Chinese migration to Thailand.

In Thailand's case, its domestic authoritarian turn and political polarization are mostly endogenous to the country itself.[79] It is a big stretch to imply that the military government's political hold on the country is because of Chinese support or through economic engagement with China as the cases of Myanmar and Cambodia, respectively, suggest. However, China has become a major talking point between those who support the authoritarian government and those who do not. Thus, the "China model" can be used to justify the military's continual control of politics because of the presumed political order and economic efficiency that authoritarian rule can bring to Thailand. For the opposition, on the other hand, they take every opportunity to criticize China and to denigrate the government for its authoritarian behavior. As long as the political polarization in Thailand continues, China will continue to be used by both sides of the political spectrum for their own political purposes.

Concluding Remarks

This chapter specifically discusses three modes of Chinese influence on authoritarian resilience in Southeast Asia. These three modes are not necessarily mutually exclusive, as the three cases discussed in the chapter show degrees of difference. Beijing has been extremely sensitive towards regime changes instigated by "foreign powers," which explains why it has offered shelter and protection for some notorious rogue regimes, such as the military junta in Myanmar. In the Myanmar case, Beijing's explicit support and recognition helped the SPDC survive when it was under Western sanctions. Although Beijing's intention is not necessarily to prolong the military government in Myanmar, its actions have achieved that result, nonetheless. In Cambodia's case, the China effect is more in terms of economic engagement, which helped to improve Hun Sen's regime governance. Finally, in Thailand's case, Chinese influence on authoritarianism in the country is more perfuse, and China's influence is more of a reference model the military uses to justify its continual rule.

However, China is an authoritarian state, and given its perceived efforts in prolonging its authoritarian neighbors, Beijing has become a target of domestic opposition forces and the public in general in a few Southeast

Asian countries. Particularly, in Myanmar's case there is strong anti-China sentiment, especially in the aftermath of the recent military coup. Beijing often seems to think its interests are best served by working closely with incumbents. This might be the case in most places, but in Myanmar, this approach probably will no longer work. As the country has descended into prolonged conflicts with popular resistance towards the military, Myanmar's perceived strategic value has also dwindled. Beijing should see that the key to its continued access to Myanmar, is Myanmar's domestic stability. Thus, Beijing should work together with the NUG to foster the country's regime transition, which would better serve bilateral relations for the longer term.

3

Trade, Investment, and Economic Influence

Introduction

The brand-new Vientiane railway station is glistening gold in the afternoon sun. The construction of the railway line linking the Lao Capital Vientiane and the Lao-China border town Boten was recently completed and was already in operation during the peak of the COVID-19 pandemic. This railway is Laos's first, and it was built by China Railway Group as part of China's BRI to increase infrastructure connectivity between Laos and Southeast Asia. Traveling at 160 km per hour, the high-speed rail (HSR) train can travel from Vientiane to Luang Prabang in less than two hours, a journey that previously would take a day or two on the winding mountainous roads. When the border officially opens after Beijing ends its zero-Covid policy, more tourists are expected to visit Laos and travel on this transitional railway linking China's Yunnan province with this land-locked country. Ultimately, the plan is to have the section in Thailand completed so that the HSR will be able to reach Bangkok, if not further down south to Kuala Lumpur or even Singapore.[1]

The HSR would certainly revolutionize how people understand geography and distance in Laos as well as provide connectivity with China and the rest of mainland Southeast Asia. Yet, in one of the least developed countries in the world, the railway project would certainly put heavy fiscal pressure on the Lao government to raise funds to pay for the project. Reports have shown that Laos has become heavily debt-dependent on China, and half of its external public debt, which was already at 66 percent of its GDP in 2021, is owed to China alone.[2] With talks about further Chinese economic investment in Laos, there is worry that Laos will become a vassal state of its northern neighbor.

Indeed, many Southeast Asian countries have seen the benefits of furthering economic cooperation with China. Economic engagement with

The Ripple Effect. Enze Han, Oxford University Press. © Oxford University Press 2024.
DOI: 10.1093/oso/9780197696583.003.0003

China, the dynamite engine of economic growth in the region, has been the dominant foreign policy choice for many regional governments in recent decades. China has been the largest trading partner for almost all countries in Southeast Asia as well as one of their main FDI sources. China's BRI and its push for infrastructure investment and connectivity has also been welcomed since many countries in the region urgently need to upgrade their infrastructure. At the same time, they are also keenly aware of the danger of becoming overly dependent on China and have tried to diversify their partnership by taking advantage of the ongoing competition between the United States and China. Indeed, many countries have become beneficiaries of the ongoing trade war between the two superpowers when the relocation of manufacturers' supply chains and the patterns of capital flows have now centered on Southeast Asia.

This chapter provides a general overview of China's economic influence in Southeast Asia, with a focus on the overall trade patterns between the two as well as the ongoing trend for Chinese investment in Southeast Asia, particularly in infrastructure development and a few key industries. It looks at a few prominent infrastructure projects that China has pushed in the region, such as the HSRs in Laos, Thailand, as well as Malaysia. It also examines how Chinese investments in Southeast Asia take advantage of special economic zones (SEZs) that some regional governments have set up with a detailed discussion of the Rayong Industrial Park (RIP) in Thailand. Although much Chinese investment might be the relocation of manufacturing from China to Southeast Asia, as a result of its upgrade of the industrial value chain and to bypass the ongoing trade war between Beijing and Washington, there are also certain key industries that we can see clearly that Chinese capital envisions expanding to Southeast Asia, such as electric vehicles (EV) industry. What we are witnessing, despite the slump during COVID-19, is an increasingly more integrated China-Southeast Asia in terms of economic cooperation.

Trade Integration between China and ASEAN

In 2008–2009, mainland China became ASEAN's largest trading partner, overtaking Japan, the European Union (EU), and the United States. This event fits the overall global trend when made-in-China products flooded markets around the world. However, in 2020, for the first time the ten ASEAN countries as a whole became China's largest trading partner. As we can see from Figure 3.1, by 2020, the total trade volume between ASEAN and China was nearly equivalent to all of ASEAN's entire trade with the United States, EU, and Japan combined. As we can also see from Figures 3.2 and 3.3, there has been a noticeable increase in imports from Southeast Asia to China compared to Chinese exports to Southeast Asia. This import data indicates that bilateral trade is much more balanced and perhaps more beneficial to Southeast Asia than China's trade with the West in general.

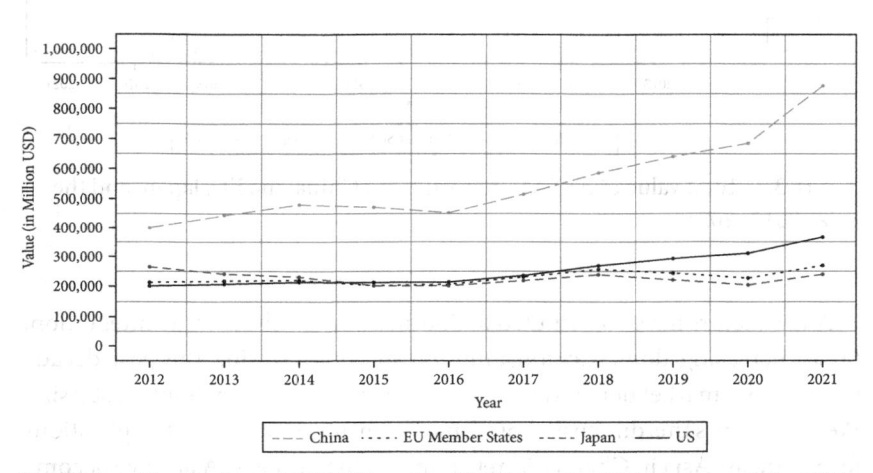

Figure 3.1 Total value of ASEAN trade with China, the EU, Japan, and the USA, 2012–2021

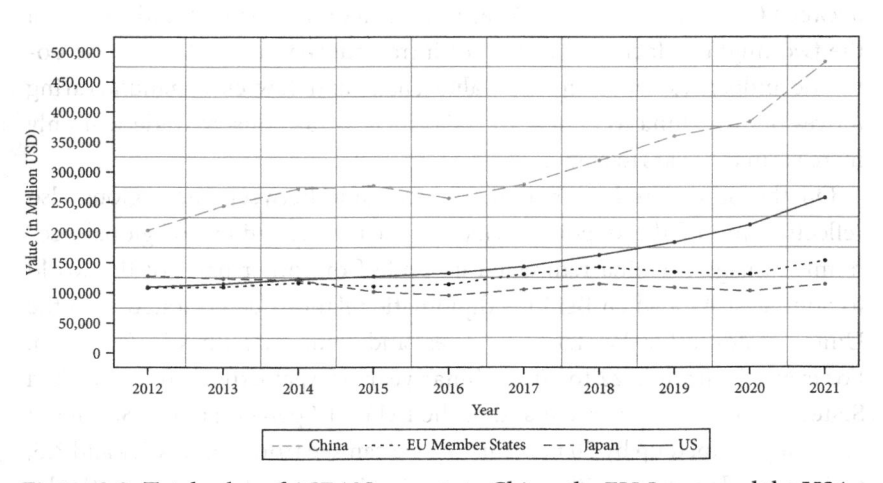

Figure 3.2 Total value of ASEAN exports to China, the EU, Japan, and the USA, 2012–2021

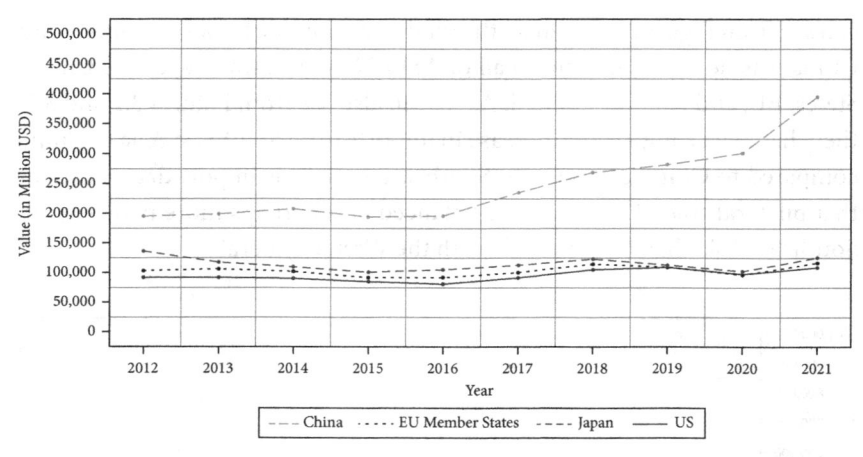

Figure 3.3 Total value of ASEAN imports from China, the EU, Japan, and the USA, 2012–2021

A few factors have contributed to Southeast Asia-China trade integration. First, increasing domestic consumption in China during the past decade means more market demand for agricultural products from Southeast Asia.[3] We will discuss this dimension of Chinese consumption-related implications for Southeast Asia in Chapter 5. Yet countries in Southeast Asia have become major suppliers of raw materials and energy for China's industrial sectors. Furthermore, there is an ongoing momentum to integrate the supply-chain between China and Southeast Asia, and much of the bilateral trade between the two might in fact be this kind of intra-industry trade. As Chinese domestic industries move up the value chain and low-end manufacturing moves out of China to Southeast Asia, such intra-industry trade will only increase in the years to come.

On the other hand, increased trade volume between the regions also reflects some of the ongoing dynamics in the reshuffling of global economic linkages.[4] China redirected its trade from other parts of the world to Southeast Asia when Beijing's diplomatic relations deteriorated with the United States, other Western countries, and some U.S.-allies in East Asia. For example, from 2022 to 2021 China's year-on-year exports to the United States dropped by 19 percent and to the EU by 17 percent; but to Southeast Asia they jumped up by 20 percent.[5] As we can see from Figures 3.4 and 3.5, Chinese trade volume with Vietnam, Malaysia, and Indonesia in particular

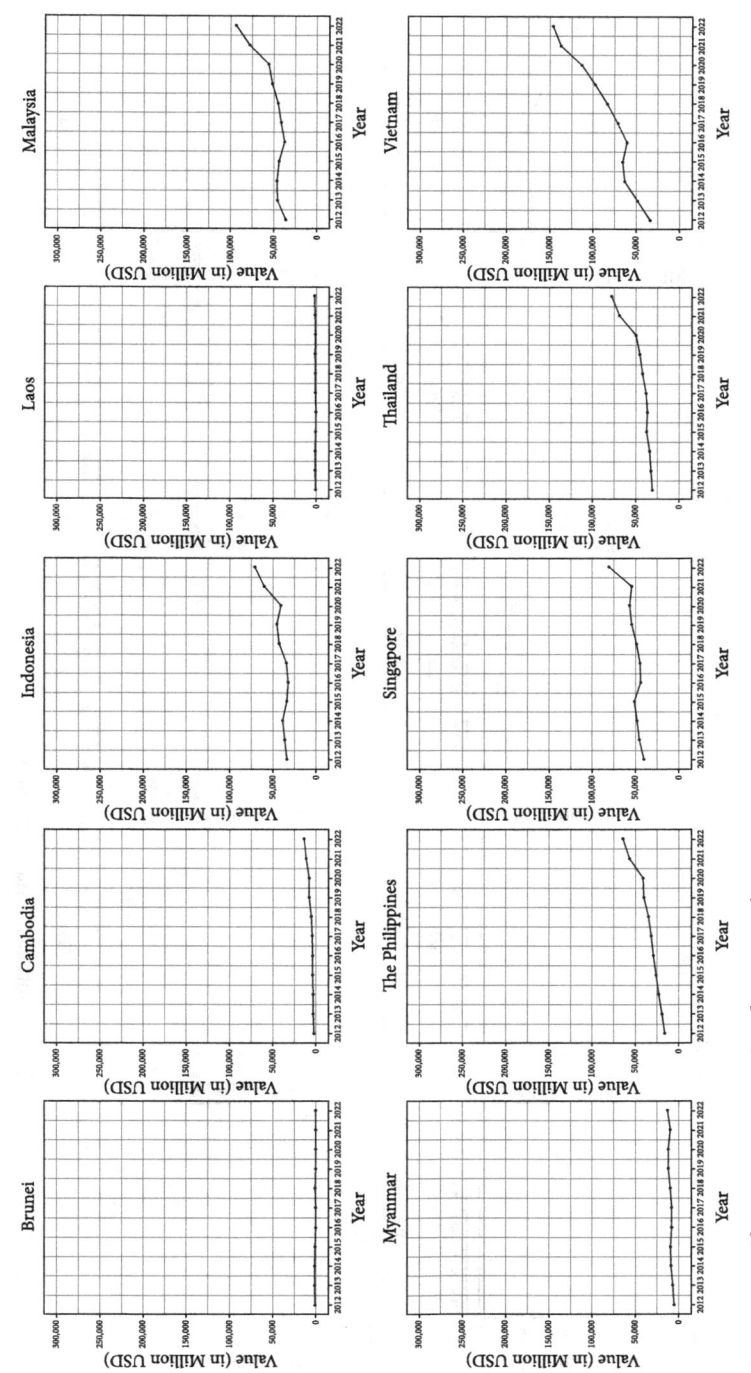

Figure 3.4 Chinese exports to Southeast Asia by country

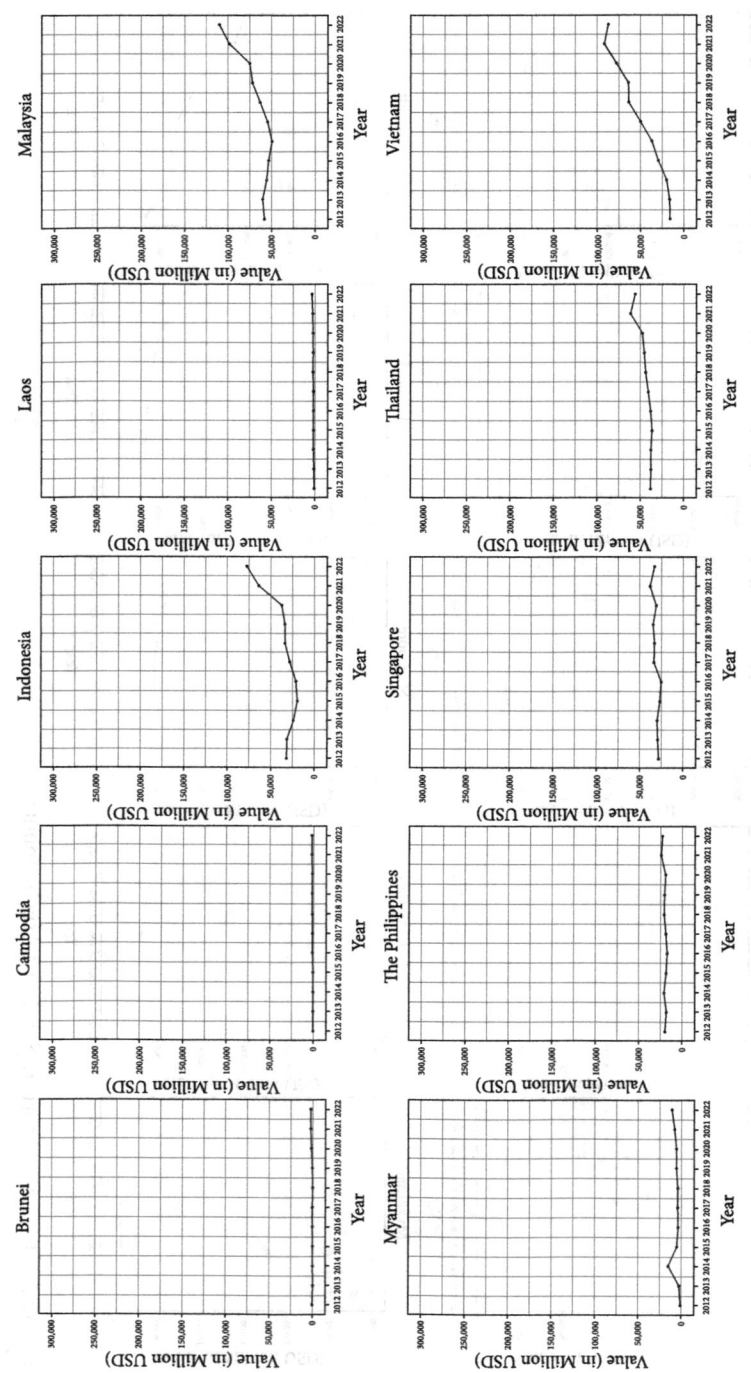

Figure 3.5 Chinese imports from Southeast Asia by country

has picked up considerably in the last few years. Indeed, currently, Vietnam is China's largest trading partner within Southeast Asia.

At least two trade-related issues are manifestations of deteriorating relations between China and the United States, in particular. The first is the ongoing sanctions on agricultural products from Xinjiang, such as cotton. The other is the trade war and the additional tariffs on Chinese trade to the United States imposed since the Trump administration. These two issues have led to a rerouting of Chinese products to Southeast Asia where they will be re-exported to the West; Vietnam is a popular destination for such practices.

One type of re-exporting, called "cotton laundering," occurs when Xinjiang cotton is exported to a third country to be re-exported to the United States or Europe to evade sanctions.[6] After the U.S. Congress passed the Uyghur Forced Labor Prevention Act effective as of December 2021, any products made in Xinjiang are presumed to be made through "forced labor of the Muslim minority" and, therefore, it is the duty of downstream manufacturers and retailers to apply due diligence to verify the origins of the cotton used.[7] In Southeast Asia, Vietnam has been a leading importer of Xinjiang cotton for the garment industries in the country. And it seems that many companies would evade U.S. law by mixing Xinjiang cotton with other cottons, which would be extremely difficult to verify.

Many manufacturers in Southeast Asia rely upon unfinished cotton products from China. According to a report prepared by Sheffield Hallam University in the United Kingdom, although the United States remained the largest consumer of finished apparel from China, China exports large quantities of raw cotton, yarn, and fabric to Southeast Asian countries such as Cambodia, Indonesia, the Philippines, and Vietnam. As importers of semi-finished cotton goods from China, manufacturers in these countries serve as intermediaries in finishing cotton-based apparel by attaching a different label on the finished products.[8] For example, the finished apparel will be labeled "Made in Vietnam," obfuscating the cotton's origin. Yet it is difficult to establish how much Xinjiang cotton or other products are re-exported to the West via Southeast Asia.

Similarly, when the Trump administration imposed across-the-board additional tariffs on Chinese products to the United States, there were reports that Chinese goods were rerouted through Southeast Asia to dodge those tariffs.[9] In fact, trade-rerouting has been a common practice for Chinese companies dealing with Western countries' anti-dumping duties. This practice refers to the indirect export of goods via a third country with an illegal change in the certificate of origin from China to that country to evade tariffs.[10]

Vietnam, for example, has been a frequent transit site for relabeled Chinese goods. Its customs highlighted "textiles, fisheries, farm products, tiles, honey, iron, steel and plywood" as among the most frequently relabeled products.[11] The Vietnamese government even passed Resolution 199 to deal with combatting and preventing such origin fraud and illegal transshipment through Vietnam. According to a Vietnamese government report, in the first six months of 2020, one-third of exporters were found to violate regulations on rules of origin, and a total of US$1.42 million in sanctions were imposed on those violators.[12]

Many violations are also reported in other Southeast Asian countries. Particularly, where there is a concentration of Chinese investment, some companies are probably there just to transship goods from China, not for manufacturing. For example, in the Sihanoukville SEZ in Cambodia, many Chinese companies that supposedly invested there are in fact engaged in the transshipment of China-made products camouflaged as Cambodia-made.[13] A few companies were put under investigation by U.S. Customs and Border Protection for possible evasion of U.S. tariffs and other anti-dumping measures targeted at China. As the trade war between the two countries has not seen any sign of easing under the Biden administration, such practices will continue, and they perhaps even account for some of the increased volume of trade between China and ASEAN countries in recent years. Thus, one can argue that the trade war has had the effect of redirecting Chinese trade to the United States via ASEAN.

At the same time, the Regional Comprehensive Economic Partnership (RCEP), which includes all ASEAN countries, China, South Korea, and Japan as well as Australia and New Zealand, came into effect in 2022. As the largest free trade agreement in the world, although its long-term effect in liberalizing regional trade is not yet apparent, the RCEP potentially has the effect of mitigating the effect of the ongoing U.S.-China trade war. According to a working paper on the topic, the RCEP will reorient trade and economic ties among member states and will "make larger contributions to global and regional welfare in the context of a trade war than under business-as-before assumptions."[14] Thus, China and Southeast Asia will experience further trade integration in the years to come.

Investment, BRI, and Infrastructure Connectivity

In addition to trade integration, China has also become one of the largest FDI sources for Southeast Asia for the past decade, as we can see from Figure 3.6.[15] Although the top three FDI sources for Southeast Asia continue to be the United States, EU, and Japan, Chinese FDI has been catching up its share in select countries in the region. By the end of 2020, six of the top twenty Chinese FDI destination countries were in Southeast Asia, including Singapore (fifth position), Indonesia (eighth), Malaysia (sixteenth), Laos (seventeenth), Thailand (nineteenth), and Vietnam (twentieth).[16] The lion's share of such FDI was in financial and insurance activities (24%), real estate (21%), and manufacturing (16.2%) from 2016 to 2020.

As we can see from Figure 3.7, the larger economies in Southeast Asia tend to receive more Chinese FDI. The significant fluctuations in the out-flow of Chinese capital might have more to do with domestic politics and capital control within China than with the country's relations with Southeast Asia. Other than Myanmar, Chinese FDI seems to have an overall upward trajectory. As the political crisis in Myanmar continues, Chinese FDI to the country will certainly see a descending trend in the years to come. Other than Singapore, it seems that more Chinese FDI has gone to Indonesia, Malaysia, Thailand, and Vietnam in recent years, which perhaps indicates some indus-trial relocation from China to these countries. Also notable is Laos, which

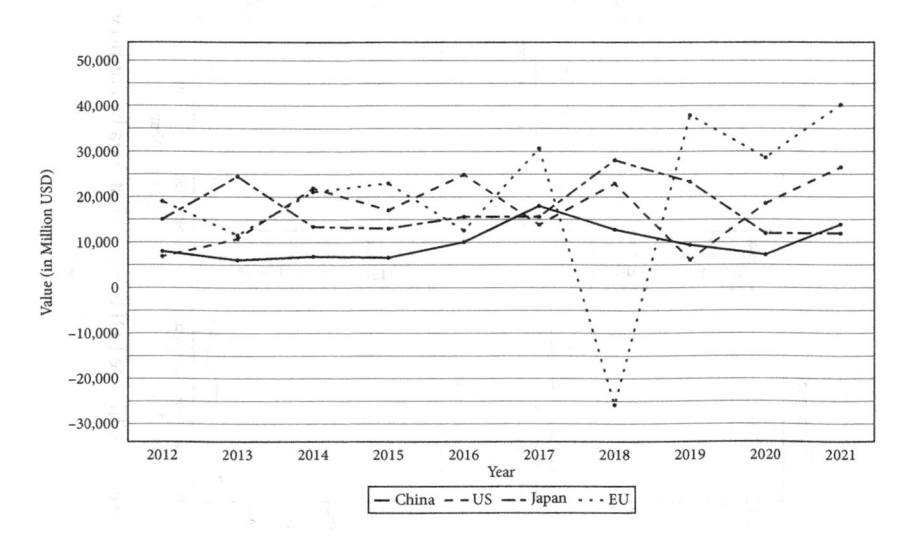

Figure 3.6 FDI to Southeast Asia

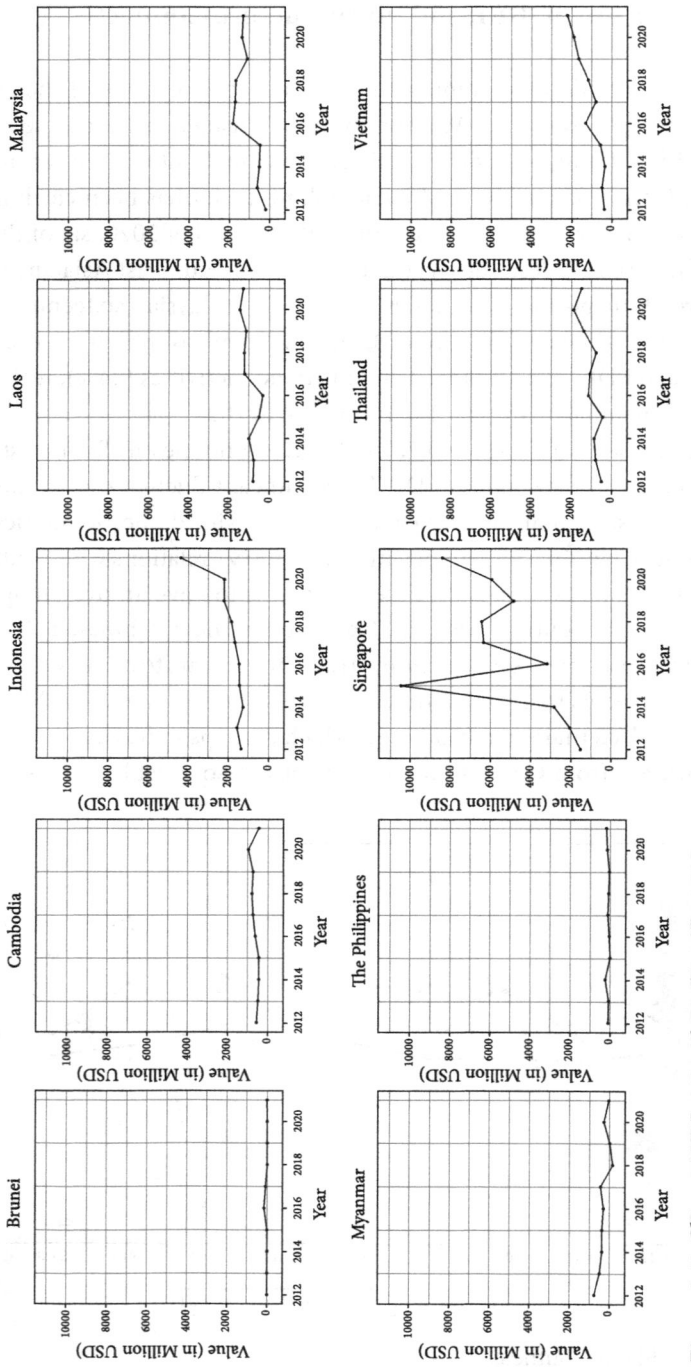

Figure 3.7 Chinese FDI to Southeast Asia by country

as a small economy received significant amounts of Chinese FDI, obviously including the China-Laos railway project but also other investment opportunities in the country.

As the financial center of Southeast Asia, Singapore is a top choice for Chinese FDI in the region. In fact, FDI from Hong Kong to Singapore is higher than from mainland China, which historically has been the case, and Hong Kong is also a transitory point for mainland Chinese capital. For example, in 2021, FDI from Hong Kong to Singapore was 91,179.6 million SGD, while FDI from the Chinese mainland was 50,073.5 million SGD.[17] Yet it seems that the FDI flow from Hong Kong to Singapore accelerated after 2019, perhaps driven by the political unrest in the city that year. Rumor has it that much of the capital flight from Hong Kong was in fact private mainland Chinese capital that feared Beijing's tightening control of Hong Kong. At the same time, many Chinese companies use offshore accounts in the Cayman Islands and British Virgin Islands to invest in Singapore. Indeed, these two offshore territories ranked second and third on the list of FDI sources for Singapore. It is no surprise that two Chinese tech giants, Alibaba and Tencent, which have invested heavily in Singapore, are both incorporated in the Cayman Islands. Therefore, although there is no exact data, the actual amount of mainland Chinese FDI to Singapore should be much higher than the official statistics.

Many Chinese companies chose Singapore for its geographical location and the country's professional knowledge to access the Southeast Asian region. Particularly for many of China's BRI projects in Southeast Asia, Singapore is clearly the place to go for financial services, such as risk management and fund raising from private capital.[18] Given that 60 percent of ASEAN projects are financed through Singapore-based banks, Chinese banks, such as the China Construction Bank and Bank of China, have issued bonds through their Singapore branches.[19] As the largest offshore RMB clearing center, Singapore is thus the ideal place to act as the intermediary for Chinese investment expansion throughout Southeast Asia.

Meanwhile, a few leading Chinese private tech companies have also chosen Singapore as their regional headquarters for Southeast Asia, among them Alibaba, Tencent, and ByteDance. Alibaba acquired control of Singapore-based Lazada in 2016, which is the largest e-commerce platform in the Southeast Asian region, covering Malaysia, the Philippines, Singapore, Thailand, and Vietnam.[20] This acquisition integrated the e-commerce market within Alibaba's ecosystem by linking Chinese merchants with their customers in Southeast Asia. Tencent also set up regional headquarters in Singapore and invested in game development and digital banking.[21] ByteDance, which owns TikTok, also uses Singapore as a beachhead for other parts of Asia.[22]

The expansion of these Chinese tech companies to Singapore can be interpreted in two ways. First, they are private companies, and have in fact faced Beijing's political pressure in cracking down on the tech industry. Alibaba in particular, once touted as the most successful example of a Chinese tech company, became the target of a political purge, due to the perceived threat it posed to China's state-owned banks and its monetary authority.[23] On the other hand, other Chinese tech companies chose Singapore when their business expansion in the West became targeted by political pressure from Washington because of its relatively neutral stance between China and the United States, particularly on issues such as data security. Thus, with the intensification of great power competition, Singapore's unique international status is arguably more attractive for Chinese firms to diversify and even move away from places such as Hong Kong, which is now considered as having already lost some of its presumed autonomy from Beijing.

Unlike Singapore, already a developed economy, other Southeast Asian countries need Chinese investment more, particularly in the infrastructure sector. According to Ho, within Southeast Asia, there is a general "agreement with the idea that infrastructure brings progress, development and modernization."[24] This understanding is why Southeast Asia as a whole has occupied an important position in China's overall BRI strategy for its so-called "Maritime Silkroad."[25] Although the BRI in many instances has taken on additional meanings or has been used too literally as almost equivalent to Chinese foreign policy in general,[26] in Southeast Asia, China's focus on infrastructure investment has made solid progress. Indeed, China has invested in or shown interest in investing in many infrastructure projects, ranging from railway to highway, and ports to hydroelectric dams. The most ambitious of all is the so-called Pan-Asian Railway, which aims to connect Kunming in China's Southwestern Yunnan Province with Singapore via Laos, Thailand, and Malaysia. Despite many uncertainties and hiccups along the way, there has been solid progress towards making the future of transnational railway connectivity in mainland Southeast Asia a possibility.

Among the Pan-Asian Railway countries, Laos has been the most enthusiastic about the railway project as its ruling communist party aims to transform the country from a land-locked to a land-linked economy.[27] However, the potential cost of such a large infrastructure project is prohibitive for a poor country such as Laos, and much of it would have to be financed through loans.[28] The total cost of the Lao section of the railway is estimated at around US$6 billion, of which 40 percent will be provided by a joint-venture company by both the Chinese and Lao governments, while the remaining 60 percent will be loaned from the Export-Import Bank of China. Additionally, within the joint venture, the Lao counterpart holds a 30 percent stake, while three Chinese SOEs hold the other 70 percent. Even within the Lao government's stake, a further US$480 million was borrowed from the Export-Import Bank of China, with its natural resources used as collateral.[29] Such heavy borrowing thus adds significant pressure to Laos's national budget, and has led to speculation that Laos is falling under China's "debt-trap."

Despite all the external criticisms since the start of construction and the shock of the COVID-19 pandemic, the railway project somehow finished on time. On the opening day of the railway on December 3, 2021, Thongloun Sisoulith, general secretary of the Lao People's Revolutionary Party (LPRP) and president of Laos, expressed his hope that the project would bring positive changes to his country:

Thanks to China's strong support, Laos has finally bid farewell to the days without trains and now has a modern railway. The Laos-China Railway is a bond deeply docking the Laos' development strategy to convert itself from a land-locked country to a land-linked country with the Belt and Road Initiative, and an important milestone in Laos' modern infrastructure construction. The railway will greatly promote Laos' national economic and social development.[30]

A few months later, when Thongloun took a ride of the train from Vientiane to Boten, he offered a positive evaluation of the experience and his hope that it would facilitate people-to-people exchanges between Laos and China and that the Lao people would feel proud of such achievement.[31]

However, because of the border restrictions during the COVID-19 pandemic, during the first year of the China-Laos railway's operation, passenger trains operated in two separate sections, one within the Chinese border and the other within the Lao border. There are also differences in the number of trains in operation every day. For example, the Chinese section is in operation with an average of thirty-six trains per day, while the Lao section operates only six to eight trains per day.[32] So far, passenger trains within China's Yunnan province are more frequent than within Laos itself. For example, in September 2022, 5.87 million passengers rode the train within the Chinese section but only 840,000 in the Lao section. This certainly reflects the demographic differences between the two countries, but also the reality of cross-border passenger travel while China's zero-COVID policy was still in place. Thus, with the lifting of China's border restriction policy, it is expected that cross-border passenger volume will surely pick up. Finally, the cross-border passenger trains started in April 2023.

On the other hand, domestic train ridership is constrained by Laos's relatively small population, but tourists from Lao's neighbor Thailand have made use of the new railway to visit popular tourist destinations within Laos.[33] With Thailand open for international tourism after a short interval of border closure, we will probably see tourists from outside the region using the railway to visit Laos. It is also expected that after the border opening, more Chinese tourists will also travel to Thailand via the railway in Laos, further boosting its passenger volume.

As well as passenger trains, the railway also operates cross-border cargo trains between Laos and China. According to a World Bank report, the railway will significantly reduce land transport price by 40 percent to 50 percent between Kunming and Vientiane and by 32 percent between Kunming and the Port of Laem Chabang in Thailand.[34] Given that 20 percent of Laos's exported goods are agricultural products, such as cassava, banana, and rubber, the cargo trains linking with China would considerably reduce logistical costs for Laos's export sector. It is also expected that the mineral sector will witness a major boost with the easing of transportation bottlenecks within mountainous Laos.[35]

Because cargo trains were not as affected by the pandemic as passenger trains, their operation has boosted cross-border trade between China and Thailand via Laos. For example, Thailand shipped its first agricultural products of 1,000 tons of glutinous rice in January 2022 and shipped 500 tons of durian in April 2022.[36] In fact, a special cold-chain train for fruits came into operation in December 2022, which would further increase Thai fruit exports to China over land, reducing the transportation time by sea and maintaining freshness.[37] Given the overall larger trade volume between China and Thailand, the cargo trains would be more useful to Thailand than Laos itself.

Although the railway in Laos was already in operation, the proposed Thai section connecting Bangkok with the Thai border city Nong Khai and then the Lao section is facing many delays. The negotiation of the Thai section with the Chinese has been particularly cumbersome. As Oh points out, in a few Southeast Asian countries' negotiations with China on railway projects, "the bargaining outcome will depend on whether outside options are available, the differing patience levels of the negotiating partners, and domestic political constraints."[38] These factors have slowed the project's progress.

For example, the Thai government understood from the very beginning that the Chinese wanted this railway more than themselves. Especially after the Lao section's construction, Bangkok clearly had the upper hand because the Lao section has limited value if it is not connected with Thailand. At the time of the negotiation with Beijing, the Thai government was simultaneously negotiating with Japan on a separate high-speed railway linking Bangkok and Chiang Mai, which they used as a pressure point to bargain with the Chinese.[39] Finally, the government led by PM Prayuth had to balance a few competing interests among its coalition parties and faced more domestic opposition.

In the end, Thailand managed to reach a deal with China without financing from the latter, and thus is the project's sole investor. Instead, China would provide the technology and offer advice on the railway system's operation. One significant politically sensitive issue was the use of Chinese labor, and Chinese workers will not be used in the construction after all.[40] Although an agreement was reached in 2016, Thai counterparts have repeatedly tried to renegotiate and have dragged their feet on construction. For example, the construction of the 609 km railway has been divided into two phases, which each phase further divided into more than ten contracts.[41] It almost seems that the Thai government is awarding different contracts to various special interests to make everyone happy in this huge and lucrative project.

Yet so far, only 3.5 km of the first phase linking Bangkok to Nakhon Ratchasima has been completed. The Thai government gives various reasons for delays, such as environmental impact analysis, the need to find bidders, and so on. But ultimately, the Thai side lacks commitment to the project, influenced by the project's high costs and the danger of being too closely intertwined with China.[42] This is, of course, the Thai tradition to seek balance in its foreign policy.[43] But ultimately, the railway if built cannot be easily removed, and for such sunk costs the Thai government would have to decide when the Chinese pressure comes to bear.

Indeed, the Chinese seem impatient with the lack of progress in the railway's Thai section. In July 2022, after Chinese State Councilor Wang Yi's visit to Bangkok, Thai PM Prayuth finally announced that the target year for railway project to be in operation is 2028. Whether it will be finished by then is anyone's guess. At the time of writing, a new national election is called for May 2023, and depending on the line up of political parties and the special interests that they represent, the future of the railway is far from certain.

Compared with the slow progress of the Thai section, there is no answer to whether the railway will ever be extended south of Bangkok and what will happen with the Malaysian section. The Malaysian section, the 688 km East Coast Rail Link, was supposed to connect Port Klang in the Strait of Malacca with Kota Bharu in northeast Peninsular Malaysia. Although the governments of China and Malaysia had reached an agreement, Malaysia's 2018 election led to a major shift in political power. The project's legitimacy was contested because of its high cost, and the public was mobilized against the Chinese investment.[44] After Mahathir won the election and became the new prime minister, he announced the suspension of the railway project. Indeed, this case has been portrayed as an example of a developing country pushing back against China's "debt-driven" BRI.[45]

However, the suspension was merely a tactic to pressure the Chinese to renegotiate. In April 2019, the Malaysian government managed to sign a revised deal with China to cut the project's cost from $16 billion to $11 billion. Mahathir claimed that "we chose to go back to the negotiation table and call for a more equitable deal, whereby the needs of Malaysian people would be prioritized."[46] Although there have been a few changes to the Malaysian government with party reshuffling and a new national election in 2022, it seems now that construction work for the railway is making reasonable progress. According to news reports, about 37 percent of the work was completed by December 2022, and it is expected to start operating in January 2027.[47]

Therefore, it seems overall that China's plan for railway connectivity on the Southeast Asian mainland will probably be realized one day, albeit later and slower than originally planned. For such large infrastructure projects, perhaps it is not reasonable to use profitability to judge their value, and we will have to see the long-term effect they will bring for increased domestic and transnational connectivity. Once complete, the flow of goods and people across national boundaries among these countries would probably be unprecedented, and there would be further economic integration. While some people might benefit from such integration between Southeast Asian countries and China, others might worry about their over-dependence on China and the issue of demographic pressure caused by the arrivals of more Chinese tourists and other types of migrants. This will be further discussed in Chapter 7.

Special Economic Zones

Other than investing in infrastructure, Chinese companies, both state-owned and private, have participated in the development of SEZs in the region. The SEZs, including industrial parks, special export processing zones, technology parks, and innovation areas, remain an attractive policy tool for many developing economies, including Southeast Asian ones. Indeed, almost all Southeast Asian countries have expanded the number of SEZs to attract business investment. For example, since 2015, Thailand has started development of ten SEZs; Indonesia has thirteen, the Philippines has twelve, and Cambodia has thirty-one SEZs.[48] Some SEZs are specifically designated for Chinese investors.

As for China, SEZs have been critical to its own economic development story, and have been attributed, in part, to China's industrial policy success for the past few decades.[49] Yet recently the Chinese government and domestic industries have been actively involved in setting up many SEZs abroad, which have been associated with several strategic objectives put forth by the Chinese government. Generally, other than the specific geostrategic intention attached to the BRI, economically these zones have been envisioned to help increase demand for Chinese machinery and equipment as well as provide post-sale support. During trade friction, these overseas SEZs can provide exports to Europe and North America to bypass trade barriers imposed on China, which happened during the trade war between the United States and China discussed earlier. They can also help restructure the Chinese domestic industrial value chain by moving low-end productions abroad and can provide opportunities for small and medium enterprises to go abroad to create economies of scale for overseas investment. Further, in some situations, overseas SEZs can also provide a working model based on China's own success story of economic growth for other developing economies to learn from.[50]

For these purposes, the Chinese government has selected a list of SEZs in Southeast Asia as targeted destinations for investment, including Kawasan

Industri Terpadu Indonesia-China, Sihanoukville Special Economic Zone in Cambodia, Thailand-China Rayong Industrial Park, Longjiang Industrial Park in Vietnam, Vientiane Saysettha Development Zone in Laos, and Malaysia-China Kuantan Industrial Park.[51] Generally, these SEZs have a variety of models regarding local partnerships; level of financial commitments; managerial, development, and marketing roles; and openness to non-Chinese companies. Here, I will focus on the Rayong Thai-China Industrial Park (RIP) in Thailand, which is located within Thailand's Eastern Economic Corridor (EEC) as an example.

As the first Chinese overseas industrial site in Thailand, the RIP was officially launched on July 1, 2005, when the China Holley Group and the Thailand Amata Group signed an agreement to develop an industrial site at Rayong Province in Eastern Thailand. The project covers the construction of an area approximately 12 square kilometers. The industrial zone was envisioned to become an overseas "industrial Chinatown," offering Chinese enterprises a way to access the world stage while furthering economic cooperation between the two countries. The new site is expected to accommodate more than 300 companies and will create upwards of 100,000 jobs in Thailand.[52]

In line with the BRI's emphasis on sustainable development, the RIP adopted a rule mandating that all enterprises build their facilities in accordance with ISO environmental management standards as well as local environmental standards.[53] And to reduce Chinese firms' investment risk in Thailand, a team of both Chinese and Thai experts was assembled to provide professional services such as target market research and policy consulting. The RIP has since become China's largest industrial cluster center and manufacturing export base in Thailand.[54] As of late 2018, the industrial park has attracted a total investment of US$3.5 billion and is home to more than 120 Chinese-owned companies. The zone's gross industrial output value reached $12 billion by the end of 2018, and it employs more than 35,000 people, mostly Thai nationals.[55]

A few key factors have been instrumental in incentivizing investment by Chinese manufacturers in the RIP. First, to avoid anti-dumping and anti-subsidy probes by Western countries, companies relocate part of their production lines from China to Thailand to help them secure more export orders and continue selling to the U.S. market without paying extra tariffs imposed during the trade war, as mentioned earlier. Second, these companies can take advantage of local natural resources and human capital. Third, some Chinese companies are intending to expand into the Southeast Asian market, so they are moving their production lines to boost capacity and to be closer to their market in the region.

The RIP is also part of Thailand's Development Strategy of Thailand 4.0 that centers on an EEC development concept. On February 1, 2018, the Thai parliament passed a legislative act officially declaring the EEC open for trade and investment.[56] The EEC straddles three eastern provinces of Thailand— Chonburi, Rayong, and Chachoengsao—and spans a total of 13,285 square kilometers. The Thai government has identified four pivotal areas essential in making the EEC a highly productive economic zone: (1) increased and improved infrastructure; (2) business, industrial clusters, and innovation hubs; (3) tourism; and (4) the creation of new cities through smart urban planning.[57] Overall, the EEC aims to attract approximately US$50 billion in foreign investment focused on the key "S-curve" industries of next genera- tion automotive, aviation and logistics, smart electronics, medical tourism, food, robotics, agriculture, and biotechnology. As of April 2018, 259 direct investments in the EEC region totaling close to US$10 billion have been approved: 133 projects in Chonburi valued at US$3.76 billion, ninety-three projects in Rayong valued at US$5.22 billion, and thirty-three projects in Chachoengsao valued at US$970 million.[58]

Indeed, there is significant synergy between the EEC and some Chinese companies' goal of expanding their export markets in Thailand and beyond. For example, Chinese e-commerce giant Alibaba is amongst the prominent investors in the EEC, committing more than US$320 million to set up a "digital hub" in the zone that aims to make Thailand the logistics base for e- commerce, linking small and medium enterprises from Thailand and neigh- boring countries with the Chinese market and the global market.[59] Similarly, China's second-biggest e-commerce firm JD.com has also partnered with Thailand's Central Group for a US$500 million joint venture on e-commerce and fintech.[60] Given the level of sophistication of China's e-commerce, there is huge potential for their expansion in mainland Southeast Asia using Thailand as a hub.

Expansion of Chinese EV Industry in Southeast Asia

Chinese companies are also expanding rapidly in Thailand's EV industry. Given that Thailand is already the production hub for the largest number of commercial vehicles in ASEAN, there is great production capacity for Thailand to switch to the EV industry as well. The Thai government has already set a goal of ensuring that by 2030, 30 percent of its total auto production output is EVs, and by 2035 all new cars will be EVs. Thailand is also already the leading market for EVs in Southeast Asia.[61] To achieve this goal, the Thai government has recently provided tax incentives to attract EV makers to invest in the country.

At the same time, the Chinese EV industry has caught up quickly and is now one of the leading players in the world. In some parts of the world, Chinese EV exports have already surpassed other competitors. The push to set up EV production centers in Thailand can not only increase exports within Southeast Asia but also lessen their exposure to geopolitical conflict between China and the United States. In September 2022, the Chinese company BYD, the largest EV maker in the world, concluded a deal with WHA Group, a Thailand industrial estates developer, to produce and sell EVs in Thailand. The deal involves using Thai plants with an annual capacity of 150,000 vehicles to produce BYD EVs.[62] Separately, BYD also announced a partnership with Thailand car retailer Rever to sell EV for Thai domestic use.[63] The US$491 million facility will be located in Rayong and will begin manufacturing in 2024.

Other than BYD, a few other Chinese EV makers are also making waves in Thailand. For example, China's Great Wall Motor (GWM) acquired a production plant in Rayong from General Motors in 2020 and has since started producing EVs in Thailand. Between January and September 2022, GWM reportedly sold 8,094 EVs in Thailand, making it the country's largest EV seller in terms of sales volume.[64] In December 2022, another Chinese EV maker Aiways won an order for up to 150,000 EVs from a Thai e-mobility service provider Phoenix EV to be delivered in the coming five years, marking the largest EV order from Chinese carmakers and setting a strong foundation for its Southeast Asian strategy.[65] It seems that there is a consensus among major Chinese EV makers that Thailand is a good place to start and base their operations within Southeast Asia.

Indeed, the EV market in Southeast Asia is booming, and according to a forecast by the International Renewable Agency, the EV market in Southeast Asia will have 10 million units by 2025.[66] For such a large market, the comparative advantage of Chinese EVs is their relatively low price, which is important given Southeast Asia's overall relatively low income level. Currently, Japanese cars dominate the combustion vehicle market while American brand Tesla is more of a high-end product. Thus, a huge vacuum exists in the affordable EV market that the Chinese are dominating. Such price competitiveness is partly due to the Chinese government's supportive policy that "backed the production of smaller, affordable EVs and their most expensive component, batteries."[67] Thus, as a whole, the Chinese EV industry is very competitive for the developing world market, such as in Southeast Asia, where it faces few competitors.

Indeed, Chinese EV exports to Southeast Asia have soared during the past five years. In 2017, for example, the value of Chinese EV exports to Southeast Asia for private transport was only US$6.9 million; export value has since increased almost 100 times to US$645 million in 2022, of which Thailand took the lion's share of US$456.6 million.[68] Other than Thailand, the main Chinese EV exports destinations are Singapore at US$84.6 million, the Philippines at US$41.9 million, and Malaysia at US$20 million in 2022. Other than private transport, China also exports EV busses to Southeast Asia valued at US$96.5 million in 2022, of which US$73 million also went to Thailand.

Meanwhile, many Southeast Asian countries, in addition to Thailand, have made policy changes to attract Chinese EV makers' investment. Other countries are also trying to benefit from the EV industry and its supply chains. Indonesia, for example, is eyeing becoming a major player due to its massive reserves of nickel, a key material for EV batteries. In fact, in 2020, the Indonesian government banned the export of nickel ore, which has led many Chinese companies to invest in Indonesia to produce core EV battery components locally.[69] The Indonesian government thus encouraged Chinese investments in the EV industries that would uplift the entire value chain of the country's auto industry, as pointed out by Indonesia's Coordinating Minister for Economic Affairs Airlangga Hartarto.[70]

The Cambodian Government is another one encouraging investment in EV assembly plants, and the country's Long-Term Strategy for Carbon Neutrality in 2022 includes a commitment to have 40 percent of EV cars and busses, and 70 percent of electric motorbikes by 2050.[71] So far, the government has reduced import duties on EVs in 2021 to about 50 percent lower than those on combustion vehicles, and an inter-ministerial working group has been established to discuss strategies to increase the use of EVs in Cambodia.[72] Its neighboring state, Laos, has also introduced tax relief to increase the use of EVs in the country, which include zero percent tariffs, an excise tax of only 3 percent and a value-added tax of 7 percent to lower the prices of EVs.[73] In February 2022, the Malaysian government also announced that all EVs will be exempt from road tax for four years. Such is the regional trend to reduce carbon emission by encouraging EV usage in Southeast Asia, and Chinese EV industries are going to occupy a major share of the market.

Conclusion

Despite the global economic slump during the COVID-19 pandemic, China's economic relations with Southeast Asia have arguably deepened. The intensifying geostrategic competition between the United States and China has led to discernable economic decoupling between the two, and Southeast Asia has benefited from the trade redirection as well as from investments from China during the past few years. Indeed, if China's relations with the United States and the West in general were to worsen, Southeast Asia as a region would witness more Chinese industries relocating there to diversify their risks.

As the country's zero-COVID policy finally came to an end in January 2023, the suspended tourism market from China to Southeast Asia will also pick up soon. With tens of millions of Chinese eager to get out of the country after being stuck inside for so long, we will definitely see a spike in Chinese consumption in Southeast Asia. Many Chinese tourists will probably travel to Laos and onwards to Thailand via the newly constructed HSR. We will have to wait and see if this will lead to changes in the downstream tourism market. But the overall pattern of economic integration between the two will persist and ideally will bring more mutual benefits in the years to come. Therefore, in this sense, Chinese economic influence in Southeast Asia will only deepen in the years to come.

4

Contesting "Re-Sinicization"

Introduction

The Sirindhorn Chinese Language and Culture Center is located in Mae Fah Luang University in Thailand's northern-most Chiang Rai province. Named after the popular princesses during Rama IX King Bhumibol's reign, the center was a gift made by the People's Republic of China to honor her contribution in the promotion of bilateral cultural exchanges between China and Thailand. Styled in a traditional Chinese garden structure with courtyards, ponds, and pavilions, it also hosts a Confucius Institute (CI) that provides Chinese language education to both university students and the public in general. Formed as a partnership between Mae Fah Luang University and Xiamen University, the CI provides Chinese language education for more than 4,000 students annually. Through this base for bilateral cultural exchange in northern Thailand, the Chinese government aims to use the promotion of the Chinese language and culture to showcase its "soft power" in a borderland region formerly known as the "Golden Triangle," infamous for its history of opium production and drug trafficking.

"Soft power" is perhaps one of those terminologies in international relations that have been used so often to be almost a cliché. Originally coined by Joseph Nye, soft power refers to a state's ability to gain favor so that it can then get what it wants without the need to use coercion or payment.[1] Although one might question whether soft power can be totally independent of hard power, it seems commonplace these days that many world countries have spent enormous resources to promote their own cultures abroad. Language in particular has been treated as one of the main sources of soft power promotion because of its assumed representation of national identity and its embodiment of national culture. Thus, from the British Council to the Goethe Institute to the Institut Français, all are institutions that have been designated by national governments as promoters of their respective languages and cultures.

The Ripple Effect. Enze Han, Oxford University Press. © Oxford University Press 2024.
DOI: 10.1093/oso/9780197696583.003.0004

Although English can be seen as the *lingua franca* in the international arena, as a rising power, the Chinese government challenges the dominance of English by devoting tremendous institutional and monetary resources to promote the study of Mandarin Chinese abroad. Through the establishment of the CI, the Chinese government intended to learn from the experiences of other countries who have undertaken similar language promotion abroad, but it also aims to use the CIs as vehicles through which to promote a better national image for China. In fact, as expressed by the former Minister of Propaganda Li Changchun, "The Confucius Institute is an appealing brand for expanding our culture abroad . . . It has made an important contribution toward improving our soft power. The 'Confucius' brand has a natural attractiveness. Using the excuse of teaching Chinese language, everything looks reasonable and logical."[2]

It seems China's efforts at spreading Chinese soft power, or propaganda—whatever way one wants to describe it—have met a significant amount of resistance in the West. Comparable to a witch hunt, many CIs have been accused of infiltrating American classrooms while hampering academic freedom, and an unprecedented number of such CIs have been closed down in the United States and several other Western countries. However, in Southeast Asia, the CIs have not witnessed the same types of pushbacks; in Thailand in particular, we have seen one of the biggest efforts at promoting the learning of the Chinese language in the royal kingdom.

This chapter focuses on the promotion of Chinese language education in Thailand and examines how the Chinese government has targeted Thailand in its overall export of Chinese culture. At the same time, it demonstrates how, through the promotion of its language and culture, the Chinese government aims to propagate its own versions of political history, particularly on issues that relate to the "One China Principle" and others that affect China's perceived national interests. To illustrate this dynamic, in this chapter I discusses how Beijing competes with Taipei in education outreach to the Yunnanese Kuomintang (KMT) community in Northern Thailand, and contextualizes the phenomenon of "re-Sinicization," as well as pointing out some of the contestations against the Chinese government's re-territorialization of the overseas Chinese community in Southeast Asia. The conclusion of the chapter explores the widespread implications China's effort at "social, cultural, and geopolitical reterritorialization" has for the broad Sinosphere.[3] Here, Sinosphere is defined loosely as countries/territories/people in East and Southeast Asia that are part of China's cultural sphere of inference, yet with different levels of political relations with contemporary mainland China.[4]

Promotion of Chinese Language and Culture in Thailand

Starting from 2004, the Chinese government launched the Confucius Institute program under the Office of Chinese language Council International (Hanban) to promote Chinese language education outside China. Thailand's Ministry of Education signed an agreement with Hanban in 2006 to promote Chinese language education, which led to an agreement on education cooperation between the two countries in 2009.[5] As one of the first countries in Southeast Asia to establish CIs, Thailand currently hosts sixteen CIs, which makes it the country with the highest number of CIs in Asia and the highest number per capita in the world.[6] Covering almost all the major universities and different geographical regions in the country, the CIs in Thailand overall have contributed to the popularity of Chinese language education among the Thai population.

The CIs have brought resources and manpower for teaching Chinese to Thailand. They not only provide official bilingual teaching materials in both Chinese and Thai but have also produced textbooks that have been localized to accommodate Thai students' needs. At the same time, the Chinese government provided needed manpower to teach Chinese in Thailand by offering a volunteer teacher program, wherein Hanban bears the financial responsibility for their room and board, as well as a stipend for living costs. These teachers have become the main force of native Chinese speakers to teach in host societies. Since 2003, more than 10,000 Chinese volunteer teachers have been teaching in Thailand at all educational levels.[7] Furthermore, since 2013, the Overseas Chinese Affairs Office launched an Implementation Plan for a Chinese language Teacher Certificate, and many Thai teachers have been invited to teacher training in China.[8] Teachers who receive such certificates and trainings also include those Chinese language instructors at universities and in many private Chinese learning centers in Thailand. Thus, overall, the qualities of Chinese language teaching have improved in recent years.

Provision of these resources for Chinese language teaching matches with a strong local demand. There are many reasons why such a demand is high in Thailand. On the one hand, there is a large number of Sino-Thai who previously did not have access to a proper Chinese education due to Thailand's prior policy to limit it. Thus, for many Sino-Thai to learn Chinese—albeit in Mandarin rather than their ancestral dialects such as Teochew or Hainan—it means a reconnection to their "roots" and might fit into the overall phenomenon of re-Sinicization that has been going on in Southeast Asia, which will be discussed in more detail below. On the other hand, as related elsewhere in the book, there are strong economic incentives in Thailand for people to learn Chinese due to abundant business opportunities, and it is relatively cheaper and easier to learn Chinese for Thai speakers than, for example, English. As both Chinese and Thai are tonal languages that share many linguistic similarities, Mandarin is not a hard language to learn for Thai speakers. Therefore, commodifying Chinese language education provides "more accessible and affordable educational opportunities for learners, especially those from low-income families, and at the same time [such] language proficiency can broaden learners' career choices and provide employees with additional value in industries, such as tourism, commerce, and services."[9]

A record number of Thai students have therefore been learning Chinese in both the public and private school systems in Thailand. According to a 2010 estimate, nearly half a million students in primary and secondary schools were learning Chinese, with that number increasing over the past decade.[10] According to a 2019 YouGov Cambridge Globalism Project poll, 76 percent of participants in Thailand agreed on the importance of learning Mandarin, which was significantly higher than people in other countries outside China.[11] We can tell from the poll that although it seems most Western countries are not convinced of the need to learn Mandarin, in Thailand there is a clear understanding of the value of learning this economically important language. This is also reflected in the growing number of Thai students who take Chinese as part of the Professional Aptitude Test, which is a national foreign language test for admission to tertiary education in Thailand.[12]

In addition to the CIs, the Chinese government established a cultural center in Bangkok in 2012. Not only is it the first and the biggest of such centers established by China in Southeast Asia, its unveiling ceremony was attended by former Chinese Premier Wen Jiabao and the Thai Prime Minister Yingluck Shinawatra, indicating the import both governments placed on bilateral cultural ties.[13] In addition to Chinese language, the center organizes regular classes in a variety of Chinese cultural activities, such as calligraphy, Chinese painting, music, dance, tai chi, and cooking, among others. Further, its theater hosts performing troupes visiting from China and holds yearly Chinese film festivals and other exhibitions.

The Chinese government also made it clear that the promotion of its language education and culture abroad is to better serve Chinese state policies. For example, at the meeting entitled "Strategies Engagement of the Confucius Institutes in Thailand under Thailand 4.0" at Mae Fah Luang University, the Chinese government pointed out that "the Confucius Institutes will use Chinese language as a medium of enhancing an effective communication and understanding of China's policy and strategy. The good communication and understanding will indeed usher in supporting the Thailand 4.0 policy and government's operations as well as strengthening smooth cooperation between the two countries."[14] It seems clear that both Thai and Chinese government are strategically utilizing each other in the promotion of national development priorities by linking the CI with Thailand 4.0, which is a Thai national strategy promoted by the incumbent Prayut Chan-o-cha government.

The Competition for Chinese Education Provision in Northern Thailand

Although the Chinese government's overall Chinese language education and cultural outreach seems harmless enough, the reality is that Beijing is not the only regional government that offers Chinese education in Thailand. The Republic of China (ROC) government in Taiwan has been in support of the KMT settlement community in northern Thailand ever since the Cold War. The Chinese language schools dotted throughout mountainous KMT villages were all set up with the support of Taipei.

When the People's Liberation Army (PLA) entered the southwestern Yunnan province in early 1950, a section of the KMT army retreated south and crossed the border into what was then Burma, now Myanmar. The Communist victory in China, together with military developments in the Korean War (1950–1953), led to the change in U.S. strategic priorities in East Asia towards the containment of communism. As a result, the U.S. decided to support the KMT troops in Burma, hoping to harass militarily the Chinese communist regime in its Southwest borderland and thereby divert attention from Korea. After repeated protests by the Burmese government and under international pressure, since 1953, several rounds of withdrawal of these soldiers and their families were carried out. Finally, after the 1960 joint military action by the PLA and Burmese government troops, the KMT troops were finally expelled from Burma. However, many decided not to go to Taiwan but instead chose to settle in the borderland area between Thailand and Burma, with more than eighty villages in Chiang Mai, Chiang Rai, and Mae Hong Son.[15] The Thai government at the time perceived a strategic value in having the KMT settlements act as a buffer zone as well as to use them to patrol the borderland area from communist infiltrations. Many of these settlements were later granted Thai citizenship, and they remain there today.[16]

As a result of this turbulent history, these Yunnanese Chinese have held strong anti-communist views towards Beijing and keep a close association with Taiwan.[17] Different from most other overseas Chinese communities who have migrated to Thailand earlier and from provinces such as Guangdong or Fujian, these Yunnanese Chinese came much later, most after the 1950s. By then, the out-migration routes from coastal provinces in China had already stopped. At the same time, their special circumstances as war refugees in a special settlement area along the border meant that the Thai government lent them significant autonomy.

More importantly, this community owed much of its existence to the KMT government in Taiwan. Throughout the Cold War, the community maintained a close connection with Taipei in their military activities in the Thai-Burma borderland area. Since the 1980s, the ROC's Chinese Association for Relief and Ensuing Services (*zhonghua jiuzhu zonghui*) provided assistance in terms of Chinese language education and economic development.[18] Specifically, in terms of education, Taiwan provided textbooks, teachers, and teacher training for local schools, from primary to high school levels. The ROC government also certified these schools, so that students graduating from them were qualified for university entrance in Taiwan, if they passed the Overseas Examination (*haiwai lianzhao*). There were also periodic visits by ROC government officials to these communities as part of their Overseas Chinese/Compatriot work, because arguably they had been the most loyal towards the ROC, particularly during the time when the KMT was still the ruling party.

After the PRC and Thailand established diplomatic relations in 1975, most other Overseas Chinese communities in Thailand reconnected with the Chinese mainland.[19] However, the Yunnanese in Northern Thailand were the last to reconcile with Beijing because of their peculiar history. To this day, the memorial hall in Mae Salong still displays name plates of these soldiers who died throughout the border wars, paying tribute to their anti-communist sacrifices and their loyalty towards the ROC. The Chinese language school systems among the Yunnanese continue to use the curriculum and teaching materials from Taiwan, and the dominant form of Chinese used is the traditional rather than the simplified Chinese characters from the Chinese mainland.

However, these Yunnanese communities became the target of a diplomatic tug-of-war between Beijing and Taipei in recent years. Although close, the relationship between the Yunnanese and the ROC government became tenuous when the Democratic Progressive Party (DPP) came into power. The DPP government, with its intention to de-Sinicize Taiwan, does not have an affinity with these Yunnanese, whose loyalty is clearly towards the KMT, now the main opposition party. Therefore, funding support for the Yunnanese community in northern Thailand has been gradually cut since the new millennium, including educational support for the Chinese schools there. In fact, the Chinese Association for Relief and Ensuing Services, which was previously instrumental in providing financial support for the Yunnanese in northern Thailand, was branded as a KMT party asset and got its finances frozen by the DPP government in 2020.

On the other hand, the Beijing government has made it clear that it wants to win over these former "Cold War warriors." In June 2006, Peng Rendong, the Chinese Consul-General in Chiang Mai, made a visit to two Yunnanese villages, where he made donations to local schools. This was the first time the Chinese Consul-General had visited the Yunnanese community since the establishment of the Chiang Mai consulate in 1991. This event was interpreted by the Taipei government, under DDP President Chen Shui-bian at the time, as a betrayal by the local Yunnanese community. Taiwan subsequently cut educational assistance to the schools that received these donations.[20] Indeed, it seems that Taipei, at least under the DPP, does not seem to be interested in continuing the former Cold War battle with Beijing in northern Thailand.

Since then, the Beijing government has made headway in convincing some schools in northern Thailand to switch curricula and teaching materials from those provided by Taiwan. In 2011, with the support of the Chinese government, Jiaolian High School was founded in Chiang Mai. This was the first high school to use the mainland Chinese educational curriculum, with textbooks and computers donated by Hanban and the Yunnan Overseas Chinese Affairs office. Currently, it enrolls 1,300 students and employs thirty-seven teachers, and many of students have received scholarships to study abroad in China. Since then, quite a few other Chinese schools in the area have followed suit by switching sides. In 2019, another Jiaolian Teachers College was set up in partnership with mainland Chinese universities to nurture local talents for Chinese education in northern Thailand.[21]

With the mainland Chinese government making more inroads among the Yunnanese community in northern Thailand, not only have the teaching materials for the Chinese language in these schools changed, but also the political meaning of being Chinese in the context of cross-strait relations between the PRC and ROC. Specifically, the Chinese government has targeted the Yunnanese community in its battle with Taiwan on the "One China Principle." In January 2019, the Chinese Consul-General in Chiang Mai attended the 10th Chinese Culture Festival Opening Ceremony, where he made a speech that encouraged the Yunnanese community not only to carry on their Chinese cultural traditions but also to support the peaceful unification of the "homeland," that is, between the Chinese mainland and Taiwan.[22] In March 2021, the Chinese Consul-General paid a visit to Yunnan Association (*Yunnan Huiguan*), which has been one of the most staunch anti-communist and pro-ROC associations in northern Thailand; previously it was very resistant to any outreach from the Chinese consulate.[23] Wu Zhiwu, the Consul-General, expressed willingness to increase contact with the Yunnan Association but also emphasized the hope that the Yunnanese would fight against Taiwanese independence and make a contribution to the early unification of China.[24]

The diplomatic battle between Beijing and Taipei for the heart and mind of the overseas Chinese community has been going on ever since the start of the Cold War.[25] As a result of the shifting balance of power across the Taiwan Strait and, more importantly, as a domestic identity change in Taiwan, Beijing is increasingly gaining the upper hand in its outreach among the Yunnanese community in northern Thailand. Its push to change the educational materials in some of the Chinese schools in the region has resulted in students singing songs about the red flag with five stars instead of songs praising the "Three Principles of People." There are, however, many people in the Yunnanese community who remain loyal to Taiwan; such close relations mean many local people continue to have family ties there, and some even hold ROC citizenship. However, the trend is clear that with more resources at Beijing's disposal, the balance of power is shifting in its favor. Yet, as Beijing is gaining momentum in exporting its own version of culture and political values, ultimately that meets with push back and contestations, particularly on the "One China Principle."

"Re-Sinicization" and Its Discontents

With Beijing investing such a wealth of resources in promoting Chinese language and culture abroad, more people around the world have shown an interest in learning Mandarin Chinese. For many overseas Chinese in Southeast Asia, this indicates a deeper connection with China and, more specifically, it has signaled a reconnection with their ancestral "homeland." Indeed, in Thailand as well as throughout Southeast Asia, a so-called phenomenon of re-Sinicization has been happening for some time.[26]

Caroline Hau defined re-Sinicization as "the revival of hitherto devalued, occluded, or repressed 'Chineseness,' and more generally to the phenomenon of increasing visibility, acceptability, and self-assertiveness of ethnic Chinese in Southeast Asia and elsewhere."[27] Such re-Sinicization has occurred across much of Southeast Asia. As Hau points out, this phenomenon entails a departure from the past when "Southeast Asian 'Chinese' were viewed and treated as economically dominant, culturally different, and politically disloyal Others to be 'de-Sinicized' through nation-building discourses and policies."[28]

In Thailand's case, the Sino-Thai community that had long been well assimilated has in recent decades embarked on efforts to rediscover and preserve its Chinese roots.[29] It is certainly the case that these processes are deeply embedded in the context of Thai society and its form of "Chineseness" has distinct traces of the history of Chinese migration to the royal kingdom. Thus, even though this re-Sinicization process might have coincided with the rise of China and the push by the Chinese government to export its language and culture abroad, it might not be correct to say that the re-Sinicization was simply caused by the rise of China. One might argue that the rise of China has created a more permissive environment for such re-Sinicization to occur in more prominent forms, but one did not necessarily cause the other.

For Hau, Sinicization and re-Sinicization should not be understood as a singular "mainland [China] state-centered and driven process of remaking the world in its own image," but rather [as] multiple sites where different actors have "created, reinvented, and transformed received meanings associated with 'China,' 'Chinese,' and 'Chineseness.'"[30] Thus, Hau finds multiple "Chinas" and a loosely defined Sinosphere inclusive of Hong Kong and Taiwan that projects a different conceptualization of the meaning to be "Chinese."

However, with a continued mainland Chinese push to export its language and culture to Southeast Asia in conjunction with its own political values, contestations have occurred over the meanings of such re-Sinicization. Increasingly, such contentions manifest in different forms of identification with the concept of China and its current authoritarian government versus that of such democratic and more liberal counterparts within the broad Sinosphere as Hong Kong and Taiwan. This is why sometimes the target of such backlash is the People's Republic of China and its cultural forms as a whole; other times it is more representative of divisions within the broad Sinosphere (e.g., southern China vs. northern China) or among different language groups (e.g., Cantonese, Hokkien, and Mandarin speakers) or ultimately contestations of what means to be "Chinese."[31] Previously in Southeast Asia, the cultural influence of Hong Kong and Taiwan was much larger during the Cold War. However, since the advent of the new millennium, the increasing cultural imprint in Southeast Asia is more prominently from the Chinese mainland because of its growing political and economic influence.

Therefore, the disputations within the Sinosphere, with mainland China's increasing attempts to dominate and Hong Kong's and Taiwan's resistance to being identified with that perceived image of China, indicate that similar contention is also being found among overseas Chinese communities in Thailand and Southeast Asia. In this sense, the phenomenon of re-Sinicization carries with it strong implications for different geographies of the Sinosphere, in terms of "spatial, social, political, and economic order throughout the region, reconfiguring leisure spaces and economies, transportation infrastructure, popular political discourse, and geopolitical imaginaries."[32]

As we have seen in this chapter, recent attempts to promote the teaching of Chinese language and culture in Thailand and Southeast Asia as whole come predominantly from mainland China. Although Taiwan also indicates an interest in promoting its version of Chinese language abroad, the number of resources and the scale of its outreach are dwarfed in comparison with those from the Chinese mainland. These patterns indicate that the meaning of being Chinese in Thailand has been increasingly tied to what is culturally and linguistically mainland Chinese.

Clearly, as noted earlier, the Sino-Thai community has been considered a relatively successful case of assimilation in Southeast Asia, thanks to a series of Thai government policies, incentives, and pressures,[33] or as a byproduct of some misunderstanding of what constitutes proper assimilation in the Thai context.[34] Assimilation has resulted in two to three generations of Sino-Thai lacking access to a formal Chinese education. Although some can communicate in "kitchen" Teochew Chinese, most can neither read nor write Chinese characters or speak proper Mandarin, which is now the *lingua franca* for the mainland Chinese diaspora community. This new need/interest in Chinese cultural heritage has generated debates about the phenomenon of re-Sinicization that scholars have explored in the Southeast Asian context.

Re-Sinicization is not a unilateral process but rather is driven by a variety of interests within Southeast Asia. In Thailand's case, this re-Sinicization coincides with the broader trend within Thailand that has seen the Sino-Thai community try to reconnect with their Chinese heritage in the age of the rise of China.[35] For some people, this re-Sinicization "has become one of the defining characteristics of Southeast Asian communities at a time when China's economic and cultural clout is growing."[36] Moreover, Liu suggests that re-Sinicization is driven primarily by the overseas Chinese community as a strategy to cope with the rising economic opportunities presented by China's presence in Southeast Asia, in addition to the desire for the community to reclaim ethnic pride in the process.[37] Of course, the Chinese government's efforts to actively engage and promote the Chinese language and culture in the region have also played a significant role.

In Thailand's case, the spoken Chinese being taught as the official *lingua franca* is Mandarin Chinese instead of the ancestral Teochew, Cantonese, or Hokkien spoken in the overseas Chinse community for centuries prior. Of course, teaching Mandarin Chinese has been a common practice in other parts of Southeast Asia such as Malaysia and Singapore. Indeed, in Singapore, the government officially banned the teaching of other Chinese dialects in favor of Mandarin Chinese, and that does not seem to have much to do with the rise of China. The "Speak Mandarin Campaign" started in 1979 when China was much poorer and had limited influence in Southeast Asia. Yet, even in Singapore's case, the government officially adopted simplified Chinese characters as well as *hanyu pinyin* to romanize Mandarin in the way done in mainland China rather than those used in either Hong Kong or Taiwan, where traditional Chinese has been in use. Therefore, the teaching of Mandarin in Southeast Asia overall indicates the intention of the overseas Chinese community to make sense of its cultural heritage and to re-connect with its ancestral homeland.

Although it might be a stretch to equate learning Mandarin with mainland China's effort to "reterritorialize" the overseas Chinese cultural space in its own contemporary image,[38] for a country such as Thailand—where previously Chinese education was heavily restricted—the recent growth of interests and access to such Mandarin language education are facilitated by the rise of China's economic and political prominence. Meanwhile, there is a lucrative market opportunity for export of cultural products to China. For example, Thailand's entertainment industry has gained popularity internationally in recent years.[39] Thai pop music, TV dramas, and movies are consumed increasingly by a regional audience in East and Southeast Asia.[40] In the Chinese market, Thai music and in particular TV and movie genres, such as horror or boy-love, have wide followings.[41] By appealing to Chinese audiences, more and more Chinese elements have been used in Thai pop-culture exports. For example, it is common to come across Thai pop singers who release a song in Mandarin or develop characters for television shows and movies with a Chinese connection. One such recent TV series, *I Told Sunset About You*, is a case in point, with extensive content about learning Mandarin and active participation in many cultural activities associated with the language and cultural outreach discussed above.[42] Part of the rationale is commercial, because it allows the Thai entertainment industry access to the vast Chinese market. Yet, inevitably, these changes indicate an appreciation within Thai society of the Chinese cultural appeal, which is part of the overall trend of re-Sinicization that is ongoing in Thailand.

Increasing Contestations of Re-Sinicization

On the other hand, because of Thailand's domestic authoritarian turn, the close association between Beijing and Bangkok has been interpreted as empowering the country's military government, which we have discussed in Chapter 3. Thus, the prominent displays of "Chineseness," in terms of language and culture promoted by mainland China in Thailand, have become targets of such contestation. This is because many younger-generation Thais have subscribed to a more liberal form of international platform that promotes democracy and freedom in Asia, which adds to their growing aversion towards the authoritarian Chinese mainland under the rule of the CCP.

The overall trend of re-Sinicization in Thailand notwithstanding, the PRC government's authoritarian nature under the leadership of the CCP, as well as modern "irredentist" Chinese nationalism, have created an additional dimension for contention. There is an undercurrent that questions and contests this overt identification of a particular version of "Chineseness" and the close association with the PRC as the representative state of China. Such contestations have occurred in multiple forms, some more subtle than others and, depending on the nature of such disputes, some have become politicized and moved into high politics at the state-to-state level.

When discussing re-Sinicization—in particular the cultural and linguistic influences that originated from the Chinese mainland—we need to be aware of the multiple sites of "Chineseness," which is in fact a transnational phenomenon and mediated by different dialect/language groups and the prominent economic and cultural appeals of other offshore "Chinese" polities of Hong Kong, Taiwan, and even Singapore.[43] Previously, when the Chinese mainland was closed to the outside world and assumed to be a backwater of poverty (at least before the 2000s), the offshore Chinese outposts represented forms of Chinese modernity dating back to the start of the Cold War. For Southeast Asia in particular, the Chinese cultural mediums, such as songs and movies, that dominated within the region's overseas Chinese community almost exclusively came from these localities, and were made in different dialects/languages of either Cantonese or Taiwanese Mandarin.[44] This situation led Hau to state that "in practice, no single political entity/regime embodies or exercises ultimate authority on 'China,' 'Chinese,' and 'Chineseness.'"[45] And indeed, she noted that the "economic rise of China and the market-driven Mandarinization of 'Chineseness'" have not "substantially reduced or simplified the multi-sited claims and belongings exercised by the ethnic 'Chinese' in Southeast Asia."[46]

However, within the Sinosphere, contestations over the meanings of "China," "Chinese" and "Chineseness" have become increasingly heated, while the issue has become polarized because of the geopolitical reshuffling of power dynamics in the region and China's increasing nationalistic and assertive "irredentist" policies.[47] For both Hong Kong and Taiwan, the mainland Chinese government's demand of the "One China Principle" has met with sustained resistance. In Taiwan, the current government, led by the DPP, has pursued a determined route for a distinct "Taiwanese" identity for the island within the international system.[48] Not only have there been persistent efforts at de-Sinicization throughout its political and cultural system,[49] but the Taiwanese government has also actively sought international recognition as Taiwan instead of Republic of China, and has deepened its dependence on the United States to push back against the Chinese mainland government.[50]

Meanwhile, Hong Kong's self-identification as part of China has also been heavily politicized in recent years. As a result of rising localism and the rejection of Chinese rule over Hong Kong, ways of how being Chinese should be manifested have also become controversial.[51] Ever since the Umbrella Movement in 2014, but more explicitly with the recent Anti-Extradition Bill protest movement since the summer of 2019, a significant sector of Hong Kong society no longer identifies as part of China and has openly defied Beijing's rule through increasingly radical resistance towards the "One Country Two Systems" model.[52] Furthermore, the cultural politics of being Chinese are heavily politicized in Hong Kong. There has been a movement to write Cantonese in newly invented scripts, and there was also periodic violence targeting Mandarin speakers, particularly during the 2019 protest movement.

Although most of these intense contestations are being played out in Taiwan and Hong Kong, Thailand has not been immune to the spread of this contestation. In some ways, such conflicts within the Sinosphere are not new. In the early twentieth century, ideological divisions between supporters of the KMT and the CCP created strong divisions within the overseas Chinese communities in Southeast Asia, including Thailand.[53] Although previously such divisions, particularly during the Cold War, were mainly ideological, today they manifest mostly as negative political response against the CCP and contradictions among forms of nationalism that pit the Chinese mainland against such territories as Hong Kong and Taiwan. Indeed, the contestation between the "One China Principle" and its antagonists has opened fissures within overseas Chinese communities in Southeast Asia. A recent example is the Malaysian Chinese singer Namewee, who partnered with another singer in Taiwan, mocked nationalists in mainland China, ridiculed China's "One China Principle," and called for self-determination by Taiwan and Hong Kong.[54]

Such controversy has also spread to Thailand. In October 2019, one of Thailand's opposition politicians, Thanathorn Juangroongruangkit, the former leader of the now-dissolved Future Forward Party, waded into Hong Kong's political turmoil. At an Open Future Festival, Thanathorn met with Hong Kong activist Joshua Wong, who later tweeted, "Under the hard-line authoritarian suppression, we stand in solidarity" with a picture of them together.[55] The political context within Thailand at that time highlighted why this meeting was controversial. The Future Forward Party, a relatively new political party founded by the young tycoon Thanathorn, emerged as one of the victorious opposition parties in the May 2019 Thai national election. The party's electoral success drew support from many young, liberal, and progressive voters in urban areas such as Bangkok, but became the target of suppression by Thailand's military-affiliated government.[56] The party was forced to dissolve, and Thanathorn has since been embroiled in a series of politically charged legal cases.[57]

Thanathorn's meeting with Joshua Wong was thus interpreted as the two sharing similar experiences of resistance towards authoritarian forces. The tweet by Wong went viral, leading to a huge online show of support for both politicians in Hong Kong and Thailand. This ultimately led the Chinese government to intervene. The Chinese Embassy in Bangkok issued a statement condemning the incident, stating that, "Certain Thai politicians have been in touch with the group calling for Hong Kong's independence from China, acting in favor of it . . . The action is extremely wrong and irresponsible. China hopes the relevant individuals can recognize the facts about the Hong Kong issue, be cautious, and do what is beneficial for the friendship between China and Thailand."[58] The Chinese government's ire ultimately compelled Thanathorn to issue a statement denying his relationship with Joshua Wong and claiming that he has always supported China playing a bigger role regionally and globally.[59]

If Thanathorn's incident was indeed an accident, another recent online battle between Chinese and Thai netizens exposed the existing political divisions among sectors of each society on the thorny issue of the "One China Principle." In April 2020, an online spat between supposedly Chinese and Thai netizens occurred on Twitter. At the time, the girlfriend of a lead actor in a popular Thai TV series, *2gether*, tweeted a conspiracy story about COVID-19 and Wuhan. However, it was not simply the COVID tweet that infuriated the Chinese nationalists online, but that they discovered she and the TV star had also "inappropriately" called Hong Kong and Taiwan "countries" in some of their online postings.[60] It is this violation of the "One China Principle" that prompted the Chinese netizens to threaten to boycott the show and the TV stars, which led to a bitter online spat with their Thai counterparts, aided by many "keyboard warriors" from Hong Kong and Taiwan. The incident quickly spiraled out of control, transforming from an incident involving TV stars in Thailand into an online battle between Hong Kong and Taiwan pro-democracy/pro-independence supporters and mainland Chinese nationalists.

This incident occurred in the context of almost a year of protest movement in Hong Kong. The original protests were against the Extradition Bill to mainland China but transformed into a broader anti-China and pro-Hong Kong localism/independence movement. At the same time, the Taiwanese state and society were combative in their perception of the Chinese government's suppression of Taiwan's international status. President Tsai Ing-wen of the DPP party linked the failure of the "One Country Two Systems" in Hong Kong to Taiwan's need to maintain independence from mainland China in the lead-up to the island's election in January 2020. Therefore, online "keyboard warriors" from Taiwan and Hong Kong were extremely active on social media, particularly given that platforms such as Twitter, Instagram, and Facebook are blocked on the Chinese mainland. The incident involving Thai netizens provided a venue through which political activists in Hong Kong and Taiwan expanded their united anti-China front to include Thailand. Subsequently, an online "Milk Tea Alliance" was founded on the basis that people from Hong Kong, Taiwan, and Thailand all have the same drink of milk tea. This commonality ties online activists together against authoritarianism in the region and against Chinese suppression in particular.[61]

For many in Thailand, the strong anti-China sentiment that emerged online represented Thai society's younger generation, who are dissatisfied with the country's political situation because of the long military rule since the 2014 coup. There is a perception that the Chinese communist government is a party that tacitly condones the military in Thailand. Yet many in Thailand were also sympathetic towards the protest movement in Hong Kong and drew comparisons between Chinese suppression of the movement and a similar political movement demanding more democracy at home. Hence, this empathy tied the Thai political activists to those activists in Hong Kong and Taiwan. Finally, the Chinese government's heavy-handed promotion of Chinese language and culture and its insistence on the "One China Principle" have also caused a backlash within Thai society. Here one can argue for a clash over different interpretations of the meaning of "China," "Chinese," and "Chineseness." The cultural politics of modern-day Chinese nationalism have come into direct confrontation with resistances within the Sinosphere, into which Thailand has ultimately been pulled.

For example, some of the younger generations of the Sino-Thai community do not want to be associated with a China that is authoritarian and increasingly imperialistic, particularly vis-à-vis Taiwan and Hong Kong. According to Netiwit Chotiphatphaisal, a political activist who wrote for the *Thai Enquirer*, "Among Thai people of Chinese descent like myself, we have grown up with the idea that China was a bastion of culture and political independence with a history worthy of being recognized and elevated but the China of today is a far cry from those idyllic daydreams."[62] He further drew similarities between Thailand with Hong Kong in claiming that if people do not oppose Chinese imperialism, "what is happening in Hong Kong will eventually happen at home." Similar to the Thanathorn incident, the Thai "Milk Tea Alliance" activists and their online solidarity with Hong Kong drew a statement from the Chinese embassy in Bangkok reaffirming that "China and Thailand are one family" and the "One China Principle" should not be violated.[63] Although, of course, such a description of China and Thailand as one family, as brothers, is again contested and ridiculed by many of these netizens.[64]

It is certainly a stretch to argue that it is China's push for education and culture export to Thailand that has caused the negative sentiment in the country against the authoritarian Chinese government and its "One China Principle." However, I argue this overall cultural outreach provided the permissive condition for such contestations of re-Sinicization. As more mainland Chinese cultural influences are felt, together with rising authoritarianism within Thailand itself, there is a tendency to conflate the link between the two.

Conclusion

Culture is political. The forms of language and culture that are promoted as official have strong political connotations behind them. As a result of the rise of China, Beijing has accumulated the resources necessary to export Mandarin Chinese education and other cultural forms abroad. Although it might be an independent phenomenon that has been ongoing in Southeast Asia for some time, the rise of China has certainly put a "mainland hue" on re-Sinicization. However, as we have seen in this chapter, resistance towards this re-Sinicization has also built up steam recently, but these are mostly towards the political meanings of what is "China," how to define who is "Chinese," and who has the right and power to define such "Chineseness." In particular, given the contested nature of the "One China Principle" within the Sinosphere, such contestation has also spread to Southeast Asia, including Thailand, in recent years. Indeed, it seems there is no sign such contention will subside any time soon, particularly given the internationalization of the "One China Principle" as part of the great power competition between China and the United States, and Taiwan and Hong Kong's crucial strategic value in this competition. We will definitely witness more of such conflicts and fissures to move through Southeast Asia, where the phenomenon of re-Sinicization will inform political debates within the region at large.

5

Chinese Consumption

Introduction

The green hillslopes were dazzling under the sun when my plane descended towards Lashio airport in the summer of 2019. The rugged, northern Shan State with its rolling hills—where one can see lush mountains stretching across the horizon in all directions—was in sharp contrast to the flat landscape of lower Myanmar. Later, when I was leaving the airport, it dawned on me that the hillslopes were made green not by trees but by rows and rows of maize. In fact, wherever I went throughout the northern Shan State, roadside hillslopes all seemed to have been cleared for maize planting. And village homes had piles and piles of harvest maize dried and ready for sale. Other than some paddy rice fields in relatively flat areas, maize had become the dominant crop for the rugged Shan State.

Indeed, maize production in Myanmar as well as other parts of highland Southeast Asia has been booming for almost a decade.[1] As a result of the global commodity price surge around 2011–2012, many parts of highland Southeast Asia, in Myanmar, Laos, Thailand and Vietnam, all increased maize production. Meanwhile, domestic Chinese demand for maize was also booming. Thus, given its geographical proximity to the Chinese border, northern Myanmar's maize became a perfect fit for China's domestic burgeoning animal feed market. But this is not a singular case: throughout northern Myanmar, many areas have entered the Chinese supply chain of cash crops destined for its consumer market, such as tropical fruits and all-season vegetables. In addition, a live cattle trade is developing in Myanmar because of the changing Chinese palate for beef in its ubiquitous hotpot restaurants. I saw truckloads of live cattle lining the road from Mandalay to Muse to be transported into Chinese slaughterhouses across the border.

Such is the magnitude of China's phenomenal domestic consumption-driven growth and shifting demographics for the past couple of decades. Unless COVID-19 finally changed these dynamics, the country's growing middle class and the sheer volume of its 1.4 billion population will continue

The Ripple Effect. Enze Han, Oxford University Press. © Oxford University Press 2024.
DOI: 10.1093/oso/9780197696583.003.0005

to maintain a high demand for non-subsistence food items in the years ahead. China's middle-class growth translates into not only an overall increase in food consumption but also changes in the structure of that consumption.[2] In particular, the demand for quality food—meat, dairy, vegetables, and fruits— is set to increase further due to the shift away from subsistence consumption of grains. Because of its tropical weather and easy transportation links, mainland Southeast Asia has become one of the main sources for Chinese demand for fresh fruits such as durian, longan, mango, watermelon, and banana. According to recent statistics, China imports almost half the fruits and vegetables produced in Myanmar, Thailand, and Vietnam.[3] Many countries in Southeast Asia have increasingly become dependent on the Chinese market for agricultural products.

These kinds of business opportunities have led to a growing Chinese presence in Southeast Asia's agribusiness sector. The Chinese government's "going out" strategy to encourage domestic businesses to seek investment opportunities abroad has led many businesses to go to Southeast Asia.[4] For the Chinese FDI to Southeast Asia, the lion's share of these FDI goes to sectors such as energy, mining, industrial parks, infrastructure, etc., and agriculture accounts for but a small percentage.[5] Many studies have looked at cases of Chinese agricultural investment in Africa,[6] but now, more attention is being paid to Southeast Asia, where the Chinese presence in the agribusiness sector has been growing.[7]

These shifts have certainly brought economic benefits to Southeast Asian farmers and related businesses. The cross-border trade between China and its neighboring states in Southeast Asia has become a major lifeline for many. However, other externalities must be considered. In particular, new farming practices have transformed the agricultural frontiers and introduced environmental challenges and degradation, like deforestation and pollution. The demand for beef has also generated a chain reaction for transnational cattle smuggling. Finally, Chinese demand for specific types of tropical fruits has also pushed up prices for these fruits at the cost of local consumers in Southeast Asia. At the same time, because of the associated high profit in the fruit business, many Chinese have gone to the Southeast to procure and even produce these fruits. The result is a more integrated fresh fruit supply chain dominated by the Chinese at the expense of local actors.

This chapter thus provides a few snapshots of China's domestic consumption's ripple effects in mainland Southeast Asia. First, it analyzes the effects of the maize boom in northern Myanmar on its ecological system by showing how rising demand for maize in China has led to an accelerated rate of deforestation. The chapter then presents the story of how China's demand for beef has led to a transnational network of live cattle smuggling. It then looks at the case of Chinese demand for durian and watermelon and its implications for business networks in Thailand and Myanmar. Finally, the chapter examines Chinese businesses' commercial banana plantation in Laos and their environmental externalities. The chapter will conclude with some reflections about the closure of the Chinese border due to COVID-19 on borderland economies.

Maize Plantation and Deforestation

Global commodity prices tend to fluctuate, and whenever there are significant changes, there are often unforeseen consequences. For example, scholars have examined how drought in China in 2011 led to China's increased purchase of wheat from the international market, which drove up the price. The wheat price shock arguably contributed to domestic political discontent in the Middle East and led to the Arab Spring in Egypt.[8] Indeed, the period between 2010 and 2012 has been known as the 2010–2012 world food price crisis, when prices for a list of grains soared across the world. For maize, its price sharply increased by 57 percent between 2010 and 2011. The price continued to increase in 2012 to almost 300 USD per metric ton. The maize price surge was caused by an incredibly dry summer in the United States and Europe in 2011. At the same time, maize was also one of the main crops used in biofuel production, in part due to higher oil prices, particularly in the United States.[9] As for Myanmar, the global surge of maize prices was coupled with increasing demand in China, its northern neighbor.

For China, although it remains one of the largest maize producers in the world, its domestic output can no longer match rising demand. And in 2008, the country turned from a net exporter of maize into a net importer.[10] The main cause for the increase of domestic demand for maize in China was its fast economic development and the subsequent rise of meat consumption, resulting in the rapid growth of its animal feed market. This increase, in turn, required supplies of maize that could not be satisfied by domestic production alone.

Furthermore, the domestic market price for maize in China has been consistently higher than international ones. Thus, the high price in the Chinese maize market, together with the geographical proximity between the two countries, which share a long 2,000 km border, makes China the ideal export candidate for Myanmar's maize. Indeed, Myanmar's domestic production responded to such incentives. Since 2010 to 2011, the country's maize production has continued to rise, which is highly correlated with the rise of global maize prices as well as increasing Chinese demand.

To see a temporal correlation between maize plantation and deforestation, I have collaborated with a geographer at the Smithsonian Institution of the United States.[11] We examined a quantified deforestation pattern in the Shan State, by using the Myanmar Forest Change dataset produced by TerraPulse and the Smithsonian Conservation Biology Institute.[12] This dataset allows us to quantify the forest cover in Myanmar in the year 2000 as the baseline so as to calculate the annual percentage loss of forest between 2000 and 2019. To maintain a consistent comparison, the annual deforestation rate in each area of interest is summarized, as a percentage of the changes from the baseline forest cover in 2000. We further truncated our data to look at the three subregions of Shan State: Eastern Shan (Shan (E)), Northern Shan (Shan (N)), and Southern Shan (Shan (S)).

From Figure 5.1 we can see that northern Shan State has experienced more deforestation than either the southern or eastern parts. Northern Shan State lost more than 15 percent of its forest during 2000–2019. On the other hand, we can also see that, temporarily, all three regions experienced deforestation differently. For the eastern and southern parts of Shan State, the peak

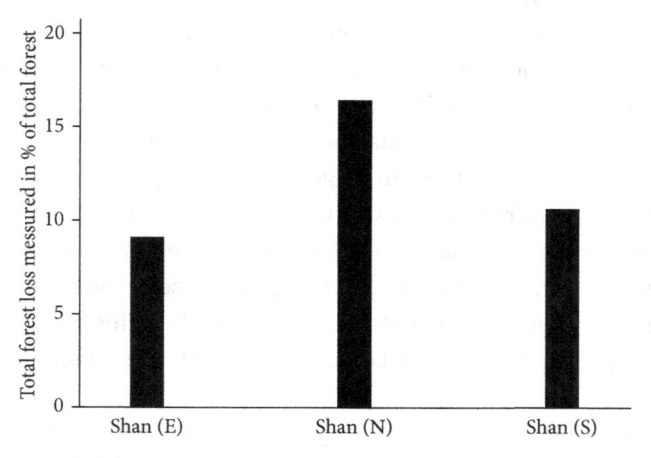

Figure 5.1   Total deforestation in parts of Shan State, 2000–2019

of deforestation occurred in the mid-2000s, while for northern Shan State it occurred after 2010 (Figure 5.2). Overall, it appears that after 2010 there has been an uptick of deforestation in all three regions, coinciding with the surge in maize price.

To further confirm the correlation between maize planation and deforestation, an interview from a villager outside Lashio is telling. The villager related:

> There is a limited supply of land within our village. Particularly the existing rice paddies have to be kept because we need the rice to survive. So, when people started to look for space to expand cultivation of maize, we would have to go to the previously bushy hillsides to clear this land. As maize is a quite tough plant, it can grow easily on hill slopes. They are also not as picky as rice so we do not need to work on them very much. Most labor are only needed in the initial period of clearing the bushes and preparing the land for cultivation, as well as during the harvest period.

Indeed, throughout interviews around Lashio, villagers who cultivate maize commonly acknowledged that they have all engaged in activities that led to

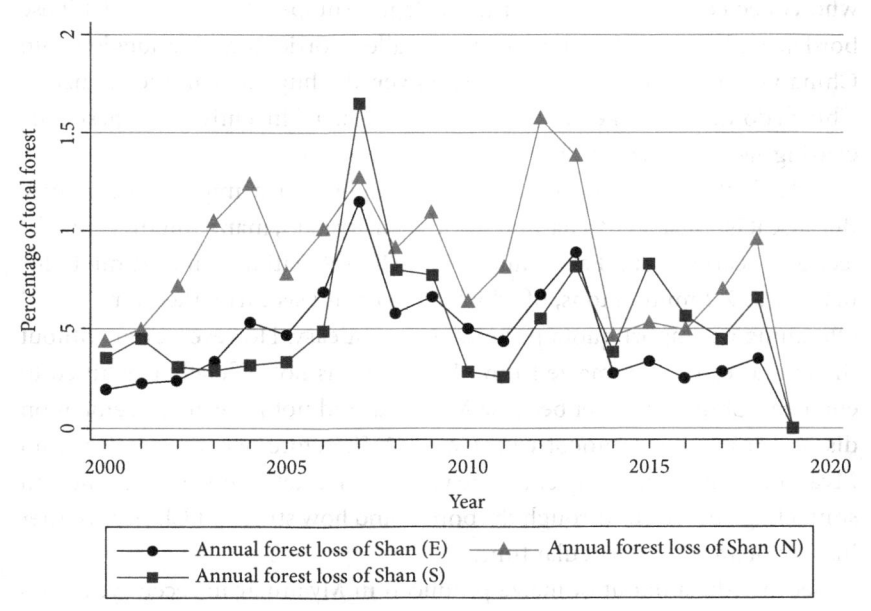

Figure 5.2 Percentage of yearly forest loss in different parts of Shan State

the clearing of the hillsides around villages. In this part of Myanmar's Shan State, flat land for rice paddy cultivation has always been limited due to the landscape's rugged nature. Thus, opening up the hillsides for agricultural cultivation, called *taungya* in Burmese, has been a familiar practice among local villagers. The only difference is the scale of these practices in northern Shan State during the past decade. Many villagers realize how much of the forest along the hillslopes has been cleared, but for them, this is inevitable: the monetary incentives created by Chinese demand have been enough to make clearing these lands profitable.

While many farmers have engaged in expanded maize planation across Shan State, the profit margins remained relatively small. At the same time, in order to buy seeds from seedling companies in the hopes of a better harvest the following year, many farmers have also engaged in various financing schemes that exposed them to further risks.[13] However, the most uncertain aspects for maize plantation and selling the year's harvest is the unpredictable border customs between China and Myanmar.

The unpredictable border customs relationship arises because, officially, China does not allow maize to be imported from Myanmar. All the harvests from northern Shan State would have to be smuggled across the border into China. Thus, farmers would usually sell their harvests to purchasing agents who collected bags of maize in the villages, shipped them to the Chinese border, and then redistributed into smaller portions and smuggled into China via the loose and long border. Given the huge demand for maize in China's domestic market, there are strong financial incentives for these purchasing agents to bypass Chinese border inspection.

Indeed, the Chinese government has tight maize import restrictions. Because it is considered a national food security item, maize imports are subject to a yearly quota. For example, in 2020, the national import quota for maize was 7.2 million tons, of which 60 percent was earmarked for SOEs.[14] Obtaining an import quota permission is not easy. However, even without the quota restriction, maize from Myanmar was not officially permitted to enter the Chinese market because Myanmar did not have an agreement on disease inspection protocol with China.[15] Therefore, whether maize from Myanmar can successfully enter the Chinese market ultimately depends on smuggling operations through the border and how stringent Chinese border inspections are at a particular time.

Because the amount of maize produced in Myanmar in recent years has increased significantly, the amount that illegally entered the Chinese market has grown accordingly. The Chinese border patrol has increased their inspections of smuggled maize crops in recent years, making it difficult for local farmers in northern Shan State to sell their harvest in time. Thus, although commodities smuggling along the Sino-Myanmar border has been ongoing for decades, China's periodic anti-smuggling campaigns inject occasional uncertainty for local farmers whose livelihood depends on easy access to the Chinese market.[16] But in January 2022, the Chinese government signed an agreement with Myanmar, the Sanitary and Phytosanitary Protocol for biosecurity, paving the way for Myanmar to legally ship maize to China on a trial run.[17]

Live Cattle Smuggling

The long and porous border between China and Myanmar is the site for all kinds of smuggling. One peculiar case was the live cattle trade that has boomed for the past decade.[18] The case not only reflected domestic consumption changes in China, but also tied together a complex web of borderland political economy and Myanmar's domestic political fragmentation.

Critically, China has become the second largest beef consuming market in the world in recent years.[19] Its combination of large population plus improving living standards has led to a surge in beef consumption in the country. With all kinds of hotpot places and steakhouses springing up across China's urban spaces, the Chinese appetite for red meat has become insatiable. Such burgeoning demand for beef in China has become so huge that it cannot easily be met by domestic supply. At the same time, the domestic beef price tended to be double that of the international price, which generated high profit for the beef import industry. For example, in early 2020, the domestic beef price was about 80 RMB per kg, while imported beef remained around 45 RMB per kg. Because the Chinese government must satisfy domestic demand while keeping the price at a reasonable level, in recent years China has permitted more foreign beef to be imported. For example, the amount of beef officially imported to China reached 1.65 million tons in 2019, which was twenty times of the 2012 amount. As we can see from Figure 5.3, China became the largest beef importer in the world, accounting for about 30 percent of the global total.

Because of the price difference and the huge domestic demand, beef smuggling is a major source of China's foreign beef. According to some

TOP 5 GLOBAL BEEF IMPORTERS
Carcass Weight Data. '000 MT. Source: USDA/FAS

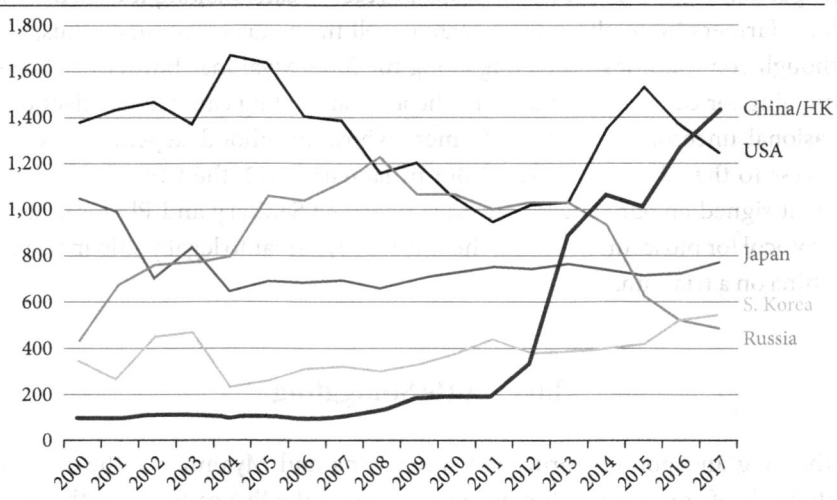

Figure 5.3 Rising Chinese beef imports

estimates, for the 1.65 million tons of officially imported beef, another 1 million tons were smuggled into China. And of the beef smuggled into China, frozen meat is usually smuggled through southern coastal cities, in particular via Hong Kong. However, Chinese consumers also have a thing about freshly slaughtered beef: it is considered a delicacy, particularly in many hotpot places. Thus, live cattle smuggling has been a prominent phenomenon along China's southwestern border provinces of Yunnan and Guangxi, which share a long border with Myanmar, Laos, and Vietnam.

Myanmar has the largest cattle herd in mainland Southeast Asia, but beef consumption is not high due to religious reasons and people's tendency to consider cattle as crucial farming animals. Before 2017, the Myanmar government officially forbid export of live cattle under the 2012 Major Commodity and Service Law. However, due to the lack of enforcement mechanisms, the cattle trade between the two countries consisted of live animals smuggled through the border into China. Some estimates are that in 2015, well in excess of half a million cattle were smuggled from Myanmar into China.[20]

However, to cross the borderland into China requires access to areas under the control of various EAGs.[21] In both Kachin and Shan states, there is a plethora of EAGs, many of which depend upon taxing cross-border trade for revenue.[22] Thus, before 2017, the live cattle smuggling trade was under the exclusive control of these EAGs. Cattle were collected throughout Myanmar, even including many smuggled from India or Bangladesh. The smuggled cattle were then auctioned to different traders, who then transported them close to the Chinese border. Instead of entering China through official customs, however, these cattle were herded by "human mules" across the mountainous and forested border, escaping border inspection.[23]

In 2017, Aung San Suu Kyi's government lifted the ban on cattle exports and decided to regulate the cattle trade in order to generate tax revenue for the Myanmar government. However, even though Myanmar officially allowed cattle to be exported to China, the Chinese government continue to officially ban Myanmar cattle due to disease control reasons. Just as in the maize case mentioned above, Chinese customs require certain standards for disease inspection and quarantine that Myanmar cannot easily meet. Thus, Myanmar's cattle cannot officially be imported into China, so instead they continue to be transported through illegal channels.

The Chinese authorities initially turned a blind eye towards the illegal cattle trade, perhaps because it prevented high beef prices but also due to bribes from local governments. However, the reality was that more and more Myanmar cattle were smuggled into the country, which realistically raised issues about disease inspection and food safety. So, both countries had tried to negotiate a deal to allow Myanmar cattle to be legally imported into China.[24] In January 2020, during Chinese President Xi Jinping's state visit to Myanmar, the Agreement on the Inspection and Sanitary Certification of Slaughter Cattle was signed, which cleared the legal hurdle for Myanmar cattle to be imported to China.

But by this time, significant Chinese business interests were invested in the live cattle import and meat-processing industries. Local governments along the border in Yunnan, for example Baoshan, Lincang, and Dehong, all wanted to have meat-processing industries invest in their locales. There was also substantial competition among them to lure the cattle trade to slaughterhouses in their respective border crossings. Dakang, which is an agribusiness conglomerate in China, invested millions of dollars in the borderland area, hoping to create a value chain for live cattle raising, slaughterhouses, and then meat processing.[25] Thus, there were strong push factors from the Chinese side to formalize this live cattle business, and many interested parties all wanted to have a share of the profitable meat-processing business.

At the same time, the Myanmar government was also responding positively to many of China's geostrategic and economic initiatives. Suu Kyi's government saw clearly that its domestic development necessitated working together with China, and signed onto a few of China's multilateral initiatives, for example the BRI, the China-Myanmar Economic Corridor, and the RCEP.[26] In the end, both countries agreed to set up a few cattle quarantine stations along the border so that cattle could be inspected and quarantined before being shipped across the border to be slaughtered.[27]

However, the legalization of the live cattle trade through official border crossing points into China undermined the profit of the EAGs, who had previously dominated the smuggling routes. This change was particularly serious for many smaller militias in the Shan State that do not control access to other revenue-generating natural resources or drugs.[28] This led several EAGs to attack the cattle trucks along the Mandalay-Muse highway while demanding payment from traders.[29] On the other hand, national peace negotiations with the EAGs had not yet achieved any concrete outcomes, and fighting between government forces and the EAGs had even intensified in the recent past.[30] Because of the Myanmar government military's inability to suppress these EAGs, cattle traders were caught in the crossfire between the two. Many traders had to protect their safety by paying double duties to both the government customs and the EAGs.

Therefore, it seems that in the end, the profitable live cattle trade has intensified conflicts between the Myanmar government and the EAGs, as the former tried to formalize the legal trade. For many traders, however, going through formal channels not only reduces their profit margins but also increases uncertainty over their trucks' passage through EAG-controlled territories along the borderland area. As reported in a *Frontier Myanmar* article, one trader said, "Even though we were paying tax to the government, it failed to protect us from armed groups . . . so eventually cattle exporters chose to go back to the old ways, where they just have to pay tax only to armed groups— at least the illegal routes are safe."[31]

Tropical Fruits

Like the stories of increasing meat consumption, Chinese demand for tropical fruits has also injected new business incentives in Southeast Asia. As China became a major importer, it increasingly dominated the market for

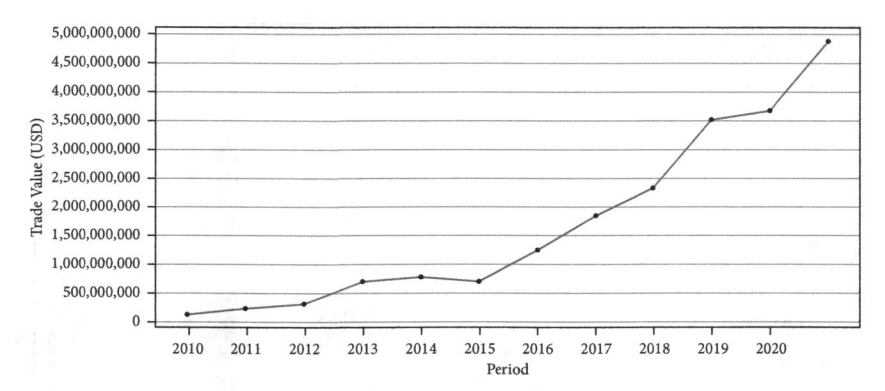

Figure 5.4 Total value of tropical fruit exports from ASEAN member states to China, 2010–2021

Southeast Asian countries in their supply of tropical fruits.[32] Although the exact numbers are difficult to ascertain, partly due to smuggling along the land border as discussed with respect to the cattle trade above, and partly due to different trade data report regimes, it is commonly acknowledged that the Chinese market, including Hong Kong, occupies a disproportionally large share of Southeast Asian fruits. And in Hong Kong's case, many of these imports would be re-exported to the Chinese mainland anyway. As we can see from Figure 5.4, the total for tropical fruits exported from ASEAN to China has consistently grown for the past decade, and particularly picked up speed after 2015. At the same time, Thailand remains the largest source of tropical fruit exports to China from ASEAN, followed by the Philippines, Vietnam, and Myanmar (Figure 5.5).

China has become the biggest market for tropical fruits from Southeast Asia for many reasons. The free trade agreement China established with ASEAN during the past decade has eliminated many trade barriers between them. Then again, geographical proximity certainly makes it easier for countries to transport fresh fruits to China, particularly easily perishable ones. Thus, the fact that watermelon exports to China accounted for almost 100 percent of exports from Vietnam and Myanmar in 2018 was precisely due to such factors.[33] But special fruits like durian have a distinct "stinky" flavor—an acquired taste cherished by Chinese consumers. This type of niche fruit thus has become highly dependent on the Chinese market.

Officially, Thailand is the only country in Southeast Asia where fresh durian is allowed to be imported into China. Malaysia can only export frozen

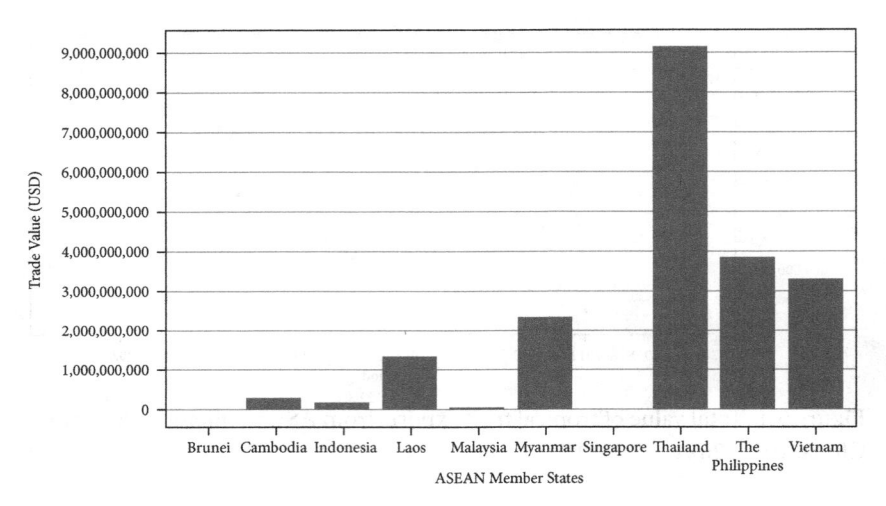

Figure 5.5 Total value of tropical fruit exports from ASEAN member states to China by country, 2010–2021

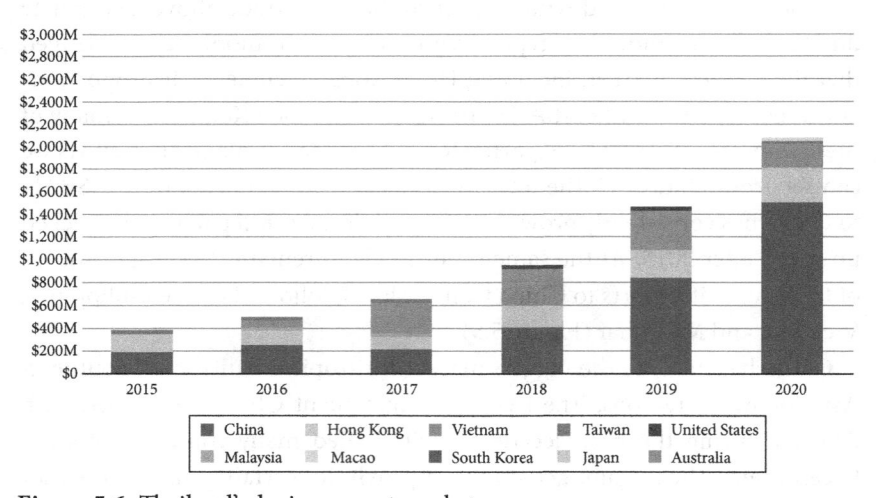

Figure 5.6 Thailand's durian export markets

ones to China.[34] As we can see from Figure 5.6, most of Thailand's durian exports go to mainland China and Hong Kong, and even the sizable exports to Vietnam are destined for re-export to China over land.[35] It seems that China's demand for durian relative to other countries has steadily increased since 2015, with a clear spike in 2020. While China seems to occupy around

50 percent of Thai durian exports in 2015, the proportion rose to almost 70 percent in 2020. In 2021, Thailand exported 875,097 tons of durian to China, totaling 109.2 billion baht, which was about 40 percent of China's market share.[36] Because of the high demand from China, the durian price has also shot up to record high numbers. Anticipation of high profits has drawn many farmers to join the boom for the "golden" cash crop. According to the Thai Office of Agricultural Economics, durian farmlands expanded from just 96,000 hectares in 2012 to 152,000 hectares in 2019.[37] And a record number of farmers have shifted from planting other cash crops (e.g., rubber) to durian in recent years.

Thailand's boom in durian exports, a result of its over-concentration on the Chinese market, has invited a call for caution. When so many farmers switch their land to durian farming, it creates a large number of sunken costs in land use. A sudden disruption on the demand side could lead to significant financial losses for farmers. Although it is easy to sound the alarm given the over-dependency on a single market, it is much harder to find alternative markets for durian comparable to China's. Because of its distinct taste, durian is unlikely to become a popular fruit in most Western markets; and its relatively high price means that durian is an expensive fruit, which further limits its marketing potential. In fact, because of its high price, durian has become increasingly unaffordable in Thailand. For example, it is reported that from 2010 to 2017, Thai domestic consumption of durian fell to 20 percent of what it used to be because of the booming export demand, while the domestic durian price increased tenfold.[38] Thus, there is also significant discontent among domestic consumers about the unaffordability of their favorite fruit.

Meanwhile, the durian trade's high profits have brought many Chinese businesses to enter Thailand to procure and process the fruit from the source. The Chinese fresh fruit business model is distinct from that of its Western counterparts. In general, the oligopolistic pattern tends to dominate in Europe and North America, where large supermarkets play a dominant role in the governance of fresh fruit imports.[39] However, for the Chinese, many small-to-medium enterprises are involved in the more decentralized logistics and distribution of fresh fruits throughout the country. In the case of durian, Chinese entrepreneurs are increasingly involved in the purchase and construction of new packing houses, while undercutting Thai counterparts by buying directly from the farmers.[40]

However, the Chinese are not directly involved in durian farming because it requires special techniques unfamiliar to the Chinese. This is not the case with Chinese investment in other fruit farming, such as watermelons in Myanmar, where they are involved in land rental from local villagers, management of these farms, and distribution back to China.[41] On the other hand, Myanmar villagers do not have the tradition to practice horticulture; instead, they mainly engage in subsistence farming of rice and legumes. Living in one of the least developed countries in the world, many Myanmar villagers are unable to afford the relatively high investment cost, or acquire the farming skills or easy access to market.[42] Therefore, Chinese businesses have expanded their presence in northern Myanmar to cultivate both tropical fruits like mangos, but also out-of-season fruits like watermelons (see Figure 5.7).

Generally speaking, Chinese watermelon season is usually during the summer months, so Myanmar watermelons are mostly exported to China from October to May.[43] Chinese entrepreneurs have dominated the watermelon trade with Myanmar, often leasing land from local villagers by amassing smaller plots into large tracts of land in order to farm at scale. They also bring agrotechnicians from China to supervise watermelon cultivation, and pair them with Burmese translators to advise in watermelon farming practices.[44] But since watermelon is perishable, easy and quick access to China's marketing system is crucial. Thus, northern Myanmar's geographical proximity to the Chinese border makes investment in watermelon farming profitable for many Chinese businesses. Aside from watermelon, many other fruits such as avocado, passion fruit, mango, and mandarin oranges have recently become popular items as well.

Chinese businesses' prominent role in Southeast Asia's fresh tropical fruit has many implications. With an integrated supply chain in both procurement

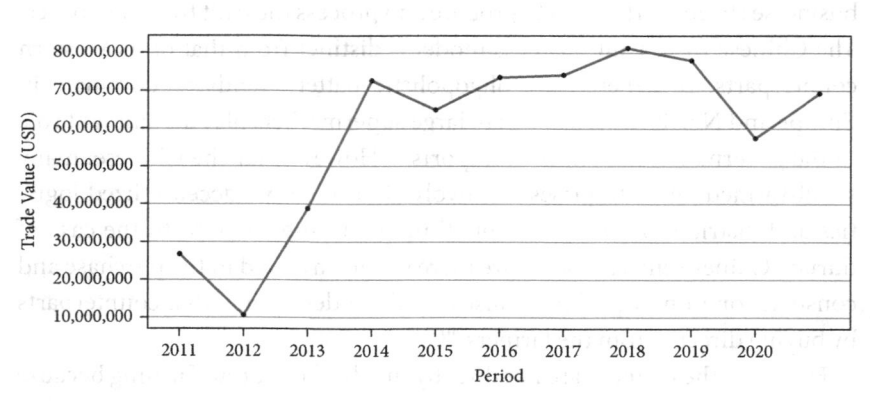

Figure 5.7 Total value of Myanmar's watermelon exports to China, 2011–2021

and distribution, Chinese businesses have clear advantages over local counterparts. These advantages are even more prominent in poorer countries like Myanmar, unlike Thailand. Therefore, more Chinese business incursions into Southeast Asia are likely to generate local business grievances against certain practices by their Chinese counterparts. And with the arrival of the platform economy and the ubiquitous online shopping within China through portals such as Taobao, these Chinese platforms have also branched out to link Chinese consumers directly with sellers in Southeast Asia.[45] So, for fruit businesses in Southeast Asia, if they want to have access to the Chinese market, they must be increasingly integrated into the Chinese platform economy.

Banana Plantation

The increasing domination of Chinese investments in tropical fruits in Southeast Asia has been an ongoing phenomenon. We have so far discussed how Chinese market mechanisms have led to business practices changes in mainland Southeast Asia. In addition, in recent years, many civil society organizations have focused on the banana plantation boom from Chinese investments in Laos, but mainly on how these practices have led to environmental degradation in the country. Although China itself is a major banana producer, many small-to-medium enterprises have also gone to China's borderland area with Laos and Myanmar to lease land for banana farming.[46] Chinese government policies have played a major role in enterprises going to the borderlands: Beijing's goal of reducing drug trafficking from the Gold Triangle area provided additional financial incentive for such investments.[47]

The Golden Triangle area, which is the borderland region of Laos, Myanmar, and Thailand, has been the center of global opium production for decades.[48] Cold War geopolitics made the area peripheral for regional governments and thus deprived it of economic development.[49] Poverty is often blamed for the region's continued poppy plantations. And due to the area's proximity to the Chinese border, the Chinese government has long tried to find a way to reduce opium production in the region since drug trafficking and heroin use have affected Chinese users, leading Beijing to deem them a major non-conventional security issue.[50] One initiative since the year 2000 was to create a poppy substitution development program for Myanmar and Laos. A special fund was set up by the Yunnan provincial government to subsidize Chinese businesses to cultivate cash crops across the border, such as rubber and banana, which could be imported to China without tariffs.[51] Although the program has achieved some positive outcomes in reducing the region's poppy plantations, its reception has been uneven because the program has mostly benefited Chinese businesses at the expense of local farmers.

For northern Laos, which borders China, there are easy transportation links to sell those bananas to China. Asian Highway 3, connected through the construction of the 4th Thai-Lao Friendship Bridge in 2012, connected China's Yunnan province to the Thai-Lao border in Chiang Khong. Thus, many small-to-medium Chinese companies have come to northern Laos to invest in banana plantations. A report published by Plan International in 2017, for example, noted that Chinese banana companies expanded to cover over 11,000 hectares in Bokeo province, where they employed thousands of workers and their families.[52] Already, China has become a main importer of bananas from Laos. In 2014, Laos exported 43,000 tons of bananas to China with a value of US$31 million. This number rose to 220,000 tons in 2017 with a value of US$162 million.[53] By the end of 2021, banana exports to China from Laos reached US$225 million.[54] Overall, as Figure 5.8 shows, bananas account for a large share of Laos's agricultural exports to China and have been overall profitable financially for the Lao economy.[55]

Chinese banana plantation practices in mainland Southeast Asia have distinct characteristics.[56] Because of the relatively limited scale of their investments, they are neither large planation estates nor family style banana farms. Instead, most Chinese banana plantations tend to use a "shifting plantation" production system, whereby land rental is relatively short term and

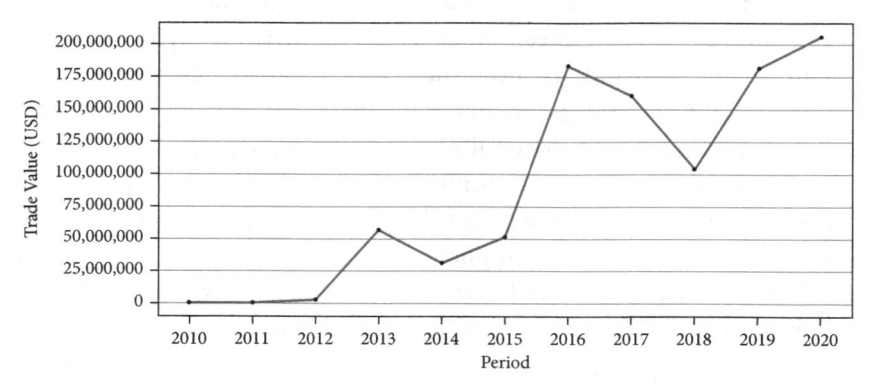

Figure 5.8 Total value of Laos's banana exports to China, 2010–2020

the company usually moves on to another plot after land yields dwindle after a few years of intensive cultivation.[57] The companies often utilize loose forms of contractual agreement with local farmers, and have managed to access large stretches of farmland through brokerage with local village headmen.[58] Land leases tend to be from six to ten years, after which the companies move to other locations because of soil depletion and pest infestation.[59] Such short-term land arrangements do not consider long-term consequences, and these banana companies would try to maximize the output by using extensive fertilizers, pesticides, and other chemicals. Thus, the long-term costs of land contamination or disruption of livelihoods would be borne by local farmers.[60]

Indeed, many recent studies have focused on how such shifting planation practices have generated socioeconomic and environmental consequences for local communities. Although no concrete data are available to determine the scale of the problem, many media reports and policy analyses have noted the widespread negative implications. For example, reports have pointed out that chemicals used in the banana plantations have affected water quality and created hazardous working conditions for workers on the farms.[61] According to a study by Laos's National Agriculture and Forestry Institute in 2016, 63 percent of the plantation workers in northern Laos were sick over a six-month period, with 35 percent reporting illness in the same period from the central and southern parts of the country.[62] With widespread reports of illness of Lao workers at these farms, it seems the health risks posed by these farms are quite high.

With mounting public pressure, the Lao central government was forced to act by issuing a ban on new licenses for banana plantations while ordering an inspection of existing ones. At the time, authorities in Bokeo province suspended the operations of eighteen Chinese-backed banana plantations after discovering violations.[63] However, this proved unpopular for local authorities, who saw their export volume drop; it was reported that in Bokeo province the banana exports fell by more than 180 percent during the first nine months of 2018 compared to the same period the previous year.[64] With the local economy dependent upon these banana exports, with farms employing wage workers, ultimately this ban was lifted in late 2018. The Lao government allowed these banana plantations to expand on the condition that they meet the United Nations Food and Agriculture Organization's Good Agricultural Practices.[65] The government can require compliance with these environmental standards but enforcement remains difficult, so many banana plantations continue to pollute. A Lao agricultural consultant commented on this problem, "[t]he legislation and policies are good, but as we all know enforcement in Laos is very weak . . . officials inspect for the use of chemicals on the plantations, the investors just give them 'white envelopes' [containing bribes] in exchange for their approval."[66]

In fact, local and international media continue to report on the banana farms' malpractice, and stories abound on how farm workers got sick and how waterways around these farms became contaminated. However, either because of local corruption or the Lao state's inability to enforce inspection of these farms, little has been done to ameliorate the problems. On the one hand, the banana boom brought economic payoffs for the Lao state, but on the other it created unforeseen environmental degradation for local communities. Such negative environmental consequences highlight the pitfalls of economic development in institutionally weak countries. As the Plan International report pointed out, it has often been the case that Laos's "provincial and district government officials have not had the capacity over the past few years to deal with the rapid expansion of bananas."[67] Without effective institutional mechanisms and the capacity to monitor and regulate, Laos fell prey to predatorial and exploitative business practices brought by the expansion of the Chinese consumer market and the scale of Chinese banana plantations in the country.

Conclusion

The COVID-19 pandemic closed China's land borders with Southeast Asia. In the initial days of the pandemic, it was reported that fruits and vegetables were left rotting in the fields and at the border crossings.[68] When Beijing further tightened domestic disease control through the so-called "Dynamic Zero" policy, it became a top priority for China's local governments along the Southeast Asian border area to prevent the virus from entering China. To do that, a long border fence was built to keep out illegal crossings from neighboring states that might sabotage its stringent domestic COVID control.[69] Periodic lockdowns of border cities have also significantly dampened local business confidence and economic dynamism.[70]

For local communities along the border, these drastic measures bode ill for their economic livelihood, as their previous transborder mobility is no longer there. As we have discussed in this chapter, there has been extensive smuggling along the Chinese border with Southeast Asian countries for decades. Yet it seems that the harsh border closure and digitized COVID control in China has also hit the smuggling network hard.[71] Thus, the Chinese border closure would mean the disruption of the previous trade networks across mainland Southeast Asia. While the China market in normal times might mean good business, it also means that countries can become exposed to its shocks if they become too dependent.

A few years ago, a *Bangkok Post* report cautioned against Thailand becoming a banana republic for Chinese investment in agriculture.[72] The worry remains whether countries in Southeast Asia would become like Central American countries, which are highly dominated and exploited by agricultural industries from the United States. There are certainly some similarities between the two. The United States, with its large consumer market, wields a huge amount of economic influence in Central America, and China occupies a similar economic position towards Southeast Asia, with a large domestic consumer base and rising purchasing power. If the COVID-19 pandemic's effect on China is temporary and the country continues to open up its economy, then perhaps a similar pattern of economic domination will occur between China and Southeast Asia as well.

6

Illicit Political Economy

Introduction

Thailand's Chiang Saen is a sleepy little town along the Mekong River. As a historical walled city, Chiang Saen used to be a major military garrison under the control of the Burmese when they ruled over the Lanna Kingdom in contemporary northern Thailand. These days, Chiang Saen is a major trading port between Thailand and upper stream countries along the Mekong. Still, it is a relatively nondescript low-rise town without many explicit signs of "development." Right across the river in the Lao city of Tonpheung, however, a massive neon-lit building complex can be seen towering over the Chiang Saen side. The Kings Romans Casino, owned by a former Chinese national/gangster Zhao Wei is a notorious gambling joint that has "long been implicated in human trafficking and drug smuggling, and caters to a predominantly Chinese high roller clientele seeking out bear-paw soup and tiger-bone wine to go with their rounds of baccarat and call girls."[1]

This massive casino is clearly visible from the Thai side of the river, yet few local people have ever ventured there. According to some of the informants that I spoke to, the Kings Romans Casino, or *jinmumian* as pronounced in Mandarin, is too expensive for the locals, and its clients are usually those who fly to Chiang Rai airport and are then chauffeured directly to the casino. Even in 2019, before the start of the COVID-19 pandemic, Kings Romans was already famous for its virtual gambling. The casino's clients placed their bets by video while their money was supposedly transferred across offshore accounts, making it difficult to trace. The seediness of the Kings Romans Casino was further exemplified by the almost autonomous status of its location within the Golden Triangle Special Economic Zone, where Zhao leased from the Lao government without much interference. In such an enclave, where Lao sovereignty has been subcontracted, being illicit is the nature of the political economy that circulates across national borders and away from state control.[2]

The Ripple Effect. Enze Han, Oxford University Press. © Oxford University Press 2024.
DOI: 10.1093/oso/9780197696583.003.0006

Transnational ethnic Chinese criminal networks occupy a crucial node of the illicit regional political economy. What is noticeable in recent years is the dramatic growth of online casinos and scamming operations, which are based in Southeast Asia but operated by these ethnic Chinese criminal networks. With the availability of widespread internet coverage and smartphones in China, the online gambling industry has blossomed through targeting Chinese customers. Called "Spinach"—in Mandarin the homophone for gambling (*Bocai*)—the boom of online casinos has facilitated the movement of capital across national boundaries and allowed criminal networks to access the vast Chinese market.

Mostly targeting the Chinese-speaking world, these criminal networks have not only been involved in tricking money out of ordinary people's pockets but also engaged in human trafficking, abductions, and even murders. In July 2022, multiple reports surfaced of people—many of them ethnic Chinese from mainland China, Taiwan, Hong Kong, Malaysia, and even Singapore—being kidnapped, trafficked, or lured to work for scam syndicates in Cambodia and Myanmar, garnering unprecedented international media and public attention.[3] One victim recounted how they were "forced to become reluctant scammers to snare prospective victims around the world" and, if cooperation was not forthcoming, they would be "beaten and confined to a dark room for days."[4] Another described how she was "tricked" into believing she was outbound for a "typical" administrative job, only to find herself coerced to "scour the internet for victims she could trick into investing in an online scam."[5] Sihanoukville, a crime-ridden coastal city in Cambodia that houses casinos as well as many scam syndicates, was described as a "living hell" where only death and despair awaits.[6]

A few governments (such as mainland China, Taiwan, and Hong Kong SAR) have issued travel warnings, or tried to prevent their citizens from traveling to some mainland Southeast Asian countries, such as Myanmar and Cambodia. Rescue missions have also been carried out to get their citizens out from the dens of these criminal syndicates.[7] However, the criminal networks and their activities in Southeast Asia seem to show no sign of abating. In fact, many overseas Chinese communities in Southeast Asia are fearful of the rising criminality in Southeast Asia and the dangers it poses for their property and physical safety.

The ethnic Chinese criminal networks have a long history of operating in Southeast Asia. The growth of Chinese secret societies or triads were part and parcel of Chinese migration to the region during past centuries.[8] They went in disguise as benevolent associations to assist the migrants, and they were often tolerated by European colonial authorities because they could help control the local Chinese population in Southeast Asia.[9] In places where the Chinese were ruled indirectly, secret societies were more prevalent.[10]

A few prominent secret societies at the turn of the twentieth century, such as the *Tongmenhui* and *Hongmen*, played crucial roles in fomenting revolutionary changes within China, due to their extensive networks among the overseas Chinese migrants in Southeast Asia and beyond. Indeed, it was difficult to distinguish between the illicit criminal networks with the transnational secret societies among the Chinese circulating across national boundaries.[11] What was considered illicit also varied across different political jurisdictions and periods of time.

Such transnational characteristics have continued to define overseas Chinese networks throughout the years. Since the communists took over in 1949, links with the Chinese mainland were cut off, and these illicit networks became further entrenched within the overseas Chinese community within the region. For example, during the Cold War, the narcotics trading networks connected overseas the Chinese criminal networks from Burma, Thailand, Hong Kong, and Taiwan.[12] With time, many such networks have also transformed into formal business-like entities.[13] It wasn't until the 1980s, however, that triads once again proliferated within mainland China, aided by political economic changes, corruption, rapid urbanization, and the demand for illicit goods and services.[14]

As China became once again plugged into the process of globalization, it became a strong link within "the global chains of vice industries . . . and a destination for many overseas Chinese triads."[15] Chinese transnational crime spread across continents yet remained deeply embedded within Chinese diasporic networks.[16] Furthermore, as a result of the recent globalization of Chinese capital, the movement of such criminal networks has also accompanied capital flows abroad, and has become entangled with preexisting transnational overseas Chinese criminal networks in Southeast Asia.

In Chapter 3, I covered the impact of China's presence on the regional political economy, and this chapter looks at the illicit dimension of China's globalized economy in Southeast Asia.[17] Specifically, it looks at how the growth of the online casino economy has been deeply tied with Chinese capital looking for investment opportunities in Southeast Asia. Closely associated with these opportunities are the online scammers who specifically target ethnic Chinese communities across national boundaries. More often than not, these operations are located in a few seemingly legitimate SEZs in Southeast Asia. Thus, camouflaged as official Chinese investment in Southeast Asia, many operations are in fact illicit criminal networks expanding their influence in the region simultaneously.

This chapter proceeds as follows. It first describes the recent boom and bust of the online casino economies from the Philippines to Cambodia and Myanmar. It then traces how changes in government regulations have facilitated the movement of online casinos across the region. The discussion then turns to how Chinese online scamming has expanded in Southeast Asia and the ensuing violence associated with this industry. The chapter then tentatively discusses the relationship between the illicit economies and the existing SEZs in Southeast Asia, and how the lack of state regulation and capacity and rampant corruption have facilitated the growth of these illicit activities.

The Boom and Bust of Casino Economies

It is a common stereotype that the Chinese people like to gamble. However, domestically, gambling is banned except for the limited state lottery, but illegal gambling operations remain prevalent throughout the country. Depending on the political winds, the Chinese government has periodically carried out campaigns to rid the country of gambling and other illegal activities.[18] The only place close to the Chinese mainland where gambling is legal is Macau. But even there, the Chinese government has also increased its monitoring of organized crime and the use of Macau for money laundering and other illegal activities, especially during recent rounds of anti-corruption campaigns carried out by the Xi Jinping administration.[19]

Yet Chinese domestic demand for gambling is huge, and quite a few countries in the region aim to cash in by enticing Chinese gamblers to spend their money in their jurisdictions. Previously, a few enclaves along the China-Myanmar and China-Laos borders operated gambling sites to attract Chinese tourists to illegally cross the border for some fun.[20] Mongla in Myanmar and Boten in Laos used to run casinos and other entertainment operations that were illegal in China.[21] However, with issues arising concerning gambling debts and the use of violence to extort money from Chinese tourists, the Chinese government forced local authorities to close these casinos. In 2011, the Lao government shut down the Golden Boten City under pressure from Beijing.[22]

Then, the trend was for many of these casino operations to move further south, away from the Chinese border to escape direct pressure from Chinese law enforcement. Domestic political changes in some Southeast Asian countries, such as the Philippines and Cambodia, also provided more supportive policies towards the casino industry. Both countries experienced a huge demand for casinos, both onsite and online, as well as throngs of Chinese investment and tourists.

In 2016, when Rodrigo Duterte became the new president of the Philippines, he started a "Philippine Offshore Gambling Operations" (POGO) scheme that allowed online gambling to operate in the country's major cities.[23] This policy opened the floodgates for online gambling capital to move to the Philippines. The state-owned Philippine Amusement and Gaming Corporation (PAGCOR) has issued sixty licenses under POGO, and each license can be used for up to twelve "service providers" that offer different online gambling games. At the same time, because it is still a legal grey area, many gambling firms operate illegally without an official license. So far, PAGCOR has become the most profitable state enterprise in the Philippines because of the handsome licensing fees, which have been the government's third-largest source of revenue behind taxes and customs.[24] For example, PAGCOR Chairman and CEO Andrea Domingo stated that PAGCOR's past earnings averaged only 56 million peso annually from online gaming operations, but had since increased considerably: "When the current management strengthened PAGCOR's regulatory authority over Philippine offshore gaming operators (POGO), we immediately saw its significant contributions to PAGCOR's overall revenues. In 2016, POGO operations generated P657 million followed by P3.924 billion in 2017 and P7.365 billion in 2018."[25]

Most of the online casino firms that obtained their POGO licenses are Chinese. Because the target clienteles are also mostly the ethnic Chinese community at large, these casino firms need workers and other service providers who can speak Mandarin. For this reason, many Chinese and Taiwanese nationals as well as other Mandarin speakers from Southeast Asia are targeted by recruitment companies to work for the casinos in the Philippines. With promises of high salaries and generous benefits, the main criteria to work in these casinos is a person's linguistic ability to speak Mandarin. As a form of linguistic labor, ethnic Chinese workers "possess the linguistic proficiency necessary to facilitate online or onsite communication between the players and the [casino] firms."[26] Indeed, Chinese nationals became the largest work permit holders in the Philippines. According to government records, about 110,000 work permits were issued to Chinese nationals in 2018, increasing to 138,000 in April 2019.[27] Also, many people work illegally in the Philippines for these online casinos.

The large number of casino firms with huge profit margins generated a shockwave in the Filipino economy, particularly in the real estate sector. The changes arose because many online casino firms were often also involved in real estate businesses such as buying properties and leasing office buildings.[28] The casinos could outbid not only other industries for fancy office buildings but also condominiums, which they bought as residential quarters for their workers.[29] As a result, the real estate sector has soared and many other industries crucial to the Filipino economy, such as call centers that provide considerable employment for local Filipinos, have been priced out. At the same time, many ordinary Filipinos have also been forced to move out of the city center to surrounding towns in Manila because they cannot afford to pay the rising rent.

The tens of thousands of ethnic Chinese who come to work for the casinos are often called the "spinach eaters," and they have formed a unique culture and way of life distinct from local Filipinos. They tend to live together in condominiums provided by the casino companies, and they often "come as a group, leave as a group" to avoid interacting with the outside world in Manila.[30] Because of their distinct characteristics, ethnic Chinese are also often targets for robbery and thus contribute to an overall deterioration of public security. Many violent acts targeting ethnic Chinese gamblers have been committed, such as kidnappings and extortion of money, and unsolved murder cases. Even the Philippine police moonlight by also targeting the Chinese to make a quick buck.[31]

Public antipathy towards the casino industry and the growing size of the Chinese community in the Philippines has been rising. The casinos' huge profits are not evenly shared with the local community, while locals have to deal with the rising cost of living and housing. For Filipinos, "Chinese workers have changed the city, populating condominiums, regularly breaking rules, and overcrowding Metro Manila's malls."[32] Strong anti-Chinese senti- ment occurred within the context of the perceived cozying up of Duterte's government towards Beijing, and has thus fueled speculation that the casino industry has deeply implicated bilateral diplomatic relations.

Indeed, Duterte's government has been hesitant to rein in the casino industry because of the huge revenues it generates for the state, and monies that have lubricated the political economic system, despite the Chinese government's years of pressure on the Philippine government to ban online gambling. In Beijing's eyes, online gambling has undermined China's financial institutions and exacerbated crimes and social problems in China.[33] In August 2019, the Chinese Embassy in Manila issued a statement urging "concrete and effective measures to prevent and punish the Philippine casinos . . . and other forms of gambling entities for their illegal employment of Chinese citizens and crack down on related crimes that hurt the Chinese citizens."[34]

The Philippine government's response was lukewarm; it only announced a POGO application moratorium, under which it stopped issuing licenses for new online gambling firms.[35] After a meeting between Xi and Duterte in Beijing in late August 2019, PAGCOR and other Philippine government agencies stepped up raids on illegal operators but resisted carrying out a complete ban on online gambling. Duterte's government continued to defend the online gambling sector, labeling POGOs an "essential" business, despite growing domestic and foreign anger towards the online gambling sector. Although allegations arose that Duterte's government was forging closer ties with Beijing instead of with Washington, Duterte's stance in pushing back against Beijing's pressure on banning online gambling might indicate special economic/political interests among his political support base for such a policy.

Indeed, after the election of Ferdinand Marcos Jr. as the new president, the Philippine government's stance on online gambling notably changed. In September 2022, the Ministry of Justice announced a plan to shut down more than one hundred online gambling companies and deport about 40,000 Chinese nationals working in the sector.[36] This move occurred despite the estimate that a complete ban of online gambling would leave "vacant 1.05 million square meters of office space and 8.9 billion pesos ($151 million) in foregone annual rental," not to mention the potential loss of licensing fees and other levies for the government.[37] It remains to be seen how the Philippines' online gambling ban will pan out and what implications it will bring to both the Philippine economy and its relations with China.

Other than in the Philippines, the boom and bust of the casino industry fueled by illicit Chinese capital has played out more dramatically in Cambodia's seaside city of Sihanoukville. As early as 2006, a Sihanoukville Special

Economic Zone (SSEZ) was selected as a cooperative project between the two governments.[38] This project preceded by almost a decade of President Xi's official launch of the BRI in 2014, and the signing of a memorandum of understanding between China and Cambodia that indicated the latter's embrace of the BRI.[39] Thus, several major industrial and infrastructure projects, such as the SSEZ, the Phnom Penh-Sihanoukville Expressway, and the Angkor International Airport in Siem Reap were incorporated within official BRI projects.

Although the Cambodian government wants Sihanoukville to become an industrial city just like Shenzhen in China, the lure of the city only brought in Chinese illicit capital, and many criminal networks simply used the BRI as a public relations cover. Such investments concentrated in the gambling sector as well as the associated industries such as real estate, entertainment, hotels, and restaurants. With such hot money, Sihanoukville transformed literally from a sleepy little "fishing village" to a neon-lit city with large-scale construction sites, soaring rents, and deteriorating public safety.

In Cambodia, citizens are legally barred from partaking in gambling activities and thus only foreigners are allowed to bet in casinos in the country. In the capital Phnom Penh, only NagaWorld, which is a Malaysian gambling conglomerate, is allowed to operate within the city's 200 km radius. Poipet and Bavet, which are on the border between Cambodia and Thailand and Vietnam, respectively, mainly cater to cross-border gamblers from Thailand and Vietnam.[40] However, the draw of Sihanoukville was not only the onsite casinos and associated industries within the city but also online gambling firms that specifically cater to Chinese clientele.

Exact data on how many casinos are in Sihanoukville is difficult to find, but it has been reported that before the ban on online casinos in Cambodia at the end of 2019, at least eighty were in operation in the city.[41] Another estimate put the annual revenue from these casinos between US$3.5 billion and US$5 billion a year, 90 percent of which came from online gambling.[42] The Cambodian government only taxes monthly casino license fees, and the national tax revenue from casinos in 2018 was $46 million, which increased to $50 million in 2019.[43] Together with the associated industries that mushroomed in Sihanoukville and elsewhere, the gambling sector has definitely brought handsome economic benefits to Cambodia shown in its overall GDP and the fattened pockets of some of its politicians.

But the gambling sector brought with it bad elements that Cambodia probably did not want. Dubbed the "Wild Wild West," as a place to make a quick buck, Sihanoukville became the place for many Chinese criminal networks to operate across all sorts of businesses, and the city witnessed an unprecedented increase of Chinese activities. It was rumored at the time that in 2017, 300,000 Chinese were living in the city, but that number doubled in 2019.[44] It became a haven for online gambling sites targeting players in mainland China, and a base for internet scams, money laundering, and other criminal activities. The concentration of gambling activities has brought with it an unintended but staggering increase in the area's crime rate.[45] In May 2019, for example, a video clip emerged online of a Chinese gang leader allegedly from Chongqing surrounded by tattooed thugs, in which the leader warned other groups to stay away from the city and declared that his Chongqing gang alone would decide the fate of Sihanoukville.[46]

Not only was the crime rate rising, but the speculative economy on real estate brought by the Chinese migrants also made the city unlivable for ordinary Cambodians. Instead of the Chinese bringing development and economic opportunities as the BRI promised, what came instead were criminal syndicates and lawlessness. Sensing a public backlash, the Chinese Ambassador to Cambodia at the time acknowledged how Chinese criminal networks brought this negative influence to Cambodia by saying, "China supports the Cambodian government to take action against any Chinese criminals according to the law . . . We will continue to cooperate and coordinate with the Cambodian government and fight against all illegal activities."[47]

Because many victims of these online casinos and scam operations were from the Chinese mainland, in 2018 both governments reached an agreement to establish a law enforcement partnership. Pursuant to the agreement, a joint operations center, namely the National Police's Anti-Technology Crime Division, was opened in Phnom Penh in September 2019. To assist in its implementation, ninety Chinese police were deployed. On the day after its inauguration, 116 Chinese criminals were arrested, deported to China for prosecution, and prohibited from entering the Cambodian territory for three years. The center also set up a hotline for the Chinese community to report information about online gambling operations or other illicit activities in Sihanoukville.[48]

In August 2019, the Cambodian government issued a directive to ban online gambling, effective from 2020. The directive decried how online gambling had encouraged a wave of Chinese investments in casinos in the country, and the industry had been used by foreign criminals to extort money both within the country and abroad, causing a negative impact on

Cambodia's "security, public order and social order."[49] The announcement of the ban was supported by the Chinese government. Chinese Foreign Ministry Spokesperson Geng Shuang stated that the ban would "help protect both Cambodian and Chinese people's interests . . . it will also strengthen our law enforcement cooperation and friendly relations."[50]

The ban on online gambling in Cambodia dealt a deadly blow to the casino economy and its associated businesses in Sihanoukville, which led to over ten thousand Chinese nationals fleeing from Cambodia. The city's real estate bubble immediately burst. Business rentals decreased by 30 percent and hotels bookings dropped by half, returning prices to approximately the pre-online gambling boom levels.[51] The whole city became a ghost town, with more than 1,000 unfinished buildings abandoned by the departing Chinese.[52] Many people who invested in the city lost money. And the city's long-term economic prospects dimmed as a result of the double whammy of the collapse of the casino economy and the COVID-19 pandemic that followed in early 2020.

However, many Chinese nationals who fled Sihanoukville have not returned to China. The gambling operators and criminal syndicates would prefer to relocate somewhere still relatively close to the Chinese mainland but far enough away from Beijing's direct ability to pressure regional governments to ban them. Myanmar's Karen State was apparently the choice. The borderland region between Karen State and Thailand has been largely under the control by a few EAGs and various loosely managed militias that might or might not be affiliated with the Myanmar central government.[53] This region has been notorious for its lawlessness and human rights violations committed by various armed forces in control of the area.[54] The town of Shwe Kokko in the city of Myawaddy along the Thai-Myanmar border thus became the next haven to shelter Chinese-run gambling operations. Soon after the exodus began in Cambodia, Shwe Kokko saw an inflow of Chinese investment, leading to the explosive growth of the Chinese migrant population locally and the construction of buildings and casino complexes in the town's vicinity.

A few prominent companies previously based in Sihanoukville have since relocated to this part of the Myanmar borderland.[55] The most notorious is the Shwe Kokko New City project, funded by a Hong Kong-registered, Thailand-headquartered Yatai International Holdings Group. Yatai Group's owner is a mysterious person called She Zhijiang. A former Chinese national currently carrying a Cambodian passport, Mr. She is known by various pseudonyms, including She Lunkai, Dylan She, and Tang Kraing Kai.[56] He first made his fortune in the Philippines, and later the Yatai Group also invested heavily in Cambodia such as the Long Bay project in the Koh Kong province as well as other casinos and hotels. As the pressure to ban online casinos was building up in Cambodia, the Yatai Group partnered with the Karen State Border Guard Force (BGF), which ruled over the Shwe Kokko area, to invest.

The BGF, previously called the Democratic Karen Buddhist Army until its formal integration into the Myanmar national military Tatmadaw, was under the command of Colonel Saw Chit Thu.[57] Although the area is technically under the jurisdiction of the Myanmar central government, Saw Chit Thu rules as if it is his own fiefdom. Indeed, much happens on the ground outside the Myanmar central government's knowledge or supervision.

The Yatai Group announced ambitious plans for the Shwe Kokko New City project, which it claims include building a US$15 billion high-tech hub with airport, casinos, hotels, luxury housing, and entertainment complex, and the creation of a self-contained city.[58] Right on the Taung Yin river that separates Myanmar from Thailand, the Shwe Kokko New City project has since taken shape with large-scale construction, and multiple high-rise hotel buildings have already sprung up in the former paddy fields.[59]

The Yatai Group claimed that its project was associated with China's official BRI to increase its legitimacy by creating the impression that it has the Chinese government's official backing. The company also concocted various claims of connection with the Chinese government and other state entities, although many such claims are nebulous without much supporting evidence.[60] The Chinese embassy in Myanmar later issued a statement clarifying that the Shwe Kokko New City project has nothing to do with the BRI, along with the usual objection to cross-border gambling and the need for law-and-order cooperation with Myanmar.[61]

Indeed, the NLD government at the time launched an investigation into the illegal online gambling at the Shwe Kokko New City project, which caused a halt to some of the project's construction. Given this investigation, together with COVID-19, it seemed that the project would come to an end. Yet Myanmar's military coup in February 2021 led to a domestic power reshuffle that further strengthened the BGF's power amidst growing lawlessness in the country.[62] As will be discussed later, the Shwe Kokko New City project became a haven for online scamming and human trafficking. In the end, at the behest of the Chinese government, Mr She was arrested in

Thailand in August 2022.[63] But it seems that even after his arrest, nothing much changed on the ground regarding illicit operations.

In addition to the Shwe Kokko New City project, there is also the Saixigang Industrial Zone, which is headed by Wan Kuok-ku, who was arrested and convicted in 1999 in Macau for a gambling-associated murder. Saixigang's name's sake literally means surpass Sihanoukville in Mandarin Chinese.[64] Another is the Huanya International New City project, which was associated with two Sihanoukville-based ethnic Chinese businessmen and was endorsed by the Karen National Union.[65] These investment projects are all affiliated with a variety of ethnic armed groups in Myanmar's Karen State. Although technically the Myanmar central government has the authority to supervise these investment projects, in reality, armed groups and their warlords have created these havens to host these criminal networks. Despite their claims of developing some kind of SEZs in Myawaddy as part of China's BRI, most accounts were false, as most projects are predominantly involved in online gambling targeting the Chinese market. Worse still, many are also the main perpetrators of online scamming and even human trafficking.

Online Scamming and Human Trafficking

It has been reported that around 60 percent of online scammers are concentrated in Cambodia and northern Myanmar.[66] In Sihanoukville, at one point a reported total of 100,000 Chinese were stationed there to carry out scamming operations.[67] Instead of preying on non-ethnic Chinese locals in Southeast Asia, however, the scamming syndicates predominantly target ethnic Chinese, loosely defined, from mainland China, Taiwan, Hong Kong, and Southeast Asia. Linguistic affinity with various Chinese dialects is the main criteria for their scamming operations. Ethnic Chinese, in particular those from the mainland, are often the target because of regulatory loopholes, the burgeoning wealth of mainland Chinese, and the population's overall lack of financial literacy.

Operators use a few common types of online scams. One scam involves posing as personnel of Chinese public security organs, procuratorates, and courts (known collectively as *Gongjianfa*), and informing victims that unless a certain amount of money, usually laundered proceeds, credit card charges, or even an outstanding electricity bills, is paid, they will be arrested or put on trial. A recent famous case involved a ninety-year-old woman in Hong Kong who was conned out US$32 million by scammers posing as public security officers from the Chinese mainland.[68] A similar scam that became prevalent during the COVID-19 pandemic was that scammers would pose as public health bureau officers to inform victims they would be found guilty of violating testing or quarantine measures unless certain payments were made. Such scamming operations were reported in a few places where governments put in place rather stringent public health measures, such as the Chinese mainland, Hong Kong, Singapore, and Taiwan.

Another form of online scam is known as "pig-butchering" (*Shazhupan*). Pig-butchering involves "the perpetrator building a relationship, often romantic but not always, with the victim over months, akin to fattening the pig, before convincing them to invest money into a fake venture, slaughtering the animal."[69] Usually, scammers are taught using specially designed manuals, trained by their superiors, with the scripts rehearsed many times so that scammers can handle just about any conversation that they would encounter.[70] It can take some time before the target is hooked, and sweeteners are usually needed in the form of some investment returns. After gaining the victim's trust, the scammer would convince him or her to deposit more money into fraudulent online platforms until the victim one day realizes the cash deposited has been frozen and disappeared.

Many victims of pig-butchering schemes are women, especially single and divorced women. In one reported case, a group of Chinese scammers based in northern Myanmar first developed virtual intimacy and trust with their potential victims through online dating sites. Once suitable targets were identified, more senior members of the syndicate would take over. According to the investigation, more than RMB 300,000 were lost by the victims.[71] In another report, Wang, a divorced woman, "met" a Mr. Li who posed as a successful businessman in construction. After the two were connected on WeChat, a popular social networking app in China, it did not take long for Wang to fall madly in love with Li. Shortly after, Li "revealed" to Wang his plan to earn quick money, which involved making strategic bets on a "foreign" gambling site. Li and his fellow scammers first offered some sweeteners to Wang by allowing her to earn and cash out some money; afterwards, when the total amount of deposited cash reached RMB 1.4 million, they froze Wang's money. Only then did Wang realize she had been scammed.[72] Additionally, scamming operations are also common on same-sex dating sites/apps.

Some telecommunication scams have matured into sophisticated investment scams involving forex, precious metals, cryptocurrency, or Ponzi schemes that go beyond the usual "butchering the pig" practices. Scammers exploit victims' inadequate understanding of finances and investment. The Chongqing police revealed a sophisticated case of an investment scam in February 2022. There, the victim was invited to join a WeChat group when "participants," many of whom were impersonated by other scammers, actively "discussed" how to invest in cryptocurrency to earn big money. The victim, under the urging of an "instructor" in the group, then downloaded an application for cryptocurrency investment. After depositing more than RMB 1 million, she was removed from the group and could no longer log into the investment application.[73]

Most scammers are recruited from the Chinese mainland. The relatively abundant cheap labor plus the lure to make a quick buck makes it easier for scamming syndicates to recruit. In 2020 alone, it was reported that a total of 361,000 online scamming suspects were arrested and recovered at least RMB 187.6 billion in losses to fraud.[74] The Chinese government realized the dire situation of online scamming and the socioeconomic damages they caused. Therefore, in April 2021, Beijing hosted a meeting on how to combat online crimes.

A national campaign was also carried out to pressure scammers in northern Myanmar to return to China. Many local governments issued notices to those suspected of living in northern Myanmar asking them to return home lest they face heavy fines. Some local governments threatened that if they did not return in time, they would cancel their household registration (*hukou*), which is extremely important in China. Others published the scammers' names, photos, and addresses, and threatened that their family's and relatives' social welfare would be in danger.[75] According to some reports, 210,000 Chinese nationals were convinced to return to China from northern Myanmar in 2021.[76]

This campaign probably worked and many of the scamming syndicates' labor force did return to China. At the same time, because of the stringent zero-COVID policy the Chinese government put in place during 2020–2022, China's borders were closed, and its citizens were prevented from traveling abroad without sound reasons. Thus, for many of the scamming syndicates, China's border closures meant that their operations faced an unstable working force. So, the syndicates looked instead to the large overseas Chinese communities in Southeast Asia.

Indeed, recently, many reports confirm cases of human trafficking regarding ethnic Chinese from East and Southeast Asia who have been tricked and coerced into online gambling/scamming dens in Cambodia and northern Myanmar. Although the actual numbers are difficult to come by, estimates are that tens of thousands of such human trafficking cases of people from Hong Kong, Taiwan, Malaysia, Singapore, and Thailand have been held as "slaves" to work for these syndicates.[77] For example, a nineteen-year-old Malaysian Chinese was enticed by a recruitment advertisement online looking for agents to purchase luxury accessories on another's behalf. Enticed by the high salary offered during the interview, he decided to accept the offer and flew to Phnom Penh, after which he was held at gunpoint and sold to a Chinese company engaged in online scamming in Sihanoukville.[78] Likewise, according to a report, more than one hundred Singaporeans were kidnapped and held captive in the Victory Paradise Resort in Sihanoukville alone.[79]

Scamming syndicates use several tactics to trick or coerce people into working for them. Many are first attracted, or rather deceived, by lucrative job offers posted online. They then fly directly to Cambodia, Myanmar, or Thailand, only to find their identification documents and belongings confiscated upon landing and themselves taken to unidentified compounds. Such a strategy is particularly effective to lure desperate young adults who are either jobless or wanting to make a quick fortune. Many others who had previously worked in Cambodia in the manufacturing sector were later tricked into these scamming operations during COVID when the local economy came to a halt. Worse still, rumor has it that many people who were directly kidnapped in Thailand were brought across the border to Myanmar. Therefore, Chinese-speaking people were warned that they should not travel to border cities such as Mae Sot, which is right across the border from Myawaddy. If they are caught by human trafficking agents, they can be sold for at least US$20,000 to one of the scamming syndicates.

Escape is often extremely difficult for victims once in captivity. One victim from Hong Kong held captive in Myanmar informed the outside world through audio that "I have seen people who tried to escape but failed, they were shot and carried back in . . . escape is not an option."[80] Some victims were told that unless a huge ransom was paid, they would not be released. Representatives from the Malaysian Chinese Association who were involved in negotiating the release of captive Malaysian nationals indicated that some victims had to fork out up to US$20,000 in return for their release.[81] However, sometimes even after the ransom is paid, the victims can still be sold to another syndicate that does not honor the release. This outcome is why many victims can only hope for a government-organized rescue team, but so far, no major intergovernmental cooperation targeting human trafficking has occurred. Most governments so far have only warned their citizens not to travel to Cambodia or Myanmar.

Conclusion

Studying the illicit economy has been a focus in some academic fields such as human geography and political economy.[82] In recent years, scholars have focused on the illicit dimension of international political economy (IPE).[83] According to Andreas's definition, illicit international political economy is defined by "clandestine cross-border flows of people, goods, money, and information that are unauthorized by the sending or receiving country."[84] Indeed, more and more IPE scholarship has noticed how the expansion of transnational illicit networks has been aided by the globalization process, because it provides an opportunity for these non-state actors to be linked with global financial and trading networks that capitalize on the economic opportunities presented by the lack of state control in certain geographical locales.[85]

As I have demonstrated in this chapter, the illicit dimension of Chinese political economy in Southeast Asia is certainly aided by the expansion of China's global footprint. Thus, it has deep implications for how we understand China's presence in Southeast Asia. Previously, such a focus has been largely overshadowed by a disproportionate emphasis on state capitalism in China, and more recently, the geopolitical rivalry with the United States. The case of online gambling and scamming operations in Southeast Asia, largely constituted and developed by outbound and transnational Chinese criminal networks, provides a window of opportunity though which to explore the illicit dimension of Chinese political economy. At the same time, we can see that the transnational proliferation of these criminal networks takes place within and capitalizes on the dense social fabric connecting Chinese diasporas to the Chinese mainland, and has harnessed cultural and linguistic affinity as a way to hook victims. Such lingual-cultural patterning is deeply embedded within the so-called "Greater China" sphere of cultural influence.[86] In this sense, the illicit Chinese political economy's presence in Southeast Asia is highly cultured. All in all, this illicit political economy, far from being sanctioned by the Chinese state, has had wide-ranging negative implications in Southeast Asia.

7

Migration Encounters

Introduction

In recent years, a food item called "*mala*" has been trending in Thailand. Its name is essentially the transliteration of the same Chinese words. Popular in Chiang Mai and Chiang Rai beginning around 2016, *mala* has since gained increasing popularity in Bangkok and other parts of Thailand. However, the name has taken on different meanings from one country to another. *Mala* in Chinese refers only to a spicy taste and numbing effect often associated with Sichuan food. But in Thailand, *mala* has become associated specifically with a type of street barbeque with cubes of meat, seafood, and vegetables topped with spicy and numbing ingredients. This style of cooking in Chinese is often called *shaokao*, which is not necessarily associated with Sichuan food, but somehow it became known as *mala* in Thailand.

This import of a Chinese food item represents a case in point for Thai society's intensified re-encounter with a "familiar other"—the Chinese. The ethnic Chinese in Southeast Asia have been defined historically as the "familiar other," in the sense that they came en masse through migration, yet they were kept out of the local *bumiputra* political and social life while maintaining a prominent cultural and economic presence.[1] In Thailand's case, many types of contemporary "Thai" food items can trace their origin to Chinese immigration since the nineteenth century, the most famous of which would be the ubiquitous street food of boat noodles, as well as Hainanese Chicken and so forth. These foods originated from southern China in provinces such as Guangdong, Fujian, and Hainan, the regions from which most migrants to Southeast Asia originated. However, the import of *mala*, a type of food associated with the Sichuan province, which is not a traditional emigrant-sending province, represents a new trend in the movement of people from China generally to Southeast Asia, and to Thailand in particular.

Two main features can be inferred from such a trend. First—at least before the start of the COVID-19 pandemic—there had been extensive movement

The Ripple Effect. Enze Han, Oxford University Press. © Oxford University Press 2024.
DOI: 10.1093/oso/9780197696583.003.0007

of people back and forth between the PRC and Thailand. China is now the biggest tourism market for Southeast Asia, and during the past decade it has become the largest tourist source for Thailand as well. With close to 10 million people visiting Thailand annually, the Chinese accounted for one quarter of Thailand's foreign tourist arrivals over this time. Although tourists by nature are short term, and thus cannot be considered in the same category as longer-term migrants, they nonetheless bring with them numerous opportunities to interact with the local population, particularly in big cities and popular tourist destinations. In many ways, the Thai people's general idea of the Chinese is often based on accounts of Chinese tourists simply because of their numbers and what is perceived as their peculiar behavior.[2]

Second, longer-term migrants from China, or the so-called *xinyimin*, are once again coming to Southeast Asia and to Thailand.[3] However, unlike previous generations of Chinese migration to Southeast Asia, these migrants are not coming only from the traditional emigrant-sending provinces, but from all of China. At the same time, they come to Thailand for a variety of purposes, such as work, study, business, and even retirement. They also tend to possess more resources and have closer political and economic relations with networks back in China. Still, these new migrants usually have a strong national identification with China and subscribe to particular versions of Chinese nationalism with strong political connotations.[4] Along with tourists, they bring Chinese cultural imprints to Thailand, through their predominant use of Mandarin Chinese and their culinary preferences, as well as other cultural practices that are distinctively mainland Chinese.

As a result of such large-scale population movement between China and Southeast Asia, there have been extensive interactions on a personal level. Although Chinese tourists and migrants bring with them economic benefits and business opportunities for local communities, their reception has been highly uneven. In many instances, "uncivilized" Chinese behavior has caused public uproar, with the Chinese often becoming laughing stocks and the target of ridicule. The image of the Chinese as the *nouveau riche* with their lavish spending might on the one hand create the impression among Southeast Asian societies that China now is wealthy. But more often than not, there is an underlying contempt rather than admiration. One might argue that more intensive interactions between local communities and Chinese migrants have in fact worsened their relations and perhaps have indirectly led to negative perceptions towards China and its foreign policy objectives in Southeast Asia.

Thus in this chapter I address the issue of how the mass movement of people from China in recent years has left unintended consequences on host countries and their local communities. The chapter is organized in four sections, using Thailand as its main focus, although set within the broader patterns of such movement of people between China and Southeast Asia. First, it places this mass movement of people within the context of the long history of migration from China to Southeast Asia, while emphasizing the similarities and differences between these different waves of Chinese migration to the region. Second, it discusses three categories of such population movement: tourists, businesses, and students. The chapter then considers the changing perception towards the Chinese in Thailand and explore how to explain such changing perceptions with a view of the Chinese migration history to the region. The chapter concludes with reflections on how the mass movement of people has created unintended consequences for China's public diplomacy within Southeast Asia.

Re-encountering the "Familiar Other"

As we will discuss in more detail in Chapter 8, the long history of Chinese migration to Southeast Asia has set parameters for understanding contemporary bilateral relations between regional states and their northern neighbor. Large numbers of Chinese migrants to Southeast Asia have infused different demographic, cultural, economic, and political legacies in various countries.[5] Given the different political attitudes in Southeast Asian countries towards Chinese migrants, from assimilation to exclusion, such migration history in many ways continues to shape contemporary relations between regional states and China.

Emigration from the Chinese mainland came to an abrupt stop after the communist government rose to power in Beijing. The Cold War division cutting through East and Southeast Asia meant that there was a limited movement of people between China and Southeast Asia from the 1950s till the late 1970s.[6] Such countries in Southeast Asia as Malaysia, the Philippines, and Thailand have large overseas Chinese populations and did not recognize the Beijing government until the mid-1970s. Singapore did not recognize Beijing until 1990, and it was also in 1990 that diplomatic relations between the PRC and Indonesia were normalized after decades of suspension.[7] Thus, for many countries in Southeast Asia, the reengagement with the Chinese mainland was reset only when their relations with Beijing became much less constrained by ideological differences. The overall peaceful international environment since then has facilitated the Chinese state's domestic promotion of economic development and pushed for reconnection with the overseas Chinese communities in Southeast Asia to solicit their help.[8] How China's rising power has affected its relations with the diaspora and their current home countries will be the focus of the next chapter.

As bilateral relations improve and are facilitated by geographic proximity and convenient transportation links, more Chinese citizens have means to travel and move to Southeast Asia with ease. In terms of this movement, we can identify three main groups that constitute the modes of migration from the Chinese mainland to Thailand in recent years. The first group is tourists who, although they are not part of the long-term migration group, constitute the most prominent form of interpersonal interaction because of their sheer numbers. The second group are Chinese people who come to work and live in Thailand for business purposes. Finally, there are also a sizeable number of Chinese students who study at all levels of education in Thailand.

Tourism

The growth of China's tourism sector mirrors the phenomenal transformation of its national economy. According to the National Bureau of Statistics of China, Chinese outbound visitors reached around 169 million in 2019, recording a 12 percent per annual growth from 2005 to 2019. As we can see from Figure 7.1, the slope of this growth rate is particularly steep around 2010

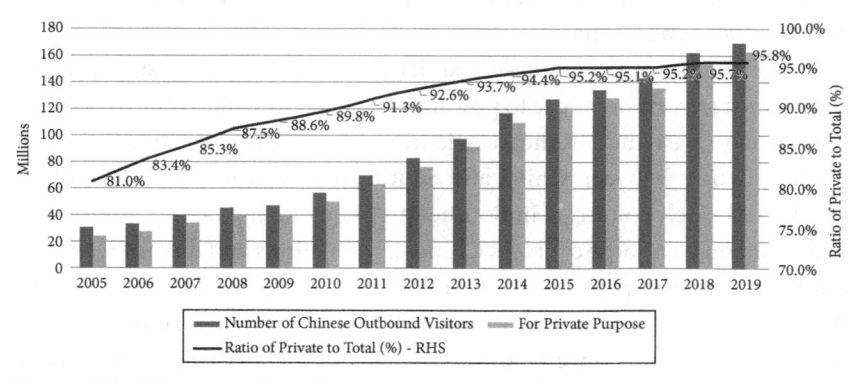

Figure 7.1 Chinese outbound tourists, 2005–2019

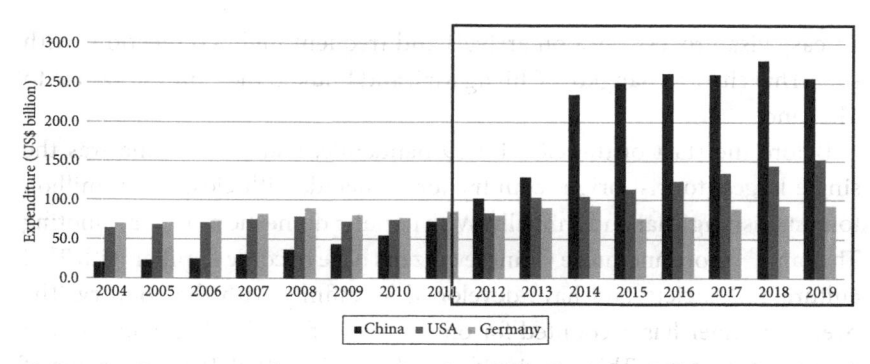

Figure 7.2 International tourism expenditure top three spenders, 2004–2019

and 2011, when outbound tourism numbers really spiked. This occurred in the context of more Chinese citizens having obtained passports to travel abroad, but also because they have had more means to go abroad for leisure. Indeed, during the same period, an average of over 90 percent of such outbound visits were for private purposes, as opposed to the previous decades when overseas tourism was restricted to only a few diplomats, officials, and athletes.[9]

Second, Chinese outbound tourists have become the biggest spenders in the world. Since 2012, China has overtaken the United States and Germany as the biggest spender in international tourism, with a total US$ 102 billion outlay. As we can see from Figure 7.2, China's international tourism expenditures have maintained double-digit growth to reach US$255 billion as of 2019, compared to the U.S.'s US$152 billion and Germany's US$93 billion in the same year.[10] The sheer number of Chinese citizens traveling abroad with their purse strings loosened has not only contributed to the destination countries' national economies, but also created an image for themselves as the *nouveau riche*—not very cultured, but with lots of cash to splash.

When considering Southeast Asia, Chinese tourists constitute the largest portion of inbound travelers to the region. According to the ASEAN-China Center, the bilateral travels between ASEAN countries and China amounted to over 55 million in 2018. Of the seventeen top destination countries for Chinese tourists, seven are ASEAN member countries, including Indonesia, Malaysia, Myanmar, the Philippines, Singapore, Thailand, and Vietnam.[11] Of these, Thailand is by far the most popular destination for Chinese tourists for its tropical beaches, delicious food, and energetic night life. Aided by an easy visa process (visa on arrival) and frequent flight connections with such Thai cities as Bangkok, Chiang Mai, and Phuket, the Chinese swarm to Thailand.

Before the start of the COVID-19 pandemic, mainland China was the single largest tourist origin country for Thailand, with close to 10 million tourists visiting Thailand annually. With popular domestic movies promoting Thailand,[12] more and more Chinese citizens have become familiar with Thai culture and society and have developed an affinity with the country. The overall number has accounted for one quarter of Thailand's foreign tourist arrivals at the time. This is a significant share, given that Thailand is one of the most popular tourist destinations in the world, and Bangkok the world's most visited city. These Chinese tourists came from all parts of the Chinese mainland. Apart from the major metropolitan areas of Beijing, Shanghai, and Guangzhou, people were flocking to Thailand from many second or third tier cities throughout the country. These tourists also represented tremendous variation in their economic and social standing; although many rich Chinese tourists are considered some of the biggest spenders in Thailand, there are also many others who go to Thailand for its affordable hotels, services, and dining opportunities.

Indeed, such large numbers of Chinese tourists have made a strong imprint on Thailand's tourist landscape. Through tourism-induced encounters, historical and contemporary China-Thailand political-economic relations have been re-enacted in the sense that Thai society overall has come to terms with the changing geopolitical landscape, with China emerging as an economic superpower in the region.[13] At the same time as the number of Chinese tourists continues to rival that of Western tourists, the cultural politics of what Thai "is" are rearticulated within the ethnic landscape of tourism, where "imaginaries of self and nation are similarly reassembled . . . where . . . Thainess is defined against, among others, the Farang [Westerners] and Chinese other."[14]

The sheer number of Chinese tourists with cash to spend has attracted many Chinese companies seeking opportunities to cater to the needs of the Chinese tourists in Thailand.[15] Many have bought/rent properties and opened businesses for such purposes. At the same time, the political economy of China's tourism sector also brought challenges to the Thai tourism industry. One of the main issues is that the Chinese online tourism market (OTM) tends to be dominated by major Chinese tourism service providers, and such major online platforms as Ctrip, Feizhu, Mafengwo, Meituan, and

Dazhongdianping have deep implications for how the Thai local tourism industry must adjust and adapt their business models.

These Chinese OTM companies tend to dominate the Chinese market because of the closed nature of Chinese cyberspace. Foreign internet service companies often cannot gain access directly to Chinese consumers or compete with their Chinese counterparts. Thus, local Thai tourist companies that intend to access the Chinese market must go through the Chinese OTM. For example, Feizhu is an app owned by Alibaba, which provides a platform for companies to set up online shops to sell tourism-related products to Chinese customers, such as day trips and cultural activities. However, few Thai tourism companies have the know-how or experience in managing these online transactions, which has led to a situation where the service provider market has become monopolized by Chinese counterparts. At the same time, these Chinese OTM companies have opened branches in Thailand and, sometimes, instead of subcontracting to local providers, they have also set up their own to compete with local providers. This practice effectively reduced profit margins for Thai companies.[16] Such business practices have contributed to the zero-dollar tourism *yitiaolong* (all in one) phenomenon, where Chinese companies would set up souvenir shops, hotels, restaurants, and day-trip activity shops in Thailand to serve Chinese tourists. Since the Chinese tourists would have made the payment through these OTMs, profit from these companies mostly stayed in China rather than going to Thailand.

This controversial practice erupted into the public sphere in the summer of 2018 when a boat carrying Chinese tourists capsized offshore in Phuket and led to the death of forty-eight Chinese nationals. Details later emerged that the boat belonged to a Chinese tour company that was set up through Thai nominees, which is against Thai regulations, and, on the day of the incident, the company ignored the high seas warnings provided by local authorities. What followed from this incident created an uproar in both Chinese and Thai media. At the time after the tragedy, Thailand's Deputy Prime Minister, Prawit Wongsuwan, was reported as blaming the whole incident on the Chinese: "Some Chinese use Thai nominees to bring Chinese tourists in . . . they did not heed warnings . . . which is why this incident happened."[17] This blame on the Chinese for the incident was factually correct but was perceived as distasteful by the Chinese public. This occurrence generated a furor within domestic Chinese media, where many called for a boycott of tourism in Thailand. Later, the Thai Foreign Minister Don Pramudwinai had to play down this comment, saying that the incident would not affect bilateral relations between Thailand and China.[18] However, tourist numbers from China dipped significantly for Phuket in the following months, leading the Thai government to introduce such new measures as waiving visa fees to coax the Chinese back to Thailand.[19] Thus one seemingly common tragedy somehow led to bilateral friction at the diplomatic level. The significant volume of Chinese tourists visiting Thailand has definitely brought economic benefits to the country, but it also can be a potential destabilizer for bilateral relations.

Business Migrants

At the same time, Thailand is experiencing a new wave of migration with Chinese coming to work and live for the long term. Generally speaking, the term *xinyimin* is used to describe post-1978 emigration from the PRC, when many Chinese migrated overseas after the country opened up, mostly to Western countries.[20] For Thailand, such migrants started to arrive in the country from the 1990s onward.[21] The pace of migration has accelerated as entrepreneurs and businesses of different sizes have started to look to Thailand as an ideal place for investment and as a gateway to mainland Southeast Asia.[22] Because of Thailand's relatively slack visa regulations, such as work permits and retirement visas for people in their fifties and older, the number of Chinese nationals now working or "retiring" in Thailand is in the hundreds of thousands. At the same time, because of the relative low cost of living in Thailand in comparison to that of China in recent years, Thailand has also become a popular destination for young people to be "drifters" for a while. Although there are no reliable statistics on how many new migrants from China have come to work and live in Thailand, one estimate in 2016 put it as between 350,000 and 400,000.[23] Another report indicates that Chinese nationals accounted for 13.3 percent of work-permit holders in Thailand in 2017, making them the second-largest expat community after the Japanese.[24]

These new migrants again have brought with them challenges and opportunities for Thailand. Particularly for the Sino-Thai community, there is ambivalence and even antipathy towards the growing size of these new Chinese migrant communities. For example, in Bangkok, a new Chinatown has emerged in the Huai Khwang district. Different from the traditional Chinatown in Yaowarat, Huai Khwang mainly attracts new migrants from the Chinese mainland. Many of these migrants operate businesses between the two countries, and in this process have created fierce competition for many small to medium Sino-Thai businesses. To understand why this is the case, we need to look at the changing status of the overseas Chinese community's "middleman" position in Southeast Asia.

Historically, the overseas Chinese community has often been described as a "middleman minority" in many colonial societies when the European rulers designated the Chinese for certain functions.[25] Other than the numerous Chinese coolie labors, some of the Chinese capitalists served as "economic and political intermediaries between the rulers and the populace but were regarded as outsiders by both."[26] In Southeast Asia, for example, European colonial authorities often gave the Chinese the responsibility of "extracting profits through port duties, market taxes and salt, opium, and gambling revenues."[27] This was the case in Siam, Thailand's old name, as well. The Chinese were hired by the Siamese court as tax farmers for opium, gambling, lotteries, and alcohol.[28] They were also heavily involved in commerce between Siam and China, and acted as middlemen traders for Western firms.[29] In fact, there were such special economic niches and monopolies that parts of the Sino-Chinese community held over the Thai economy, and this in part led to their overall economic success.

However, Sino-Thai businesses' historical middleman position has faced increasing competition from the newer arrivals from mainland China, the latter having taken over the middleman position, especially in bilateral trade between the two countries. The Sino-Thai community has settled in Thailand for generations and is highly assimilated, and their ability to access and network with the contemporary Chinese domestic business environment has weakened. In addition, the newly arrived Chinese migrants come from all corners of China, rather than from the traditional southern Guangdong or Fujian provinces, meaning they can tap into wider networks and business resources. These businesses, especially in the wholesale and retail sectors, have become competitive with their Sino-Thai-owned counterparts.

Strong competition from the new Chinese businesses has led to a perception in the Sino-Thai community of being undercut in their business operations. Such sentiment was clearly expressed by Mae Yai, an elderly Sino-Thai businesswoman in the Samyan area of Bangkok whom I met in the summer of 2018 together with my coauthor Sirada Khemanitthathai.[30] She said, "Now my trading business has mostly failed. Other trading companies also face the same difficulty. Mainland Chinese businessmen have come to open shops and offices here. They directly contact local factories. They also know many businesses back in China. In the past, they bought products from me as I am the middleman. But now they buy directly from the producers." Specifically, there is a strong perception that the mainland Chinese are more resourceful and more connected with companies back in China, giving them a strong advantage over the Sino-Thais, who cannot easily expand existing business networks there. For example, Phi Sao, a Sino-Thai owner of a fruit import-export company, lamented that, "In the past, Sino-Thai trading companies imported and export fruit with China. But now it's the mainland Chinese themselves who do this."

While the middleman position of many Sino-Thai has been challenged by the incoming mainland Chinese, there are also some others who have benefited by acting as agents, or as the Thai would call them, "nominees," for the Chinese. Nong Toy described himself as "betraying the Thai nation" because he worked as an agent helping mainland Chinese businesses in Thailand find loopholes and bribe officials to get deals done. On paper, foreign companies in Thailand have to form partnerships with Thai citizens because Thai law requires Thai ownership to be more than 51 percent.[31] But in reality, many Chinese businesses would use Thai citizens as nominees to make up the ownership structure. In this way, these Chinese companies can operate as if they were Thai firms, and they can buy land and conduct businesses in sectors where foreigners are typically excluded. Thus, facilitated by various opportunities and possible loopholes, the Chinese business community has expanded, and many people have brought their families and settled down in Thailand for the long term.

Students

Finally, Chinese students have also moved to Thailand in significant numbers during the past several years. For example, it was reported that in 2010, there were 9329 Chinese students enrolled in a Thai higher-education institution, which was 46.4 percent of the total number of foreign tertiary students in the royal kingdom.[32] The number has increased since then, and it was estimated that a total of 30,000 Chinese students were enrolled in Thai universities in 2017.[33] These students attend not only government-sponsored autonomous universities, but also the expanding number of private universities in Thailand, which mainly target the Chinese market for profit. Private universities, such as Assumption University, Rangsit

University, and Bangkok University have accepted many Chinese students in recent years.

There are many factors that led these Chinese students to pursue tertiary education in Thailand. In comparison with most Western countries, as well as other advanced economies such as Singapore or Japan, tertiary education in Thailand is much more affordable. Thus, for someone who did not do well in China's notoriously difficult national examination, Thailand might be an easy outlet. Added to that is the geographical proximity, particularly for the Southwestern provinces in China. Indeed, people from such provinces as Yunnan and Guangxi account for more than half the Chinese students who study in Thailand's universities. Finally, the prospect of further economic ties between China and Thailand under the promises of the BRI has convinced many Chinese students to take advantage of the study experience in Thailand to gain a foothold in future economic opportunities between the two countries.[34]

However, there are also pitfalls for such students. There have been reports that some private universities in Thailand, which are not as well-regulated as the state universities, sell degrees to Chinese education agents. As a result, some complain that such practices would only lower the education standard for Thai universities.[35] There are also other instances where communications between the Chinese students and Thai university instructors are a problem, because many Chinese students do not speak Thai and the Thai instructors do not speak Chinese. Some programs claim they are international and employ English instructors, but the reality is that the English level for the Chinese students is not high. Thus, often the Chinese students keep to themselves and do not interact much with their Thai counterparts on university campuses. At the same time, there are also loopholes in the Thai immigration system where student visas are much easier to obtain than work visas, which prompted many instances of Chinese migrants who come to Thailand as students but in fact work illegally.

In addition to university students, there has also been a trend for younger Chinese students to enroll in international schools in Thailand. Compared with China, international schools in Thailand are also cheaper and less competitive to get in to. International schools in Thailand are also subject to less political pressure than in China. In particular, for families who want to use Thailand as a steppingstone for further education in Western countries, it is a reasonable investment to send their kids to study at various international schools in Thailand. At the same time, it is a common practice for mothers to accompany these minors while studying abroad,[36] which is also the case in Thailand. On Chinese websites, there are many stories of such "study mothers" in cities such as Bangkok, Chiang Mai, and Phuket, who describe the pros and cons of accompanying their children to pursue international school education in Thailand.[37]

These Chinese students and their families account for a sizable body of the Chinese migrants in Thailand. Many, although not legally permitted to work, would still engage in some trading practices, such as *daigou* (purchasing on someone's behalf) or *weishang* (petty traders) on some Chinese online platforms. They would set up an online shop on a platform such as Taobao, buy Thai products, and sell them to customers in China. Additionally, many have invested in real estate, restaurants, and other business opportunities in Thailand. Indeed, it has been well established that there are agency companies that promote such migration experiences and provide networks to facilitate easy transition from China to Thailand. Thus, these students and their families tend to stay in Thailand for the long term. As their population size grows, the effects of their culinary preferences are felt. Increasingly, there are more Chinese restaurants serving Chinese food with Chinese menus open in Thailand that cover a wide range of regional cuisines from China. From my own experiences, there are many such restaurants in cities such as Bangkok, Chiang Mai, and Phuket where one can order food in only Mandarin Chinese without needing to use either Thai or English. As indicated in the chapter's opening story on the growing popularity of *mala* food in Thailand, the growing number of such Chinese restaurants has brought popular Chinese mainland culinary trends to Thailand.

Thai Society's Changing Perceptions of China and the Chinese

According to a 2014 PEW global survey on people's opinion of China, 72 percent of respondents in Thailand reported that they have a favorable view, while only 17 percent had a negative opinion.[38] In a separate Asian Barometer Survey Wave 4 on Thailand, which was also conducted in 2014, 94 percent of respondents reported that they thought China had a positive impact on Thailand, while 86 percent considered that Chinese influence in the region was positive.[39] Thus, in comparison with Western countries and some other regional neighbors, Thai public opinion towards China was mostly positive, indicating the overall good relationship between the two countries, at least in 2014.

More recent data, however, indicates more caution and anxiety towards Thailand's over-dependence on China. According to a report on the "State of Southeast Asia" published by the ISEAS-Yusof Ishak Institute in Singapore in early 2020, 86.5 percent of respondents in Thailand believe that China is the most important economy for Southeast Asia, an increase from 72.6 percent in the 2019 report who held such a view. For Thailand, China's economic impact on the country is clearly felt, and people have started to view China occupying the central economic role for the region. However, although many Thais do see China's economic prominence, 75.9 percent of the respondents also mentioned that they have concerns about China's growing economic impact on Thailand, and they are worried about the negative externalities over-dependence on China might bring.

Such anxiety towards China's growing power and the negative impact of Chinese economy on Thailand was widespread.[40] In fact, it is common to see social media posts that describe China as a threatening force for Thailand. The message is that Thailand should fear their future of subjugation under the Chinese sphere of influence because Thai people cannot compete with the Chinese.[41] This fear of China or the Chinese people in general, which are often seen as one and the same, has deep historical roots in the Thai context;[42] it ties to a historical discourse in Thailand that typically states that the Chinese are economically savvy, and if there is no check on them, they will dominate the local economy.

This was the origin of the "Jews of the Orient" label used by King Rama VI Vajiravudh to describe the Chinese a century ago. He published an essay in 1914 that invoked the rhetoric of Western anti-Semitism, denouncing the Chinese as "vampires who steadily suck dry an unfortunate victim's life-blood," referring to the economically dominant position of the Chinese, their lack of loyalty to Siam, and the fact that they sent money back to China.[43] Indeed, Skinner once commented on the ethnic division of labor between the Thai and Chinese during the nineteenth and twentieth centuries by pointing out that it was a common practice to portray the Chinese as "displaying extreme industriousness; willingness to labor long and hard, steadiness of purpose, ambition, desire for wealth and economic advancement, innovativeness, venturesomeness, and independence." In contrast, the Thai were portrayed as "indolent, unwilling to labor for more than immediate needs, content with their lot, uninterested in money or economic advancement, conservative, and satisfied with a dependent status."[44] Although such a stark differentiation of people seems overly racist, and also repeats common cultural clichés, such descriptions of the differences between the two groups of people continue to hold sway today.[45] They continue to shape the contemporary Thai society's perception of the Chinese and their anxieties towards Chinese economic domination.

Anxieties and concerns over the potential Chinese economic dominance in Thailand can be seen through the following encounters that I had in Bangkok in the summer of 2019. I met Po Sai at his coffee shop in Ari, where he recounted old stereotypes towards the Chinese and how Thai people would not be able to compete. He said when he was younger, his grandmother used to tell him about how hardworking the Chinese were, and how the Chinese migrants did lots of jobs that the Thai people didn't want to do, such as collecting sewage, night soil, and other dirty chores. He said, "there was an old saying that the Chinese people work hard for seven days but only eat well for one day. But the Thai people are the opposite; they work hard for one day but eat well for seven days!" Such a narrative also resonates with Po Bu in Bangkok's Chinatown Yaowarat, who is in his seventies and owns a rice mill factory. He said, "Chinese people have a 'fighting spirit,' that is why they have established themselves here in Thailand and many have made fortunes. Chinese people are good at 'eat bitterness' and they can eat and sleep in uncomfortable places. These are the things the Thai people cannot do."

From such accounts, we can see how the discourse of the Chinese migrants of the past can have contemporary relevance. There are certain traits that were historically associated with the Chinese, such as industriousness and being hardworking. Juxtaposed with the current rising China and its increasingly prominent economic presence in Thailand, these historical discourses again inform contemporary Thai society's anxious attitude towards China. As a result of the large number of Chinese migrants coming to do business in Thailand, many in Thai society have expressed a feeling of powerlessness to compete with them. For example, one female business owner expressed the opinion that, "There are so many Chinese people coming to Thailand now for business. They are fearless and do not obey any rules. There is no way for us to be successful because Thai people do not work hard enough."

In fact, there is a strong undercurrent of self-blame among many Thai informants regarding economic competition caused by the Chinese migrants in Thailand. When discussing the differences between the Chinese and the

Thai, one constantly hears referencing the Thai as "lazy," while describing the Chinese as "diligent."[46] Therefore, many of the economic problems facing Thai society have often been blamed on Thais not being hardworking enough. Compared with the Chinese, it seems there is this sense of resignation; the Thai people have no way of competing with them, and it is natural that the Chinese economy will dominate Thailand's. Of course, this was not the case for most of the twentieth century, when China's economy was way poorer than Thailand's. However, as soon as China's economic prominence began to be felt in Thailand, Thais' historical perceptions of earlier Chinese migrants began to frame their contemporary understanding, which in some ways offers an explanation for why China's economic development has grown so quickly in the past several decades.

Although the Thai people are impressed by China's economic success, they nonetheless uphold deep concerns of its negative consequence for Thailand. By this logic, China is to be feared not solely because of the communist party and its authoritarian political system, which of course Thai people strongly dislike. Rather, the Chinese threat in Thailand also stems from the perception of the Chinese people being too hardworking and industrious, and the natural consequence of this is Chinese economic domination. It is this connecting of the past to the present that explains the endurance of the narrative of Chinese migration, as well as the popularity of China threat stories in Thai online social spaces, which have all fed into the increasing anxiety and fear of ever-growing Chinese economic presence in Thailand.

Furthermore, we can see that intensified meetings between the Chinese and Thai people through mass movement have unfortunately and perhaps ironically led to their further estrangement. This is definitely the case with the growing unpopularity of some Chinese tourists, whom the Thai public criticizes for their "uncivilized" behavior. Generally speaking, Chinese tourists have a bad reputation abroad. According to a survey conducted among Bangkok residents, overall, people appreciate the economic contributions that the Chinese tourists bring, and they have a slightly positive perception of Chinese tourists' economic behavior (with a mean score 3.30 out of scale of 5). However, perception towards the sociocultural and environmental impacts of the Chinese tourists tends to be more on the negative side, with mean scores of 2.51 and 2.63, respectively. In particular, there are a few issues that Thai society associates with Chinese tourists: Chinese tourists tend to speak loudly, do not wait in line, and do not respect rules for photography. At the same time, there are also perceptions that the Chinese tourists are not tidy, often leave messes behind, and tend to disturb the natural environment.[47]

Indeed, negative stereotypes towards Chinese tourists are commonplace on Thai social media. In general, they are described as uncivilized, loud, and untidy, and that they tend to be rule-breakers and not respectful of local customs.[48] There are many video clips online that ridicule Chinese tourists; for example, one such clip shows how they fight each other over shrimp at a buffet in Thailand while leaving lots of food uneaten and wasted.[49] Perhaps just like the "ugly Americans" traveling in Europe during the post-World War II years, Chinese tourists have faced similar pejoratives in Southeast Asia because of the way they flaunt newly gained wealth while having a strong sense of entitlement and lack respect for local customs. It seems their behavior has lent disgrace to China's national image abroad. More Chinese traveling to Thailand has somehow caused more antipathy towards them from the locals.

The Chinese government has clearly realized how the behaviors of these tourists, although not orchestrated by the Chinese state, can have negative consequences for its public diplomacy abroad. The China National Tourism Administration (CNTA), for example, has published a guide on how to become "civilized tourists" abroad, emphasizing the need for etiquette and respect for local cultures.[50] The CNTA has also maintains a "blacklist" for tourists who behave badly overseas in response to a series of events that caused public outcries abroad. For example, one such event involved Chinese tourists who were caught drying underwear at a temple in Thailand, kicking a bell at a sacred shrine, and washing their feet in a public restroom.[51] However, despite such initiatives, the image of Chinese tourists abroad remains bad, and such negative stereotypes are difficult to overcome.

Concluding Remarks

The contemporary mass movement of people from China to Southeast Asia has a historical precedent. Thus, the long history of Chinese migration to the region has brought particular legacies that continue to shape how contemporary migrants are perceived. Although some such stereotypes persist, one might have hoped more interactions between the Chinese migrants and the local society would create more common understandings. Yet more encounters between people have led to more friction. The Chinese migrants bring with them economic opportunities but also increased competition with local communities. Further, they create a bad image for China abroad. Even though they are private entities and all these Chinese tourists traveling to Thailand are acting in their own individual capacity, somehow or other, they are often associated with the overall image of China.

The COVID-19 pandemic has put a full stop to the intensified movement of people around the world. The busy streets of Bangkok and Chiang Mai, where tourists previously outnumbered the local population, were empty during the time the country closed its borders. Chinese tourists were nowhere to be seen, and many Chinese migrants returned to China because of the country's perceived better control of the pandemic. Within Thailand, some people offered to support the Chinese in the early stage of the pandemic while laying a significant amount of the blame on China when the pandemic reached the royal Kingdom and created a huge public health crisis.[52] It might be the case that the pandemic represents an extraordinary time, and when it passes, everything will return to normal. Let us hope that to be the case for easier international travel and migration. Yet in Thailand, as well as in Southeast Asia overall, intensified encounters between the Chinese people and the locals are not necessarily friendly or positive. Just as in Hong Kong and Taiwan, more interaction with the mainland Chinese has unfortunately led to a heightened perception of cultural differences and the marking of clearer group boundaries.[53] The mass movement of people from China has thus created unintended consequences for China's public diplomacy in the region. When more Chinese migrants go abroad, they are in no way under the control of or coordinated by the Chinese state. However, sometimes, the friction they create locally have a lingering effect on the popular perception of China as a whole.

8

Diaspora Engagement

Introduction

In July 2022 at a meeting with the United Front Work Department (UFWD), Chinese President Xi Jinping laid out how the Chinese diaspora can serve the CCP's diplomatic goals and realize the rejuvenation of the Chinese nation. He said that efforts should be made to promote the unity and hard work of Chinese people at home and abroad, and to pool their strengths to fully realize the "China Dream." Indeed, the UFWD, which absorbed the Overseas Chinese Affairs Office (OCAO) from the State Council in 2018, has emphasized that the overseas Chinese should promote China's prosperous, stable, and peaceful development abroad; shape a positive image of China in their home countries; and tell the story of the CCP's good governance record.

This appeal to overseas Chinese as a patriotic force to assist the political and economic needs of the homeland has been a constant theme in modern Chinese history.[1] Maintaining and strengthening ties with the diaspora was of fundamental importance to modern Chinese nationalism and revolutionary changes.[2] Similarly, the remittances and investments of overseas Chinese have played a crucial role in the economic miracle the Chinese mainland has experienced in recent decades.[3] This is particularly the case with the overseas Chinese communities in Southeast Asia, who have played an extremely important role in political and economic developments in China.

Of course, the issue of who constitutes the Chinese diaspora can be controversial, depending on when migrants left China (before or after 1949), what citizenship they currently hold (*huaren* versus *huaqiao*), what type of social identity construction exists in the home states, the level of affinity with China as a sending "homeland," and which Chinese government we are talking about, whether it is the one in Beijing or the one in Taipei.[4] Some scholars define the Chinese diaspora broadly as referring to all migrants who left China at some point in the past and their descendants, whereas others define it more narrowly as referring only to those who left China after the founding of the PRC, and thus the estimated size of the Chinese diaspora can

The Ripple Effect. Enze Han, Oxford University Press. © Oxford University Press 2024.
DOI: 10.1093/oso/9780197696583.003.0008

vary significantly.[5] Here I take an agnostic approach to defining the Chinese diaspora, treating people as members thereof only if they ascribe to such an identification and subject themselves to diaspora governance by the contemporary PRC state.

The most recent attempts by the CCP government to mobilize the Chinese diaspora represent certain departures from past practices. What we have witnessed is a more explicit attempt by the Xi administration to emphasize the use of diaspora linkages to further China's great power ambitions.[6] As a rising great power, Beijing sees the diaspora as an asset in projecting a particular image of China on the international stage, and has thus appealed to overseas Chinese to serve its strategic interests and promote China's global soft power. However, such an explicit emphasis on diaspora linkages serving the external kin state can often encounter backlashes from various Southeast Asian states against such attempts by Beijing.

Indeed, existing research on linkages between a diaspora and its external kin state generally argues that such transnational kinship ties often tend to be securitized, a process engendered by the political dynamics among the diaspora group, the home state where the group resides, and its kin state.[7] Securitization in this context means such kinship ties would become politicized and people's loyalty to their current home state would become suspect. Yet this does not necessarily have to be the case, and in some situations such transnational kinship ties do not lead to their securitization. As the rising great power with exponential economic growth for the past few decades, China has transformed itself from a dirt-poor backwater state to the second largest economy in the world, and is also seemingly on the way to reclaiming its historical dominant status in East and Southeast Asia.[8] During this process, overseas Chinese in various home states in Southeast Asia have not experienced a uniform securitization of their kinship ties. On the contrary, one might argue that many home states have treated such transnational kinship ties with China as an asset for forging closer economic and political ties. It is thus fruitful to explore under what context such transnational ethnic kinship ties between the overseas Chinese in Southeast Asia and China have led to their securitization, and in what context they have not.

This chapter thus serves the purpose of reflecting on what factors condition different Southeast Asian states' responses to China's influence in the region, after the extensive discussion on China's complicated presence in Southeast Asia in previous chapters. It introduces a conceptualization on diaspora politics and how it affects Southeast Asian states' relations with

China.[9] Focusing on the nature of China's power in its ascent, the chapter examines how China's relations with the countries in Southeast Asia as well as the overseas Chinese communities there have been changing. On the one hand, no longer the Cold War communist foe, the PRC today represents economic opportunity and political influence for Southeast Asia. After generations "sojourning" in Southeast Asia, there is a movement to re-connect with the Chinese mainland for language learning and cultural adaptation, at least for some. Yet keeping the right balance between reconnecting with their ancestral kin state and concerns about the political sensitivities in their current home states can be a tricky business.

Focusing on how states in Southeast Asia maintain different types of relations with China, this chapter argues that the growing power of China has implications for securitization of the overseas Chinese's transnational kinship ties with China. Here we can understand the growing Chinese power in terms of military capability, economic prowess, and cultural appeal, which is comprehensively conceptualized regarding both hard and soft powers.[10] Thus, when China's power grows asymmetrically versus the home states in Southeast Asia, the degree of securitization of the overseas Chinese's transnational kinship ties depends on the threat perception of the home state towards China, as well as the power asymmetry between them.[11]

Additionally, the home state's domestic politics are equally important, and can act as a modifier for such securitization. The space of domestic political contestation condition how much public threat perception can translate into state policy. At the same time, if the home state allows more civic forms of national belonging, it should also lessen the degree of such securitization if it occurs. When threat perception towards China is lower while the space for domestic political contestation is larger in the home state, the overseas Chinese would have more space to negotiate their belonging and their relations with both states. In many cases, such transnational kinship ties might in fact become a useful asset for the home state to forge closer economic, cultural, and political ties with China.

Empirically, this chapter looks at three states of Southeast Asia— Indonesia, Myanmar and Thailand—as illustrative examples. It examines the different ways ethnic Chinese have been treated in the past, and how these experiences continue to condition the threat perception by the three home states towards China as the external kin state. With the three cases, both historical and contemporary developments are analyzed to demonstrate the broad patterns across cases and over time.

The chapter is organized as follows. First, it situates China's relations with Southeast Asia within the literature on diaspora politics. Then it reviews the history of Chinese migration to the region and the different patterns of treatment that migrants have received in the three countries in Southeast Asia, Indonesia, Myanmar, and Thailand. The chapter then analyzes China's changing diaspora governance practices in the context of its miraculous rise in recent decades, by pointing out how such changing power dynamic matters for Beijing's relations with its diaspora and the three countries in Southeast Asia. The chapter concludes with some reflections on how the dynamics of diaspora politics is one important aspect that will continue to define China is perceived by regional states in Southeast Asia and their future relations.

Diaspora Politics and Rising Power of the Kin State

The literature on diaspora politics has discussed extensively the relationship dynamics among the diaspora group, its home state, and the external kin state. Brubaker, for example, has discussed how national identity contestation can be generated within a "triadic nexus" involving these three political fields. Amidst nation-building politics in the home state, the kin state for the diaspora group often assumes the role to "monitor the condition, promote the welfare, support the activities and institutions, assert the rights, and protect the interests of 'their' ethnonational kin."[12] Thus, the politics of diaspora management often clashes with the nation-building politics in the home states, which contributes to the securitization of the diaspora group's identity and their political belonging.

Whether and how such securitization of identity occurs depends on several key structural factors. Mylonas, for instance, has shown that types of relationship between home state and the kin state matters because the former is likely to treat an ethnic minority group that is supported by an enemy kin state differently than one supported by an ally.[13] This is so because it is unlikely for the home state to tolerate support for the diaspora group by an enemy. In such a situation, the diaspora group's identity is likely to be securitized as a "fifth column" that poses a political threat to the home state's domestic cohesion and political survival. Therefore, the diaspora group is more likely to be treated with great suspicion and handled with repressive measures. On the other hand, if the home state and the kin state are friendly to each other, then the diaspora group is more likely to be tolerated and less likely to be securitized as a threat. Indeed, the diaspora group in this kind of situation can even be considered an asset for bridging friendly relations between the two states.[14]

Comparative research has also shown that the power dynamic between the home state and kin state matters for the securitization of the diaspora group. If the kin state is more powerful than the home state, then there will be consequences not only for political mobilization and identity construction among the diaspora group, but also for how the home state will react to the power asymmetry between itself and the diaspora group's more powerful kin state.[15] In such a situation, the diaspora group is likely to feel proud about its kin state, perceiving it as a feasible superior option to the current situation in the home state,[16] and would try to maintain strong linkages between itself and the kin state. Likewise, the home state, barring any third-party support or multilateral security guarantee, is also more likely to accommodate the group given the power asymmetry. There are likely to be concerns that this powerful kin state might use punitive measures for any perceived violation of the diaspora group's welfare.

However, the "triadic nexus" model, while accounting for the dynamic relations among the three political fields, generally assumes a static nature for the kin state. There is a noticeable lack of focus on the potential implications of significant transformations within the kin state itself, such as changes in economic development, geopolitical power, or cultural appeal. In the context of diaspora groups, it is not uncommon for their kin states to be initially less powerful. However, it is possible for the fortunes of the kin state to change over time. As its diaspora settles abroad, the kin state may transform from a less powerful to a more powerful entity, or from a poorer to a wealthier state, as was the case with Japan in the past.[17] Such a transformation in the kin state could have considerable implications for both the diaspora group and the home state.

When a kin state undergoes such a transformation and maintains a friendly relationship with the home state, we can expect the diaspora group to actively identify with the kin state. In this case, the home state may tolerate or even encourage this identification to foster a cordial relationship. Consequently, there would be a lower threat perception of these transnational kinship ties, resulting in limited political impetus for securitization. However, if the relationship between the home and kin states is less amicable, the home state may react cautiously and become suspicious of the intentions behind the strengthening of kinship ties. Despite this, the home state is unlikely to adopt repressive or exclusive measures towards the diaspora group, as it must consider the power dynamics between itself and the now more powerful external state, lest such actions invite punitive measures against itself.

Finally, domestic politics in the home state play a crucial role. The transformation of a kin state's power, similar to the domestic politics of the home state, is a process that unfolds over time. The manner in which diaspora communities live and negotiate their belonging, rights, and access to institutions has developed over an extended period. Historical contingencies may have led to their inclusion or exclusion, creating a path dependency that influences how diaspora communities are treated in later generations. Additionally, political regimes and domestic political institutions within the home state should serve as mediating factors for the extent of securitization of transnational kinship ties. In countries with more inclusive citizenship regulations and robust democratic measures protecting minority rights, the pressure to securitize such kinship ties should be tempered. On the other hand, if a diaspora ethnic minority group continues to face exclusion, the likelihood of securitization of the group's kinship ties would be significantly higher.

Patterns of Overseas Chinese Inclusion/Exclusion in Southeast Asia

There is a long history of Chinese migration to Southeast Asia, with seafaring junks bringing traders and workers from China to the region over the centuries.[18] Since the mid-nineteenth century outbound migration increased significantly as a result of European imperial powers opening up Chinese port cities, and the ceding of Hong Kong to Britain created further opportunity for labor to be exported to plantations and mines in Southeast Asia and beyond.[19] Domestic political chaos and famines in Southern China pushed more migrants out of the coastal provinces of Guangdong and Fujian to Southeast Asia to seek better opportunities. Warfare and revolutions in the first half of the twentieth century not only sped up the pace of emigration, but also set up competing political parties of the

Nationalist (KMT) versus the Communist (CCP). Later the two political regimes in Taipei versus Beijing competed for loyalty among the overseas Chinese community in Southeast Asia during the Cold War.[20] Nonetheless, before the late 1970s, the Chinese mainland remained closed off to the diaspora communities, and it was much poorer and more backward in comparison to the Southeast Asian economies.

At the same time, except for Thailand, anti-colonial independence movements ushered in a new age of nationalism in Southeast Asia. How to deal with the numerically significant and economically prominent minority of Chinese in their midst was one of the challenges facing different governments, from Jakarta to Rangoon and from Bangkok to Kuala Lumpur. In the end, they adopted varying policies to manage the political implications of the Chinese minority population. Other than Singapore, which was a predominantly Chinese city state that was expelled from Malaysia, the rest of regional governments have adopted policies that ranged from assimilation to exclusion of the Chinese.[21] The following three cases of Thailand, Myanmar, and Indonesia are used to illustrate the different patterns of how overseas Chinese were treated in Southeast Asia, with Thailand as the good example of how assimilation has been the dominant mode, and Myanmar and Indonesia as examples of exclusion and periodic violence.

Pressure for Assimilation in Thailand

By the early twentieth century, the number of Chinese migrants to Siam, Thailand's former name, had risen to almost 400,000. However, their numbers increased significantly in the following years, reaching three to four million by the mid-twentieth century.[22] The Thai government was particularly concerned about the Chinese immigrants' citizenship status and their loyalty to China rather than their adopted country. In 1909, the last imperial Qing government introduced the first Chinese *Nationality Law*, which granted Chinese citizenship to anyone born to a Chinese parent and allowed dual citizenship for Chinese citizens living abroad.[23] This law prompted the Siamese government to enact its own *Nationality Act* in 1913, which granted citizenship to anyone born on Siamese soil.[24]

After the collapse of the absolute monarchy in Thailand in 1932, the People's Party government intensified its assimilationist policies towards the Chinese community. A set of laws was enacted during the years

1938–1939, aimed at liberating the Thai economy from Chinese influence. The legislations included the exclusion of Chinese individuals from a variety of occupations, the prohibition of dealing in certain goods, and the denial of access to certain residential areas.[25] Additionally, the *Nationality Act* was amended in 1939, requiring all Chinese naturalization applicants to adopt Thai names, enroll their children in Thai schools, speak Thai, and renounce any allegiance to China.[26] During World War II, Chinese political activities were further restricted, as many of them were organizing against Japan's occupation of China."[27] In 1943, the Chinese were also banned from purchasing land.[28]

After the establishment of the PRC, the Thai government imposed stricter immigration quotas, making it nearly impossible for new migrants from China to enter Thailand from 1950 onwards. Consequently, those born in Thailand formed the majority of the Chinese diaspora in the country, and many faced assimilation pressure to adopt Thai culture and language.[29] In 1955, the Beijing government abandoned the *jus sanguinis* principle in its citizenship law, effectively relinquishing its claim to overseas Chinese in Southeast Asia. Subsequently, Thailand amended its *Nationality Act* to ease the naturalization process for those seeking Thai citizenship.[30]

In the meantime, the Thai government placed limitations on Chinese language education opportunities for Chinese migrants and their descendants for several decades. Through a series of *Private School Acts* (1918, 1936, and 1954), the Thai government regulated Chinese language education, including its curriculum, textbooks, and teaching hours. Many Chinese schools in the country were shut down as part of a project to promote Thai culture, and harsh measures were taken to enforce this policy. As a result of these assimilative efforts, the Chinese community in Thailand gradually became integrated into Thai society, and their cultural identity transformed to become Thai-Chinese.[31]

It's important to note that the measures implemented by the Thai government were aimed at pressuring the Chinese to assimilate and become naturalized Thai citizens, rather than excluding them from Thai society. The government did not target Chinese individuals who were already Thai citizens or introduce policies that reinforced the boundaries between the Chinese and the Thai. As a result of these assimilation efforts, including name changes, intermarriages, and various other measures, the Chinese in Thailand became so well-integrated into Thai society that they are often viewed as the most successfully assimilated Chinese diaspora in Southeast Asia.

Historical Exclusion in Myanmar/Burma

Burma, which is now known as Myanmar, was colonized by Britain after three Anglo-Burmese wars in the nineteenth century. Subsequently, Chinese migrants began arriving in large numbers, primarily through the maritime route, and settled in major port cities such as Moulmein and Rangoon.[32] By the 1920s, the Chinese population in Burma had grown significantly, reaching an estimated 149,000 individuals, which accounted for around 1.2 percent of the country's total population at that time. The Chinese migrants established themselves as an important minority community in Burma, and their presence was especially notable in the country's urban centers.[33]

However, the British colonial government tended to favor Indian migrants as Burma was incorporated into British India, and Indians tended to occupy a different economic niche than the Chinese community, with many working in white-collar professions such as clerical work and accounting. They also tended to be more politically active than the Chinese community.[34] Meanwhile, the majority Bamar population faced significant discrimination and oppression by the British colonial government. The British employed a divide-and-conquer strategy, placing the Bamar population at the bottom of the social and political ladder.[35] This systemic marginalization led to resentment towards immigrant communities, including both Chinese and Indian individuals, who were seen as benefiting from British colonial rule at the expense of the Bamar population.

The oppressive treatment of the Bamar people by the colonial government within what they believed to be their rightful land fueled the flames of Bamar nationalism.[36] Rooted in a staunchly anti-foreign and xenophobic foundation, Bamar nationalists rallied around the call of *dobama* in the 1930s, which translated to "our Burma." This phrase was used as a direct opposition to the *thudobama*, referring to those who dominated Burma during the colonial period.[37] This nationalist discourse was fraught with an "us vs. them" dynamic, serving as the bedrock for post-independence nationalistic politics. Foreigners and ethnic minorities were viewed with contempt and suspicion, perpetuating a dangerous narrative of disloyalty and undermining the unity of the newly independent nation.[38]

The deep-seated cleavages that colonialism created had significant implications for the country's post-independence nation-building efforts. The 1948 *Citizenship Act* stipulated that Burmese citizenship was only available to individuals descended from one of the eight "national races (*thanyintha*)," namely the Bamar, Chin, Kachin, Karen, Karenni, Mon, Rakhine, and Shan. These groups were supposedly residents in Burma since 1823, one year prior to British colonization. As a result, individuals of Indian, Chinese, and other foreign "races" were required to undergo naturalization as "associated citizens," a process which was often characterized by prolonged and difficult legal procedures.[39]

Following Ne Win's 1962 coup, the Burmanization of the economy led to the further expulsion of many Indians and Chinese. The government prohibited foreigners from owning land and barred them from many professions, exacerbating their marginalization and exclusion from mainstream society.[40] The amended 1982 *Citizenship Act* further complicated the citizenship process for "foreigners." The new law established different categories of citizenship, including full citizenship, associated citizenship, and naturalized citizenship. Overseas Chinese, in particular, were often categorized as associated citizens and excluded from the possibility of full citizenship.[41] Such practices continue to this day.

Discrimination and Violence in Indonesia

During the Dutch colonial period, particularly from the seventeenth century onwards, Chinese migration to what we call Indonesia today became more significant. The Dutch East India Company (VOC) actively encouraged Chinese migration as a means of promoting economic growth and development, particularly in the trading hub of Batavia, the former name of Jakarta.[42] The Chinese community in Batavia, which later became known as Jakarta's Chinatown, grew rapidly in the seventeenth and eighteenth centuries. Chinese migrants were predominantly involved in commerce, particularly as middlemen between European traders and local producers. They also played an important role in agriculture and mining, particularly in the production of sugar and tin.

However, these early Chinese migrants faced various forms of discrimination and marginalization during the colonial period.[43] They were often subject to forced labor, extortion, and violence, particularly during times of political and economic turmoil. The most notorious was the 1740 Batavia Massacre when thousands of Chinese migrants were killed.[44] Afterwards, fearing further unrest, the colonial authority issued a series of regulations aimed at segregating the Chinese and limiting their economic and political power.

Overall, the overseas Chinese population in Indonesia can be divided into two categories based on their time of immigration to the Dutch East Indies and their degree of assimilation with the local *Pribumi* community: the highly integrated *Peranakan* and the *Totok*, who maintained stronger connections to the Chinese mainland. In the 1950s, the Chinese population in Indonesia was estimated to be between 2 and 3 million, with the *Peranakan* accounting for 40 percent and the *Totok* comprising the remaining 60 percent.[45] Furthermore, ideological differences created divisions within the Chinese community, with some supporting either the KMT or CCP since the 1940s. Even after Indonesia gained independence, political allegiance towards Jakarta, Beijing, or Taipei continued to be a significant issue that divided the Chinese Indonesian community.[46]

Following Indonesia's independence in 1949, the ethnic Chinese community was intermittently subjected to communal violence during periods of economic and political unrest. Despite constituting less than 2 percent of Indonesia's population, the ethnic Chinese were often accused of having an outsized influence on the nation's economy. The Indonesian state has also persistently marginalized the ethnic Chinese community, fostering a perception of their affluence that has engendered envy and suspicion among the broader populace. As such, questions of ethnic Chinese loyalty to the nation remain prominent, complicating their place in the Indonesian social and political landscape.[47]

One of the most significant incidents in Indonesia's recent history was the mass killings of 1965, which followed the purge of the Communist Party of Indonesia.[48] After Suharto seized power, Chinese Indonesians were systematically excluded from mainstream society. Chinese schools were shuttered, Chinese-language media was banned, and the use of Chinese characters was prohibited in the name of promoting assimilation. Under the Cabinet Presidium Decision 127 of 1966, many Chinese were compelled to adopt Indonesian-sounding names. Additionally, although only a small fraction of Chinese Indonesians are wealthy, the entire community is often blamed for the country's staggering economic inequality. During the Asian Financial Crisis of the late 1990s, the New Order regime's economic troubles led to a devastating riot on May 13–14, 1998, during which ethnic Chinese Indonesians were targeted in what was one of the worst anti-Chinese outbreaks of violence in the country's history.[49]

From these three cases, we can see two overall patterns of treatment of overseas Chinese in Southeast Asia, one emphasizing assimilation and the other exclusion. Particularly during the twentieth century, as countries in the region undertook their nation-building projects, they adopted different approaches to managing the Chinese community. Meanwhile, China was experiencing internal warfare and political turmoil, which culminated in the CCP's ascent to power in 1949. The ensuing chaos and violence, coupled with China's large population, widespread poverty, and intermittent famine, made it difficult for the central government in Beijing to monitor the situation of overseas Chinese in Southeast Asia. Furthermore, many of these overseas Chinese had little or no desire to be associated with Beijing. However, this situation began to change towards the end of the twentieth century when China's economy took off. The newfound economic power of China and its great power ambition led to a shift in Beijing's approach towards the overseas Chinese. In addition, the Chinese diaspora in Southeast Asia started to become more economically integrated with mainland China, which led to increased interest and involvement from Beijing in their affairs.

Rising Chinese Power and Relations with Southeast Asia

As we have discussed so far, either intentionally or unintentionally, China's influence in Southeast Asia is impossible to ignore these days. Whether it's in the political, economic, or cultural spheres, China's presence is felt quite substantially. Over the past century, the meaning of China's involvement in Southeast Asia has undergone a significant transformation. No longer a communist adversary or an economic backwater beset by poverty and famine, China is now perceived as a great power that offers economic opportunity and political influence for the region. This shift has created a new reality for the Chinese diaspora, who once sought to escape the country's challenges. China's emergence as a major player in the region means it seeks to exert its influence over Southeast Asia, which it regards as within its sphere of influence.[50] The re-Sinicization process discussed in Chapter 4 has demonstrated that, for many members of the overseas Chinese community in Southeast Asia, China, despite its authoritarian regime, represents an opportunity for economic advancement and a potential source of ethnic and cultural pride.

Thus, as China's power has risen in the past few decades vis-à-vis the countries in Southeast Asia, how has that affected Thailand, Myanmar, and

Indonesia's relations with China? How has the issue of overseas Chinese affected such a relationship in the new era? Does the history of assimilation versus exclusion continue to condition how the Chinese diaspora is perceived in Southeast Asia?

Forging Close Relations between Thailand and China

In Thailand's case, the relative success of Chinese assimilation into Thai society and the lack of institutionalized ethnic boundaries excluding the ethnic Chinese means that "being Chinese" is not much of a political issue.[51] The thorough Thaification of the Chinese, through intermarriages and name changes, means there are few ostensible signs that separate an ethnic Chinese from the rest of the society. This has resulted in the non-politicization of being Chinese in Thai politics in the contemporary period due to the past of successful assimilation. Many Thai politicians openly profess their ethnic Chinese heritage, but such practices have not caused any political backlashes within the Thai society.[52]

As such, the Chinese diaspora's transnational kinship ties with China have not been securitized in recent years. As far as the ethnic Chinese are concerned, there has been "an observable trend towards de-ethnicisation of Thai politics."[53] Therefore, during Thailand's election seasons, no major political parties politicize or sensationalize politicians' ethnic Chinese origins, nor do political parties commonly focus on relations with China as a main campaign issue. Since the 2014 coup, although people have voiced concern about increasing Chinese influence in Thailand to criticize the military government, such concerns are mainly economic and political rather than cultural.[54] For Thailand, because of the perception of ethnic Chinese as successfully assimilated, there has not been too much concern about the new phenomenon of re-Sinicization.

At the same time, the ethnic Chinese in Thailand have played an important role in facilitating cordial relations between the two countries. One of the most famous Thai Chinese companies is Charoen Pokphand (CP), which was the first foreign business to invest in China in the post-reform era.[55] As the largest agro-business conglomerate in Thailand, CP has developed close economic relations with China, with the Chinese market becoming a key driver of CP's regional growth. CP has also developed close partnerships with some prominent Chinese enterprises. For example, CP has partnered with Chinese e-commerce giant Alibaba in 2016 to cooperate in agriculture, e-commerce, and financial products in Thailand.[56] Indeed, a couple of recent meetings in early 2023 between Jack Ma, the founder of Alibaba, and Dhanin Chearavanont, senior chairman of the CP Group, as well as his son Suphachai Chearavanont, CEO of the CP Group, in both Bangkok and Hong Kong, have generated speculations for further cooperation between the two.[57]

CP has made significant investments in China, particularly in the agriculture and food processing industries. As we have discussed in Chapter 5, Chinese consumption has seen tremendous growth in recent years and CP clearly sees itself as well positioned to link the Chinese consumer market with the food supply chains in Southeast Asia. At the same time, CP has also become the partner of choice for many Chinese companies to invest in Thailand, including infrastructure projects, automobiles, and the biopharma industries. Most notable is that the CP group has invested heavily in Sinovac, one of the most prominent COVID-19 vaccine makers from China, and it was also rumored to have facilitated the procurement of Sinovac vaccine for Thailand.[58]

CP is just one example of many such Thai Chinese companies that have forged close economic relations between the two countries. They are also the targets of public diplomacy by the Chinese government in Thailand, and they are often invited to many of the Chinese embassy's diplomatic activities in the country. On the other hand, such close engagement between China and the ethnic Chinese in Thailand has in fact been tolerated and even encouraged by the Thai government. Thus, the success of past assimilation has translated into the non-securitization of such transnational kinship ties, and has helped improve bilateral relations between the home state and the external kin state.

Securitization amidst Domestic Political Chaos in Myanmar

During recent decades, overall China's relations with Myanmar has been cordial, whether it was the military government or the democratic elected one. Throughout the 1990s and 2000s, Beijing offered diplomatic protection for the Myanmar military government while the latter was under serious sanctions by western governments.[59] After its electoral victory in 2015, Aung San Suu Kyi's government also maintained close relations with Beijing, with an understanding of the indispensable role China can play for both Myanmar's domestic economic development and the political support the great power of China can offer for Myanmar, particularly during the country's Rohingya crisis.[60] During Aung San Suu Kyi's reign, Myanmar signed onto many of China's economic initiative, such as the China-Myanmar Economic Corridor as well as China's Belt and Road Initiative. Because of the warm relations between the two countries at the time, domestically anti-Chinese sentiment subsided, and much of the attention was directed towards the Muslim minority instead.[61] Overall, China has come to dominate trading relations with Myanmar as the latter's top trading partner. China also rivals Singapore as the largest FDI source for Myanmar, with major investment projects going to the natural resources and infrastructure sectors in the country.[62]

Despite the overall close economic relations, Myanmar domestic public has always resented China's economic domination in the country.[63] Such anti-China sentiment was mostly palpable during Thein Sein's government from 2010 to 2015, during which Myanmar sought diplomatic rapprochement with the West to distance it from Beijing.[64] As a result of these factors, many of China's investment projects came under significant public and official pressure. The most famous case was the suspension of construction on the Myitsone Dam in September 2011, which the China Power Investment Corporation (CPI) built to produce electricity for the Chinese market.[65] In general, many of China's previous strategic investment plans in the country experienced severe pushback from Myanmar government amidst popular anti-Chinese sentiment.[66]

The negative perception of China has worsened after the military coup in 2021. As we discussed in Chapter 2, Beijing has been targeted as the culprit for supporting the coup because of its initial silence on the matter and refusal to condemn the military government. This has led to strong social anger towards China, and as a result, ethnic Chinese in the country have also become targets. Incidents of violence and arson directed towards Chinese textile factories located on the outskirts of Yangon have led to a climate of fear and apprehension among the Chinese community residing in Myanmar.[67] The fear of reprisals from the wider Myanmar public based on their ethnic identity has resulted in many Chinese residents either fleeing the country or concealing their identities. The Chinese New Year in 2022, which coincided with the one-year anniversary of the coup, serves as an illustrative example of this atmosphere of caution. Members of the Chinese community in Myanmar cautioned each other to refrain from overtly celebrating the festival on Facebook, fearing a potential misinterpretation of their intentions by their Myanmar neighbors.[68]

The Myanmar case illustrates that its exclusive citizenship regulations continue to marginalize ethnic Chinese from the Myanmar society. The degree to which the ethnic Chinese community's identity has been securitized is closely linked to their transnational kinship ties with China and the fluctuating nature of China-Myanmar relations throughout modern history. At certain junctures, China's increasing economic and political influence over Myanmar created a greater level of dependence. However, this dependence was perceived as a threat by the Myanmar public, leading to the ethnic Chinese becoming targets of blame. Therefore, the securitization of the ethnic Chinese identity is most pronounced during periods of domestic political uncertainty in Myanmar.

Democratization and Lessening of Securitization in Indonesia

Following the downfall of Suharto's New Order regime, domestic discriminatory practices against the Chinese community in Indonesia officially ceased as part of the country's broader democratization efforts and renewed commitment to safeguarding the civil and political rights of all its citizens.[69] One example of the positive changes that have taken place in Indonesia since the end of discriminatory practices against the Chinese community is the official designation of the Chinese New Year as a national holiday, which has been in effect since 2003. These developments have enabled the Chinese community to openly embrace their cultural heritage, leading to an increase in the public display of Chinese language and other cultural symbols. At the same time, the rise of China has fostered a greater sense of ethnic affinity with the China among some members of the ethnic Chinese community.[70]

Despite the progress made in Indonesia since the end of discriminatory practices against the Chinese community, negative attitudes towards Chinese Indonesians persist. A recent study found that 47.6 percent of Indonesian respondents agreed with the assertion that "Chinese Indonesians may still harbor loyalty towards China."[71] While there have been no overt acts of violence against ethnic Chinese in the twenty-first century, domestic political factions continue to manipulate public opinion against the community for their own gain. For instance, during Joko Widodo's presidential campaign in 2014, his opponents disseminated false information claiming that the former Mayor of Solo and Governor of Jakarta was of Chinese descent.

During Jokowi's first term in office, there were two major cases of blasphemy involving ethnic Chinese. The first case involved a Chinese woman who expressed her displeasure with the broadcast of the call to prayer, which led to an angry mob gathering outside her home and subsequently vandalizing nearby Buddhist temples as an act of revenge. The second case involved Basuki "Ahok" Tjahaja Purnama, the former Governor of Jakarta, who was accused of insulting the Quran. Major protests targeting Ahok took place, resulting in his imprisonment for two years.[72]

Despite occasional domestic political tensions, the bilateral relationship between Indonesia and China remains relatively stable, albeit not particularly close.[73] As the world's largest Muslim country, with a commitment to an independent foreign policy,[74] Indonesia seeks to maintain a workable relationship with China regarding bilateral economic exchanges as well as regional affairs. For instance, Indonesia has relied heavily on Chinese-made vaccines to combat the COVID-19 pandemic and has worked closely with China in addressing the political crisis in Myanmar.[75] Nonetheless, there remains a sense of guarded threat perception regarding China's rise and its implications for Indonesia. As such, the bilateral relationship between the two countries remains lukewarm.[76]

While ethnic Chinese in Indonesia continue to face securitization of their identity and kinship ties with China, the intensity of this securitization has arguably diminished since the country has taken steps towards greater domestic tolerance and inclusive citizenship, despite occasional domestic political incentives to do otherwise. Moreover, the stable bilateral relationship between Indonesia and China has reduced incentives to securitize such kinship ties in recent years. As such, there remains an interactive dynamic between Indonesia's domestic treatment of ethnic Chinese and its bilateral relations with China, which continue to condition the level of securitization of their external kinship ties.

Conclusion

In recent decades, Beijing has used various mechanisms to engage with its populous diaspora in Southeast Asia. The PRC's remarkable economic growth since the late 1970s has been heavily dependent on investments made by overseas Chinese communities throughout the Asia-Pacific region.[77] As a result, Beijing has dedicated significant resources to encouraging investments from these communities and has established laws to institutionalize their legal privileges in areas such as social welfare and economic well-being.[78] In more recent years, Beijing has also taken on the responsibility for safeguarding the welfare of overseas Chinese and has indicated its intention to support the diaspora community in times of political need. Finally, Beijing has also tried to make use of its diaspora to realize its great power ambitions. The Chinese diaspora is considered a crucial toolkit in the CCP's vision of promoting China's soft power abroad and raising its international standing through public diplomacy.[79] Beijing is making use of diaspora networks to strengthen its economic and technological linkages with developed economies, and is lobbying governments through prominent diaspora actors and institutions.[80] In many countries where the BRI has been promoted, Chinese diaspora communities, and diaspora leaders (*qiaoling*) in particular, are often the medium through which Chinese investments and policy initiatives are embedded.[81] Thus, diplomacy through the diaspora and by the diaspora has become an important dimension of contemporary Chinese foreign policy.[82]

It is crucial to recognize that China's changing diaspora policies will undoubtedly have significant implications for Southeast Asian countries, particularly regarding the level of securitization of the ethnic Chinese' transitional kinship ties. As this chapter has made clear, the nature of the relationship between the home state and the kin state, as well as the domestic political institutions within the home state, are crucial factors to consider. Moreover, we must also consider the transformative potential of the kin state, where increasing wealth and influence can have an impact on both the diaspora group and the home state in which they reside. The cases of Thailand, Myanmar, and Indonesia demonstrate how the overseas Chinese and their kinship ties with China can be subject to varying degrees of securitization and de-securitization. This is particularly noteworthy in light of China's growing power and influence in the region and beyond. Therefore, it is imperative that policymakers carefully consider the potential implications of China's diaspora policies and take appropriate measures to safeguard their nations' security and interests.

9

Conclusion

On March 2, 2021, I found myself on a plane departing from Hong Kong and heading towards Singapore. In the midst of a global pandemic, the journey was fraught with uncertainty and anxiety. Upon arriving in Singapore, I was faced with stringent entry quarantine requirements, which mandated a two-week isolation in a government-designated hotel. The experience was a stark contrast to the bustling airports that Hong Kong and Singapore were once known for. As international travel became most challenging, the close economic and human ties between these two cities that once defined the relationship between China and Southeast Asia seemed to come to a halt.

In the midst of the pandemic, mainland China clung stubbornly to its zero-COVID policy, effectively sealing itself off from the rest of the world, including Hong Kong SAR. Meanwhile, Singapore charted a different course, becoming the first country in the region to open up its borders. This approach proved attractive to international capital and professional talent, drawing them away from Hong Kong, which had become increasingly enmeshed with mainland China's regulatory regime. Furthermore, mainland China's zero-COVID policy has led to disruptions in trade and supply chains, with Southeast Asian countries experiencing a slowdown in exports to China.

China's strict measures to control the COVID-19 virus significantly impacted the economies of Southeast Asian countries that depend on tourism, such as Thailand and Vietnam. As discussed in Chapter 7, Chinese tourists were a crucial market segment for these countries, and the sudden drop in their numbers led to severe consequences for the tourism industry. Thailand, which heavily relied on Chinese tourists, was hit particularly hard. By October 2022, when I visited for the first time since the start of the pandemic, Bangkok's once-bustling streets were unexpectedly quiet, even as the rest of the region, such as Singapore, had started to return to normalcy. The prolonged absence of Chinese tourists had forced many businesses to close their doors, with some popular tourist destinations shutting down permanently.

The impact on relations between China and Southeast Asian countries during the pandemic was multifaceted. While the immediate economic

The Ripple Effect. Enze Han, Oxford University Press. © Oxford University Press 2024.
DOI: 10.1093/oso/9780197696583.003.0009

implication of fewer Chinese tourists was felt most acutely in the tourism sector, the repercussions extended to other industries as well. The decline in tourism revenues led to reduced consumer spending, which in turn affected retail, food, and entertainment sectors. Moreover, the situation highlighted the vulnerability of these countries' economies to external shocks, emphasizing the need for diversification to reduce overreliance on tourism from a particular country. In fact, Thailand has recently started to explore alternative tourism markets, such as India and the Middle East, to lessen its previously over-dependence on the Chinese market.[1] India emerged as the second-largest source of tourists in Thailand, following Malaysia.

In the long term, it remains to be seen whether the pandemic will lead to lasting changes in the region's tourism industry and economic ties with China. While some of the impacts are likely to be temporary, others may persist, especially if countries succeed in their efforts to diversify their economies and reduce their dependence on Chinese tourists. However, given the immense potential of the Chinese market and the historical and cultural ties between China and Southeast Asia, it is likely that both sides will continue to find ways to cooperate and build mutually beneficial relationships. Indeed, right after China ended its zero-COVID policy in January 2023, three Thai cabinet ministers even went to welcome the first plane of Chinese tourists at the Suvarnabhumi airport with flowers and gift bags.[2]

As discussed throughout this book, China currently represents the most significant and multifaceted partner for Southeast Asia in various domains. The relationship between China and Southeast Asian nations spans political, economic, and cultural dimensions, and Chinese influence in the region has been keenly felt by regional governments and people alike. This comprehensive partnership has evolved over time, and has been conditioned by historical ties, migration encounters, and geographical proximity.

From a political standpoint, China has actively engaged with Southeast Asian nations on a bilateral basis and has generally supported regional governments, regardless of their democratic or authoritarian nature. Although framed within the context of China's foreign policy rhetoric of non-interference, this approach has frequently faced criticism for providing legitimacy to authoritarian regimes, particularly the infamous military junta in Myanmar. The negative implications of this approach are evident, where resistance towards SAC has reached unprecedented levels and the NUG is pursuing international recognition as the legitimate government of the country.

Indeed, the future of Myanmar remains highly uncertain, with several possible scenarios for the country's political development. The most favorable outcome would be the NUG toppling the SAC and restoring democracy. However, considering the SAC's superior military equipment, combat capabilities, and a formidable size of its army, this scenario seems improbable in the near future, barring direct foreign military assistance or intervention. Conversely, it is also unlikely that the SAC could eliminate the NUG and the PDFs, despite its recent deployment of aerial strikes and various "four-cut" anti-insurgency strategies.

Hence, to restore political stability, some form of political dialogue and negotiation between the two parties may be necessary. At present, neither the SAC nor the NUG appears willing to engage in such discussions. In this context, China holds a unique position, as it maintains working relations with the SAC while also keeping communication channels open with the NUG. This is due to the SAC seeking political support from Beijing and the NUG pursuing relations with China, recognizing the significance of this relationship for its future governance of Myanmar. In turn, China values its relationships with both parties through the prism of its own interests, seeking the most effective way to safeguard and advance existing and future Chinese geostrategic, political, and economic interests in Myanmar. Beijing acknowledges the importance of the SAC's commitment to honor existing projects but also recognizes the potential role of the NUG and its affiliated political forces in fostering goodwill between the two countries. It is with great hope that Beijing, in collaboration with ASEAN, can promote some form of political dialogue between the SAC and NUG to achieve political stability and bring about meaningful change in Myanmar.

Economically, China has been a primary trade partner for many Southeast Asian countries, and the region is also a main destination for Chinese investment and development initiatives in recent years. At the same time, interdependence between the two has grown in recent years, with China serving as a key market for Southeast Asian exports and a critical source of imports, capital, and tourists. Although we have noted the negative externalities of China's rapacious consumption for the region's environmental and social conditions, the economic interdependence between the two regions seem most likely to deepen, especially after China's economic recovery after the COVID saga.

Beijing is likely to continue promoting regional connectivity through its BRI strategy, but it should also reevaluate the pushback it has received in recent years. The COVID-19 pandemic has caused significant economic damage domestically, making it prudent for Beijing to scale down its ambitions and concentrate on fostering genuine economic integration with Southeast Asia while addressing concerns and anxieties regarding overdependence and vulnerability to debt and other economic shocks. In countries like Cambodia, Myanmar, and the Philippines, the nefarious Chinese illicit economy has resulted in considerable socioeconomic harm. For the sake of its public image, Beijing needs to collaborate closely with these governments to tackle these detrimental elements and enhance law and order, which in turn affects its own citizens and the diaspora community in Southeast Asia.

Simultaneously, historical connections and the ongoing migration of Chinese people to Southeast Asia have brought these diverse cultures closer together. Such intensified interactions have facilitated the exchange of cultural values, traditions, and languages, fostering understanding and affinity between the people of China and Southeast Asia. However, these exchanges have also given rise to new frictions concerning individuals' cultural identities and political orientations. Beijing's promotion of Chinese culture and language is primarily aimed at the overseas Chinese community in Southeast Asia, which it views as a crucial component of its united front work. From Beijing's standpoint, its extensive diaspora community in Southeast Asia is a valuable asset for advancing its interests in the region. Nonetheless, we have also observed that the historical patterns of managing the overseas Chinese population in Southeast Asia have left a strong path-dependent legacy in regional capitals, which could potentially backfire against China's intentions.

Considering that the overseas Chinese community has historically faced discrimination and tensions with local populations, China's efforts to engage more closely with them could inadvertently exacerbate these tensions, leading to heightened friction between Chinese and local communities. It is essential for China to recognize these historical contexts to ensure that its engagement is constructive and conflict-sensitive. Simultaneously, China's endeavors to utilize its diaspora community as an instrument for promoting its interests may inadvertently escalate political tensions within Southeast Asian nations. Certain countries may view China's influence on their domestic affairs with skepticism, prompting questions about the loyalty of the overseas Chinese. Consequently, Beijing should take these political sensitivities into account when engaging with its diaspora community to maintain positive relations with Southeast Asian countries. Furthermore, Beijing's engagement might not consistently align with the priorities and aspirations of the heterogeneous

Chinese communities in Southeast Asia. This misalignment may lead many individuals to resist China's efforts or even oppose Beijing's influence in ways that run counter to China's strategic interests.

This book has primarily explored the intricacies of China's presence in Southeast Asia, examining both the intended and unintended consequences of its influence. By specifically addressing the conceptual gap in understanding China's influence through the lens of intentionality or lack thereof, the book presents a complex image of various Chinese actors, including state-affiliated and private entities, and their diverse implications for China's relations with Southeast Asia. Nevertheless, the book's focus is selective and does not offer a comprehensive analysis of China's foreign relations within the region.

The book has specifically excluded the security dimension, which encompasses China's ongoing territorial disputes and regional apprehensions related to its great power ambitions. The primary reason for this omission is the extensive coverage this topic has already received within the academic and policy-making spheres worldwide. China's security concerns include disputes over the South China Sea, where several countries in Southeast Asia contest Beijing's claims. Additionally, China's increasing military capabilities and assertiveness in the region have sparked apprehensions about its objectives and potential impact on regional stability. Most importantly, China's growing influence in Southeast Asia has raised questions about its potential to challenge the existing regional order and the balance of power.

Such is the case with the intensifying competition between China and the United States in the region. The United States has sought to maintain its strategic position and longstanding relationships with regional allies and partners, and has increasingly felt its position being challenged by the rising China. The U.S.-China rivalry manifests itself in various aspects of Southeast Asian geopolitics. In the South China Sea, for example, the United States has conducted freedom of navigation operations to push back against China on behalf of its regional allies. The U.S. also conducts joint military exercises and provides security assistance to countries in the region, such as the Philippines and Vietnam, in an effort to counterbalance China's growing military capabilities. Moreover, Washington has been promoting its vision for a free and open Indo-Pacific, which has been considered a containment strategy towards Beijing.

The Indo-Pacific strategy, driven primarily by the U.S., presents complications for ASEAN as it could undermine its centrality. The strategy's confrontational approach towards China deviates from ASEAN's emphasis on non-confrontation, consensus-building, and peaceful dispute resolution. As regional countries engage more with external powers, focus on ASEAN-led mechanisms like the ASEAN Regional Forum and East Asia Summit could diminish, weakening ASEAN's role in shaping regional agendas. The emergence of alternative frameworks, such as the Quadrilateral Security Dialogue (Quad), could divert resources from ASEAN-led initiatives, reducing their relevance. Intensified U.S.-China competition can further add pressure on ASEAN members to choose sides, threatening the organization's unity and potentially fragmenting the regional order. ASEAN's consensus-based decision-making would be in serious trouble when members adopt differing stances on the Indo-Pacific strategy. Strangio rightly points out that many Southeast Asian countries view Washington's Indo-Pacific strategy with apprehension as "motivated primarily by an American desire bid to curb and contain China, and worry that it could dislodge ASEAN's centrality and polarize the region."[3]

Beijing has been keenly aware of the issues associated with Washington's Indo-Pacific strategy, particularly in how any mention of "Asia" has been omitted from this strategy. Thus, the promotion of a "free and open Indo-Pacific" appears to prioritize American interests over those of the diverse nations that actually constitute the East and Southeast Asian region. Consequently, China perceives this policy as a direct challenge to its regional influence and an attempt by the United States to maintain its dominance in the area by diluting the importance of Asia's own cultural, historical, and geopolitical identities. This omission of "Asia" may inadvertently contribute to the perception that the strategy is designed to serve the interests of a limited group of countries, rather than fostering a more inclusive and collaborative environment for the entire region. Indeed, Beijing is most likely to capitalize on this perception by emphasizing on this Asian identity for regional states. For example, during Xi Jinping's visit to Bangkok during the APEC leaders' summit in November 2022, he specifically emphasized that the Asia-Pacific region is no one's backyard and should not become an arena for contests between big powers.[4]

Furthermore, the Indo-Pacific strategy has strong military and security undertones, with its emphasis on countering the perceived threats posed by China's growing influence in the region. This strategy often frames the region as a battleground for influence between the United States and China, sidelining the unique challenges and contributions of many regional states.

This narrow focus risks reducing the complexities of the region to a simple binary of strategic competition, which may not reflect the true dynamics and interdependencies at play in Asia. That is why the Chinese emphasis on economic development and further trade integration has met with considerable enthusiasm, as evidenced by the RCEP framework. This enthusiasm underscores the need for a more holistic approach to regional cooperation and development, which encompasses not only security concerns but also economic and socio-cultural dimensions that shape the aspirations and realities of the diverse actor in the region.

Nonetheless, the domestic consolidation of power under President Xi Jinping has elicited apprehension throughout Southeast Asian capitals. This centralization of authority, characterized by the abolition of term limits and the elevation of Xi's ideological doctrine within the CCP, has raised concerns about the implications of China's increasingly assertive stance in regional and international affairs. It is perhaps a harbinger of a more muscular Chinese foreign policy in its competition with the United States, which could exacerbate existing tensions and fuel apprehension among Southeast Asian states. Indeed, during Xi's speech on Chinese foreign policy in March 2023, he specifically emphasized that China needs to be ready to fight while maintaining a sober mind.[5] Thus, a more combative China in its dealings with the equally hawkish United States bodes ill for regional stability.

In the latest *State of Southeast Asia* survey report by Singapore's ISEAS-Yusof Ishak Institute, there are concerning indications of apprehension towards China. Notably, some countries that are usually seen as more closely aligned with China are experiencing growing negative perceptions about Beijing. For instance, in Cambodia, the 2023 survey results revealed a significant increase in respondents expressing concern about China's expanding regional economic influence, rising from 29.4 percent to 50.5 percent compared to the previous year. The numbers increased from 65.8 percent to 72.7 percent in Laos, and from 66.7 percent to 86.0 percent in Thailand, respectively.[6] Simultaneously, an overwhelming number of respondents, 95.5 percent in Thailand and 93 percent in Vietnam, expressed concern about China's increasing regional political and strategic influence.

At the same time, there persists a relatively low degree of trust among Southeast Asian respondents towards China, with a general inclination for countries in the region to align with the United States if ASEAN were compelled to choose sides. In fact, the preference for China diminished from 43 percent in 2022 to 38.9 percent in 2023, while the United States saw an increase from 57 percent to 61.1 percent.[7] It is important to acknowledge that the respondents for the State of Southeast Asia survey are not representative of national samples, but they are drawn from specific professional groups, such as policymakers, academics, business leaders, and other individuals with the capacity to influence policy. As a result, the survey does not capture the full range of public opinions but provides valuable insight into the perspectives of those who are more likely to shape regional decision-making. Additionally, their demographic distribution within ASEAN varies randomly over the years, which could potentially skew the results in favor of certain countries or groups, leading to an incomplete understanding of regional dynamics. The annual surveys conducted in the past few years have taken place during the COVID-19 pandemic, which may have had an impact on people's perceptions. Notably, the stringent lockdown measures implemented in China throughout much of 2022 could have contributed to a lack of sympathetic views from its Southeast Asian counterparts. Nevertheless, China faces a considerable challenge in winning the hearts and minds of the countries of the Southeast Asian region, despite the significant economic interdependence between them.

Notes

Chapter 1

1. "Biden Calls for the U.S. to Become More Competitive against a 'Deadly Earnest' China," *CNBC*, 29 April 2021.
2. Sebastian Strangio, *In the Dragon's Shadow: Southeast Asia in the Chinese Century* (New Haven: Yale University Press, 2020); Murray Hiebert, *Under Beijing's Shadow: Southeast Asia's China Challenge* (Washington, D.C: Center for Strategic & International Studies, 2020); David Shambaugh, *Where Great Powers Meet: America and China in Southeast Asia* (New York: Oxford University Press, 2020).
3. Patrick Buchan and Brian Harding, "Power, Norms, and Institutions: The Future of the Indo-Pacific from a Southeast Asia Perspective" (Washington, D.C: Center for Strategic & International Studies, June 2020), 1–2.
4. Buchan and Harding, "Power, Norms, and Institutions," 1–2.
5. Evelyn Goh, ed., *Rising China's Influence in Developing Asia* (New York and London: Oxford University Press, 2016); David Shambaugh, "U.S.-China Rivalry in Southeast Asia: Power Shift or Competitive Coexistence?," *International Security* 42, no. 4 (May 1, 2018): 85–127; Brantly Womack, *China and Vietnam: The Politics of Asymmetry* (Cambridge and New York: Cambridge University Press, 2006).
6. Enze Han, "Non-State Chinese Actors and Their Impact on Relations between China and Mainland Southeast Asia," *ISEAS Trends in Southeast Asia*, no. 1 (2021): 1–19; Pál Nyíri and Danielle Tan, eds., *Chinese Encounters in Southeast Asia: How People, Money, and Ideas from China Are Changing a Region* (Seattle: University of Washington Press, 2016); Yos Santasombat, ed., *The Sociology of Chinese Capitalism in Southeast Asia: Challenges and Prospects* (Singapore: Springer Singapore, 2019).
7. Robert K. Merton, "The Unanticipated Consequences of Purposive Social Action," *American Sociological Review* 1, no. 6 (1936): 894–904.
8. David C. Kang, *China Rising: Peace, Power, and Order in East Asia* (New York: Columbia University Press, 2009); Suisheng Zhao, "Rethinking the Chinese World Order: The Imperial Cycle and the Rise of China," *Journal of Contemporary China* 24, no. 96 (November 2, 2015): 961–82; Martin Jacques, *When China Rules The World: The Rise of the Middle Kingdom and the End of the Western World* (London: Penguin, 2012).
9. Susan L. Shirk, *China: The Fragile Superpower* (New York and London: Oxford University Press, 2007).
10. Shirk, *China*, 6.
11. Yukon Huang, *Cracking the China Conundrum: Why Conventional Economic Wisdom Is Wrong* (New York: Oxford University Press, 2017), 2.

12. John J. Mearsheimer, "The Gathering Storm: China's Challenge to US Power in Asia," *The Chinese Journal of International Politics* 3, no. 4 (December 1, 2010): 381–96; Thomas Christensen, *The China Challenge: Shaping the Choices of a Rising Power* (New York: W. W. Norton & Company, 2015).

13. Michael Beckley, "China's Century? Why America's Edge Will Endure," *International Security* 36, no. 3 (December 28, 2011): 41–78; Adam P. Liff and G. John Ikenberry, "Racing toward Tragedy?: China's Rise, Military Competition in the Asia Pacific, and the Security Dilemma," *International Security* 39, no. 2 (October 1, 2014): 52–91; Stephen G. Brooks and William C. Wohlforth, "The Rise and Fall of the Great Powers in the Twenty-First Century: China's Rise and the Fate of America's Global Position," *International Security* 40, no. 3 (January 1, 2016): 7–53.

14. G. John Ikenberry, *Liberal Leviathan: The Origins, Crisis, and Transformation of the American World Order: The Rise, Decline and Renewal* (Princeton: Princeton University Press, 2011); G. John Ikenberry, "The End of Liberal International Order?," *International Affairs* 94, no. 1 (January 1, 2018): 7–23.

15. Yongjin Zhang and Barry Buzan, "The Tributary System as International Society in Theory and Practice," *The Chinese Journal of International Politics* 5, no. 1 (March 1, 2012): 3–36; Peter J. Katzenstein, *Sinicization and the Rise of China: Civilizational Processes Beyond East and West* (Routledge, 2013).

16. Kang, *China Rising*.

17. Evelyn Goh, *The Struggle for Order: Hegemony, Hierarchy, and Transition in Post-Cold War East Asia* (Oxford: Oxford University Press, 2015); David A. Lake, "Domination, Authority, and the Forms of Chinese Power," *The Chinese Journal of International Politics* 10, no. 4 (December 1, 2017): 357–82.

18. Joseph Nye, *Soft Power: The Means to Success in World Politics* (New York: PublicAffairs, 2004); Yanzhong Huang and Sheng Ding, "Dragon's Underbelly: An Analysis of China's Soft Power," *East Asia* 23, no. 4 (December 1, 2006): 22–44.

19. Evelyn Goh, "Great Powers and Hierarchical Order in Southeast Asia: Analyzing Regional Security Strategies," *International Security* 32, no. 3 (2007): 113–57; Alice D. Ba, "China and ASEAN: Renavigating Relations for a 21st-Century Asia," *Asian Survey* 43, no. 4 (August 1, 2003): 622–47.

20. Ian Storey, "China's Bilateral Defense Diplomacy in Southeast Asia," *Asian Security* 8, no. 3 (September 1, 2012): 287–310.

21. Denny Roy, "Assertive China: Irredentism or Expansionism?," *Survival* 61, no. 1 (January 2, 2019): 51–74; Ketian Zhang, "Cautious Bully: Reputation, Resolve, and Beijing's Use of Coercion in the South China Sea," *International Security* 44, no. 1 (July 1, 2019): 117–59.

22. Cheng-Chwee Kuik, "The Essence of Hedging: Malaysia and Singapore's Response to a Rising China," *Contemporary Southeast Asia: A Journal of International and Strategic Affairs* 30, no. 2 (2008): 159–85; Pongphisoot Busbarat, "'Bamboo Swirling in the Wind': Thailand's Foreign Policy Imbalance between China and the United States," *Contemporary Southeast Asia; Singapore* 38, no. 2 (August 2016): 233–57; Ann Marie Murphy, "Beyond Balancing and Bandwagoning: Thailand's Response to China's Rise," *Asian Security* 6, no. 1 (January 22, 2010): 1–27.

23. Belton Fleisher, Haizheng Li, and Min Qiang Zhao, "Human Capital, Economic Growth, and Regional Inequality in China," *Journal of Development Economics* 92, no. 2 (July 1, 2010): 215–31; Yehua Dennis Wei, "Regional Inequality in China," *Progress in Human Geography* 23, no. 1 (March 1, 1999): 49–59.

24. Shahar Hameiri and Lee Jones, "Rising Powers and State Transformation: The Case of China," *European Journal of International Relations* 22, no. 1 (March 1, 2016): 74.

25. Hameiri and Jones, "Rising Powers and State Transformation," 96.

26. Ching Kwan Lee, *The Specter of Global China: Politics, Labor, and Foreign Investment in Africa* (Chicago and London: University of Chicago Press, 2018).

27. Lee, *The Specter of Global China*, xiv.

28. Yi-Chong Xu, "Chinese State-Owned Enterprises in Africa: Ambassadors or Freebooters?," *Journal of Contemporary China* 23, no. 89 (September 3, 2014): 822–40; Karl P. Sauvant and Victor Zitian Chen, "China's Regulatory Framework for Outward Foreign Direct Investment," *China Economic Journal* 7, no. 1 (January 2, 2014): 141–63.

29. Xueli Huang and Chi Renyong, "Chinese Private Firms' Outward Foreign Direct Investment: Does Firm Ownership and Size Matter?," *Thunderbird International Business Review* 56, no. 5 (2014): 393–406; Dylan Sutherland and Lutao Ning, "Exploring 'Onward-Journey' ODI Strategies in China's Private Sector Businesses," *Journal of Chinese Economic and Business Studies* 9, no. 1 (February 1, 2011): 43–65.

30. Pál Nyíri, "The Yellow Man's Burden: Chinese Migrants on a Civilizing Mission," *The China Journal*, no. 56 (2006): 83–106.

31. Lee, *The Specter of Global China*, 5.

32. Chih-shian Liou, "Rent-Seeking at Home, Capturing Market Share Abroad: The Domestic Determinants of the Transnationalization of China State Construction Engineering Corporation," *World Development* 54 (February 1, 2014): 220–31.

33. Shaun Breslin, "China and the South: Objectives, Actors and Interactions," *Development and Change* 44, no. 6 (2013): 1273–94.

34. William J. Norris, *Chinese Economic Statecraft: Commercial Actors, Grand Strategy, and State Control* (Ithaca, New York and London: Cornell University Press, 2016).

35. Lee Jones and Yizheng Zou, "Rethinking the Role of State-Owned Enterprises in China's Rise," *New Political Economy* 22, no. 6 (November 2, 2017): 743–60.

36. Kenneth G. Lieberthal and David M. Lampton, eds., *Bureaucracy, Politics, and Decision Making in Post-Mao China* (Berkeley: University of California Press, 1992).

37. Jing Gu, "China's Private Enterprises in Africa and the Implications for African Development," *The European Journal of Development Research* 21, no. 4 (September 1, 2009): 450.

38. Lee, *The Specter of Global China*.

39. Enze Han, "Mainland Southeast Asia's Environmental Challenges from China," Perspective (Singapore: ISEAS Yusof Ishak Institute, 2020).

40. Danielle Tan, "Chinese Enclaves in the Golden Triangle Borderlands: An Alternative Account of State Formation in Laos," in *Chinese Encounters in Southeast Asia: How People, Money, and Ideas from China Are Changing a Region*, ed. Pál Nyíri and Danielle Tan (Seattle: University of Washington Press, 2016), 136–56; Osman Antwi-Boateng

and Mamudu Abunga Akudugu, "Golden Migrants: The Rise and Impact of Illegal Chinese Small-Scale Mining in Ghana," *Politics & Policy* 48, no. 1 (2020): 135–67.

41. Mette Thunø and Frank N. Pieke, "Institutionalizing Recent Rural Emigration from China to Europe: New Transnational Villages in Fujian," *International Migration Review* 39, no. 2 (June 1, 2005): 485–514; Gracia Liu-Farrer, "Educationally Channeled International Labor Mobility: Contemporary Student Migration from China to Japan," *International Migration Review* 43, no. 1 (March 1, 2009): 178–204.

42. Hong Liu, "New Migrants and the Revival of Overseas Chinese Nationalism," *Journal of Contemporary China* 14, no. 43 (May 1, 2005): 291–316; Nyíri and Tan, *Chinese Encounters in Southeast Asia*.

43. Ian Rowen, "The Geopolitics of Tourism: Mobilities, Territory, and Protest in China, Taiwan, and Hong Kong," *Annals of the American Association of Geographers* 106, no. 2 (March 3, 2016): 385–93.

44. Mary Mostafanezhad, Joseph M. Cheer, and Harng Luh Sin, "Geopolitical Anxieties of Tourism: (Im)Mobilities of the COVID-19 Pandemic," *Dialogues in Human Geography* 10, no. 2 (July 2020): 182–86.

45. Clive Hamilton, *Silent Invasion: China's Influence in Australia* (Richmond, Australia: Hardie Grant, 2018).

46. Gungwu Wang, *The Chinese Overseas: From Earthbound China to the Quest for Autonomy* (Cambridge, Massachusetts: Harvard University Press, 2002); Leo Suryadinata, *Understanding the Ethnic Chinese in Southeast Asia* (Singapore: Institute of Southeast Asian Studies, 2007).

47. Leo Suryadinata, "Government Policies towards the Ethnic Chinese: A Comparison between Indonesia and Malaysia," *Southeast Asian Journal of Social Science* 13, no. 2 (1985): 15–28.

48. Kasian Tejapira, "The Misbehaving Jeks: The Evolving Regime of Thainess and Sino-Thai Challenges," *Asian Ethnicity* 10, no. 3 (October 1, 2009): 263–83.

49. David Shambaugh, *China Goes Global* (New York and London: Oxford University Press, 2013).

50. Evelyn Goh, "The Modes of China's Influence: Cases from Southeast Asia," *Asian Survey* 54, no. 5 (2014): 825–48; Goh, *Rising China's Influence in Developing Asia*.

51. Goh, "The Modes of China's Influence," 826.

52. Goh, "The Modes of China's Influence," 827.

53. Merton, "The Unanticipated Consequences of Purposive Social Action," 903.

54. Frank de Zwart, "Unintended but Not Unanticipated Consequences," *Theory and Society* 44, no. 3 (2015): 283–97.

55. Alejandro Portes, "The Hidden Abode: Sociology as Analysis of the Unexpected: 1999 Presidential Address," *American Sociological Review* 65, no. 1 (2000): 7–8.

56. Jack S. Levy, "Misperception and the Causes of War: Theoretical Linkages and Analytical Problems," *World Politics* 36 (1983): 76; Robert Jervis, *Perception and Misperception in International Politics*, 2nd edition (Princeton: Princeton University Press, 2017).

57. John J. Mearsheimer, *Why Leaders Lie: The Truth about Lying in International Politics* (London and New York: Oxford University Press, 2013).

58. Valerie M. Hudson and Benjamin S. Day, *Foreign Policy Analysis: Classic and Contemporary Theory* (Lanham: Rowman & Littlefield, 2019).

59. Portes, "The Hidden Abode," 8.

60. Cheng-Chwee Kuik, "Host-Country Agency and Hedging in Infrastructure Cooperation: Definitions, Drivers, and Determination," in *The Rise of the Infrastructure State: How US China Rivalry Shapes Politics and Place Worldwide*, ed. Seth Schindler and Jessica DiCarlo (Bristol: Bristol University Press, 2022), 2.

61. Yoon Ah Oh, "Power Asymmetry and Threat Points: Negotiating China's Infrastructure Development in Southeast Asia," *Review of International Political Economy* 25, no. 4 (July 4, 2018): 530–52; Alvin Camba, "Derailing Development: China's Railway Projects and Financing Coalitions in Indonesia, Malaysia, and the Philippines," Global China Initiative Working Paper 008 (Boston: Boston University Global Development Policy Center, 2020).

62. Womack, *China and Vietnam*.

63. Goh, "The Modes of China's Influence," 830.

64. Julia Bader, "China, Autocratic Patron? An Empirical Investigation of China as a Factor in Autocratic Survival," *International Studies Quarterly* 59, no. 1 (March 1, 2015): 23–33; Mathew Y. H. Wong, "Chinese Influence, U.S. Linkages, or Neither? Comparing Regime Changes in Myanmar and Thailand," *Democratization* 26, no. 3 (April 3, 2019): 359–81.

65. Enze Han, "Under the Shadow of China-US Competition: Myanmar and Thailand's Alignment Choices," *The Chinese Journal of International Politics* 11, no. 1 (2018): 81–104.

66. National Economic and Social Development Board, "Thailand's Special Economic Zones" (Bangkok, 2016).

67. Pál Nyíri, "Enclaves of Improvement: Sovereignty and Developmentalism in the Special Zones of the China-Lao Borderlands," *Comparative Studies in Society and History* 54, no. 3 (July 2012): 533–62.

68. Pinkaew Laungaramsri, "Commodifying Sovereignty: Special Economic Zones and the Neoliberalization of the Lao Frontier," in *Impact of China's Rise on the Mekong Region*, ed. Yos Santasombat (New York: Palgrave Macmillan, 2015), 117–46.

Chapter 2

1. Prashanth Parameswaran, "Thailand Turns to China," *The Diplomat*, December 20, 2014.

2. Enze Han, "Rumors are Flying that China is behind the Coup in Myanmar: That's Almost Certainly Wrong," *Monkey Cage at The Washington Post*, March 2, 2021.

3. Enze Han, "Overconfidence, Missteps, and Tragedy: Dynamics of Myanmar's International Relations and the Genocide of the Rohingya," *The Pacific Review* 36, no. 3 (2023): 581–602.

4. Pongphisoot Busbarat, "Thailand in 2017: Stability without Certainties," in *Southeast Asian Affairs 2018*, ed. D. Singh and M. Cook (Singapore: ISEAS–Yusof Ishak Institute, 2018), 343–62.

5. Jessica Chen Weiss, "A World Safe for Autocracy? China's Rise and the Future of Global Politics," *Foreign Affairs* 98, no. 4 (2019): 92–102.

6. Thomas Ambrosio, "Constructing a Framework of Authoritarian Diffusion: Concepts, Dynamics, and Future Research," *International Studies Perspectives* 11, no. 4 (November 1, 2010): 375–92.

7. Weiss, "A World Safe for Autocracy?"

8. Courtney J. Fung, "Separating Intervention from Regime Change: China's Diplomatic Innovations at the UN Security Council Regarding the Syria Crisis," *The China Quarterly* 235 (September 2018): 693–712.

9. Alina Polyakova and Chris Meserole, *Exporting Digital Authoritarianism: The Russian and Chinese Models* (Washington, D.C.: Brookings, 2019).

10. Julia Bader, "Propping up Dictators? Economic Cooperation from China and Its Impact on Authoritarian Persistence in Party and Non-Party Regimes," *European Journal of Political Research* 54, no. 4 (2015): 655–72.

11. Steve Hess and Richard Aidoo, "Democratic Backsliding in Sub-Saharan Africa and the Role of China's Development Assistance," *Commonwealth & Comparative Politics* 57, no. 4 (October 2, 2019): 421–44.

12. Julia Bader, "China, Autocratic Patron? An Empirical Investigation of China as a Factor in Autocratic Survival," *International Studies Quarterly* 59, no. 1 (March 1, 2015): 23–33; Christine Hackenesch, "Not as Bad as It Seems: EU and US Democracy Promotion Faces China in Africa," *Democratization* 22, no. 3 (April 16, 2015): 419–37; Jason Brownlee, "The Limited Reach of Authoritarian Powers," *Democratization* 24, no. 7 (November 10, 2017): 1326–44.

13. Inna Melnykovska, Hedwig Plamper, and Rainer Schweickert, "Do Russia and China Promote Autocracy in Central Asia?" *Asia Europe Journal* 10, no. 1 (May 1, 2012): 75–89; Mark Chou, Chengxin Pan, and Avery Poole, "The Threat of Autocracy Diffusion in Consolidated Democracies? The Case of China, Singapore and Australia," *Contemporary Politics* 23, no. 2 (April 3, 2017): 175–94.

14. Christian von Soest, "Democracy Prevention: The International Collaboration of Authoritarian Regimes," *European Journal of Political Research* 54, no. 4 (2015), 628.

15. Andrew J. Nathan, "China's Challenge," *Journal of Democracy* 26, no. 1 (2015): 156–70.

16. Benjamin Reilly, "Southeast Asia: In the Shadow of China," *Journal of Democracy* 24, no. 1 (2013): 156–64.

17. David M. Lampton, Selina Ho, and Cheng-Chwee Kuik, *Rivers of Iron: Railroads and Chinese Power in Southeast Asia* (Oakland: University of California Press, 2020).

18. Alice D. Ba, "China and ASEAN: Renavigating Relations for a 21st-Century Asia," *Asian Survey* 43, no. 4 (August 1, 2003): 622–47.

19. Nhung T. Bui, "Managing Anti-China Nationalism in Vietnam: Evidence from the Media during the 2014 Oil Rig Crisis," *The Pacific Review* 30, no. 2 (March 4, 2017): 169–87.

20. Robert Taylor, *General Ne Win: A Political Biography* (Singapore: Institute of Southeast Asian Studies, 2015).

21. Yoshihiro Nakanishi, *Strong Soldiers, Failed Revolution: The State and Military in Burma, 1962–88* (Singapore: NUS Press, 2013).

22. Maung Aung Myoe, *In the Name of Pauk-Phaw: Myanmar's China Policy since 1948* (Singapore: Institute of Southeast Asian Studies; London, 2011), 113.

23. Myoe, *In the Name of Pauk-Phaw*, 127.

24. Myoe, *In the Name of Pauk-Phaw*, 128.

25. Dan Slater, "The Elements of Surprise: Assessing Burma's Double-Edged Détente," *South East Asia Research* 22, no. 2 (June 1, 2014): 171–82.

26. John Clifford Holt, *Myanmar's Buddhist-Muslim Crisis: Rohingya, Arakanese, and Burmese Narratives of Siege and Fear* (Honolulu: University of Hawai'i Press, 2019).

27. Reuters, "China, Russia Block U.N. Council Concern about Myanmar Violence," *Reuters*, March 18, 2017.

28. Shuang Geng, "Foreign Ministry Spokesperson Geng Shuang's Regular Press Conference," September 12, 2017. Chinese Ministry of Foreign Affairs Spokesperson's media session.

29. David Brenner and Enze Han, "Forgotten Conflicts: Producing Knowledge and Ignorance in Security Studies," *Journal of Global Security Studies* 7, no. 1 (March 1, 2022): 1–17.

30. Centre for Strategic and International Studies, "Seeking Strategic Options for Myanmar: Reviewing Five-Point Consensus and Anticipating the Future of Democracy in Myanmar A Policy Paper Compendium" (Jakarta, Indonesia: Centre for Strategic and International Studies (CSIS) Pakarti Centre, 2022).

31. "Myanmar Coup: China Blocks UN Condemnation as Protest Grows," *BBC News*, February 3, 2021.

32. "Burmese Expert: China Helping Military Establish Cyber Firewall," *VOA News*, February 12, 2021.

33. Dinakar Peri, "India One of Eight Countries at Myanmar Armed Forces Day Parade," *The Hindu*, March 29, 2021.

34. "Wang Yi Holds Talks with Myanmar's Foreign Minister U Wunna Maung Lwin," *Ministry of Foreign Affairs of the People's Republic of China*, April 1, 2022.

35. "China to Work with Int'l Community to Help Restore Social Stability in Myanmar: FM," *Xinhua*, August 31, 2021.

36. "Foreign Ministry Spokesperson Zhao Lijian's Regular Press Conference on November 16, 2021," *Ministry of Foreign Affairs of the People's Republic of China*, November 16, 2021.

37. Thearith Leng, "Underlying Factors of Cambodia's Bandwagoning with China's Belt and Road Initiative," *East Asia* 36, no. 3 (September 1, 2019): 246.

38. Sovinda Po and Kearrin Sims, "The Myth of Non-Interference: Chinese Foreign Policy in Cambodia," *Asian Studies Review* 46, no. 1 (January 2, 2022), 41.

39. Lee Morgenbesser, "Cambodia's Transition to Hegemonic Authoritarianism," *Journal of Democracy* 30, no. 1 (2019): 158–71.

40. Lee Morgenbesser, "Misclassification on the Mekong: The Origins of Hun Sen's Personalist Dictatorship," *Democratization* 25, no. 2 (February 17, 2018): 191–208.

41. Po and Sims, "The Myth of Non-Interference," 41.

42. Sovinda Po and Christopher B. Primiano, "An 'Ironclad Friend': Explaining Cambodia's Bandwagoning Policy towards China," *Journal of Current Southeast Asian Affairs* 39, no. 3 (December 2020): 451.

43. David Hutt, "How Cambodia Went from Denouncing China to Being Beijing's Most Faithful Client State," *The Diplomat*, September 1, 2016.

44. Ian Storey, "China's Tightening Relationship with Cambodia," *China Brief*, April 26, 2006.

45. Tan Hui Yee, "China's Li Courts Cambodia with New Deals," *The Strait Times*, January 11, 2018.

46. Po and Sims, "The Myth of Non-Interference," 43.

47. Neil Loughlin, "Chinese Linkage, Leverage, and Cambodia's Transition to Hegemonic Authoritarianism," *Democratization* 28, no. 4 (May 19, 2021): 845.

48. Chanrith Ngin, "The Undetermined Costs and Benefits of Cambodia's Engagement with China's Belt and Road Initiative," Perspective (Singapore: ISEAS Yusof Ishak Institute, 2022), 4.

49. Ngin, "The Undetermined Costs and Benefits," 3.

50. Leng, "Underlying Factors of Cambodia's Bandwagoning," 249.

51. Ngin, "The Undetermined Costs and Benefits," 10.

52. Loughlin, "Chinese Linkage," 844.

53. David Hutt, "China Isn't the Only Reason for Cambodia's Vaccination Success," *The Diplomat*, November 4, 2021.

54. Sebastian Strangio, "What Explains Cambodia's COVID-19 Vaccine Distribution Success?" *The Diplomat*, September 8, 2021.

55. ASEAN Studies Centre, "The State of Southeast Asia: 2021 Survey Report" (Singapore: ISEAS Yusof Ishak Institute, 2021), 9–13.

56. Loughlin, "Chinese Linkage," 845.

57. Loughlin, "Chinese Linkage," 845.

58. "Cambodia's Hun Sen: 'If I Don't Rely on China, Who Will I Rely On?'" *Nikkei Asia*, May 20, 2021.

59. "Li Keqiang Holds Talks with Cambodian Prime Minister Samdech Techo Hun Sen," *The Ministry of Foreign Affairs of the People's Republic of China*, November 10, 2022.

60. Rebecca Root, "Who is Hun Manet: PM's Son Anointed as Cambodia's Next Leader," *The Guardian*, December 29, 2021.

61. Pavin Chachavalpongpun, "The Necessity of Enemies in Thailand's Troubled Politics," *Asian Survey* 51, no. 6 (2011): 1019–41.

62. Andrew MacGregor Marshall, *A Kingdom in Crisis: Thailand's Struggle for Democracy in the Twenty-First Century* (London: Zed Books, 2014); Chachavalpongpun, *Good Coup*.

63. Kanokrat Lertchoosakul, "The White Ribbon Movement: High School Students in the 2020 Thai Youth Protests," *Critical Asian Studies* 53, no. 2 (2021): 206–18.

64. "Protesters Submit Statement Opposing Absolute Monarchy to German Embassy," *Bangkok Post*, November 14, 2021, https://www.bangkokpost.com/thailand/politics/2215223/protesters-submit-statement-opposing-absolute-monarchy-to-german-embassy.

65. "Thailand: Prayuth Refuses to Resign Despite Protests," *Al Jazeera*, October 28, 2020, https://www.aljazeera.com/news/2020/10/28/thai-pm-prayuth-says-he-will-not-resign-despite-protests.

66. Enze Han, "Entrenching Authoritarian Rule and Thailand's Foreign Policy Dilemma as a Middle Power," *Asia Policy* 17, no. 4 (2022): 181–98.

67. Panithan Onthaworn, "Japan Ranked as Nation with Biggest Investment in Thailand in 2021," *Thai Enquirer*, January 31, 2022.

68. Courtney J. Fung et al., "Conditioning China's Influence: Intentionality, Intermediaries, and Institutions," *Journal of Contemporary China* 32, no. 139 (April 15, 2022): 1–16.

69. "Thai Conservatives Claim US Supports Democracy Movement," *UCA News*, April 22, 2021.

70. Amy Sawitta Lefevre," Thai Leader Cites China as Positive Example in Year-end Message," *Reuters*, December 25, 2014.

71. Kasian Tejapira, "The Sino-Thais' Right Turn towards China," *Critical Asian Studies* 49, no. 4 (October 2, 2017): 614.

72. Tejapira, "The Sino-Thais' Right Turn towards China."

73. Panu Wongcha-um and Patpicha Tanakasempipat, "China Denounces Thai Politicians for Show of Support to Hong Kong Activists," *Reuters*, October 11, 2019.

74. "Chinese Embassy in Thailand Condemns Politicians for Siding with Hong Kong Pro-Independence Group," *Channel News Asia*, October 11, 2019.

75. Thompson Chau, "Thai Opposition Leader Defends Taiwan, Vows Support for Myanmar," *Nikkei Asia*, November 12, 2022.

76. This is a collaborative project with Dr. Wilfred M. Chow at The University of Hong Kong and Dr. Sirada Khemanitthathai at Chiang Mai University.

77. Enze Han and Sirada Khemanitthathai, "Through the Prism of Migration: History of Migration and Contemporary Chinese Engagement with Thailand," *Journal of Contemporary China* 32, no. 142 (2023): 620–34.

78. In the end, the distribution between those who think democracy is either very good or good and those who think otherwise is unbalanced, with almost 90 percent in the former category.

79. Prajak Kongkirati, "From Illiberal Democracy to Military Authoritarianism: Intra-Elite Struggle and Mass-Based Conflict in Deeply Polarized Thailand," *The ANNALS of the American Academy of Political and Social Science* 681, no. 1 (January 1, 2019): 24–40; Savitri Gadavanij, "Contentious Polities and Political Polarization in Thailand: Post-Thaksin Reflections," *Discourse & Society* 31, no. 1 (January 1, 2020): 44–63.

Chapter 3

1. David M. Lampton, Selina Ho, and Cheng-Chwee Kuik, *Rivers of Iron: Railroads and Chinese Power in Southeast Asia* (Oakland: University of California Press, 2020).

2. Kearrin Sims and Emma Luce Scali, "What's Driving Laos' Debt Crisis?" *The Diplomat*, November 1, 2022.

3. Enze Han and Qiongyu Huang, "Global Commodity Markets, Chinese Demand for Maize, and Deforestation in Northern Myanmar," *Land* 10, no. 11 (November 2021): 1232.

4. Gabriel Felbermayr, Hendrik Mahlkow, and Alexander Sandkamp, "Cutting through the Value Chain: The Long-Run Effects of Decoupling the East from the West," *Empirica* 50, no. 1 (February 1, 2023): 75–108.

5. David P. Goldman, "Digital Infrastructure Propels New SE Asian Tigers," *Asia Times*, February 5, 2023.

6. Maliha Shoaib, "Wilful Ignorance or Lack of Enforcement? Chinese Suppliers Unaware of US Xinjiang Cotton Ban," *Vogue Business*, July 7, 2022.

7. Jasmin Malik Chua, "Vietnamese Exports Could Be Linked to Forced Labor," *Sourcing Journal*, March 29, 2022.

8. Laura T. Murphy et al., "Laundering Cotton: How Xinjiang Cotton Is Obscured in International Supply Chains," Helena Kennedy Centre for International Justice, Sheffield Hallam University, November 2021.

9. Keith Bradsher, "Tariff Dodgers Stand to Profit Off U.S.-China Trade Dispute," *The New York Times*, April 22, 2018.

10. Xuepeng Liu and Huimin Shi, "Anti-Dumping Duty Circumvention through Trade Rerouting: Evidence from Chinese Exporters," *The World Economy* 42, no. 5 (2019): 1427–66.

11. "Vietnam: China Companies Using Fake 'Made in Vietnam' Labels," *AP News*, June 10, 2019.

12. Chris Vale, "Vietnam: Navigate through the Rules of Origin," *Rouse*, October 22, 2020.

13. Prak Chan Thul, "U.S. Fines Firms Transhipping via Cambodia to Dodge Trump's China Tariffs," *Reuters*, June 19, 2019.

14. Peter A. Petri and Michael G. Plummer, "East Asia Decouples from the United States: Trade War, COVID-19, and East Asia's New Trade Blocs," Working Paper, Peterson Institute for International Economics, June 2020.

15. Data from: https://data.aseanstats.org/.

16. "The Growing China-ASEAN Economic Ties," HKTDC Research, January 7, 2022.

17. Department of Statistics, Singapore.

18. Sarah Chan, "Singapore–China Connectivity and Its Role in the Belt and Road Initiative," *China: An International Journal* 17, no. 4 (2019): 42.

19. Chan, "Singapore–China Connectivity," 41.

20. Lihui Tian and Xin Li, "Global Expansion with Takeovers and Value Creation with Integration in China: A Case Study of Alibaba and Lazada," *Asia Pacific Business Review* 29, no. 2 (2023): 372–91.

21. "Tencent Leads $95m Funding Round in Singapore-Based Digibank Firm," *The Straits Times*, December 9, 2021.

22. "Tiktok Owner Plans to Spend Billions in Singapore after US Ban," *The Straits Times*, September 11, 2020.

23. Canghao Chen, "The Real Cause of China's Alibaba Crackdown," *The Diplomat*, September 9, 2021.

24. Selina Ho, "Infrastructure and Chinese Power," *International Affairs* 96, no. 6 (November 1, 2020): 1474.

25. Jean-Marc F. Blanchard, "Probing China's Twenty-First-Century Maritime Silk Road Initiative (MSRI): An Examination of MSRI Narratives," *Geopolitics* 22, no. 2 (April 3, 2017): 246–68.

26. James D Sidaway et al., "Introduction: Research Agendas Raised by the Belt and Road Initiative," *Environment and Planning C: Politics and Space* 38, no. 5 (August 1, 2020): 795–802; Gustavo de L. T. Oliveira et al., "China's Belt and Road Initiative: Views from the Ground," *Political Geography*, August 3, 2020, online first, https://www.sciencedirect.com/science/article/pii/S0962629820301177?via%3Dihub.

27. Simon Rowedder, "Railroading Land-Linked Laos: China's Regional Profits, Laos' Domestic Costs?" *Eurasian Geography and Economics* 61, no. 2 (March 3, 2020): 152–61.

28. IMF, "Lao People's Democratic Republic: Staff Report for the 2016 Article IV Consultation—Debt Sustainability Analysis" (Washington, D.C.: International Monetary Fund, 2017).

29. Nick Freeman, "Can Laos Profit from China Rail Link Despite Being US$1.5 Billion in Debt?" *South China Morning Post*, December 10, 2019.

30. "Xi Jinping and General Secretary of the LPRP Central Committee and Lao President Thongloun Sisoulith Jointly Attend the Opening Ceremony of the China-Laos Railway," Ministry of Foreign Affairs of People's Republic of China, December 3, 2021.

31. "Lao Leader Speaks Highly of China-Laos Railway," *The Star*, February 11, 2022.

32. "China-Laos Railway Exceeds Expectations, Defies Critics, Injecting Momentum into Regional Prosperity as Part of the BRI," *Global Times*, September 7, 2022.

33. "Laos-China Rail a Boon for Thais," *Bangkok Post*, September 2, 2022.

34. "Transforming Lao PDR from a Land-locked to a Land-linked Economy," *The World Bank*, June 2, 2020.

35. "A Lot of Hidden Minerals in Laos, Any Possibility as a Supplier of Raw Materials?" Korea Trade-Investment Promotion Agency (KOTRA), July 29, 2022.

36. "Thailand Exports 500 Tons of Durian to China via China-Laos Railway for the First Time," *Global Times*, April 26, 2022.

37. "First Fruit Transportation Train Launched on China-Laos Railway," *The Nation Thailand*, December 3, 2022.

38. Yoon Ah Oh, "Power Asymmetry and Threat Points: Negotiating China's Infrastructure Development in Southeast Asia," *Review of International Political Economy* 25, no. 4 (July 4, 2018): 530–52.

39. Oh, "Power Asymmetry and Threat Points," 546.

40. Sivarin Lertpusit, "Long-Delayed Thailand-China High-Speed Train: A Political Game on Two Tracks," *Fulcrum Analysis on Southeast Asia*, January 5, 2023.

41. "High-Speed Train Still on Track," *Bangkok Post*, January 5, 2023.

42. Zsomber Peter, "Thailand Sets 2028 Target to Finish High-Speed Rail Link with China," *VOA News*, July 17, 2022.

43. Pongphisoot Busbarat, "'Bamboo Swirling in the Wind': Thailand's Foreign Policy Imbalance between China and the United States," *Contemporary Southeast Asia; Singapore* 38, no. 2 (August 2016): 233–57.

44. Alvin Camba, "Derailing Development: China's Railway Projects and Financing Coalitions in Indonesia, Malaysia, and the Philippines," Global China Initiative Working Paper 008 (Boston: Boston University Global Development Policy Center, 2020), 11.

45. Karen P. Y. Lai, Shaun Lin, and James D. Sidaway, "Financing the Belt and Road Initiative (BRI): Research Agendas beyond the 'Debt-Trap' Discourse," *Eurasian Geography and Economics* 61, no. 2 (March 3, 2020): 109–24.

46. "Mahathir: Malaysia Saves Billions in Renegotiated Railway Deal with China," *Radio Free Asia*, April 15, 2019.

47. Kok Leong Chan, "Malaysia's East Coast Rail Link Project to Continue Under Anwar," *Bloomberg*, December 6, 2022.

48. "Special Economic Zones in ASEAN: Opportunities for US Investors," *ASEAN Briefing*, June 5, 2020.

49. Yue-man Yeung, Joanna Lee, and Gordon Kee, "China's Special Economic Zones at 30," *Eurasian Geography and Economics* 50, no. 2 (March 1, 2009): 222–40.

50. Deborah Brautigam and Xiaoyang Tang, "China's Investment in Special Economic Zones in Africa," in *Special Economic Zones: Progress, Emerging Challenges, and Future Directions*, ed. Thomas Farole and Gokhan Akinci (Washington, D.C.: World Bank, 2011), 71.

51. For the complete list of Chinese overseas SEZs, see http://www.cocz.org/index.aspx.

52. Sophie He, "'Industrial Chinatown' Rides High on BRI," *The China Daily*, April 9, 2019.

53. Jiping Wang, "'Industrial Chinatown' Booms in Thailand," *China Report ASEAN*, April 30, 2017.

54. Nuomin Bao, "Thai-Chinese Rayong Industrial Zone Enters 'Fast Lane,'" *Xinhua Silk Road Information Service*, March 4, 2019.

55. He, "'Industrial Chinatown' Rides High on BRI."

56. Apornrath Phoonphongphiphat, "Thai Parliament Passes Eastern Economic Corridor Law," *Asian Nikkei Review*, February 9, 2018.

57. Aksornsri Phanishsarn, "The Link Between the EEC of Thailand 4.0 Model and China's BRI: A New Chapter of Thailand-China Economic Relations," in *Exchanges and Mutual Learning Among Asian Civilizations*, ed. Linggui Wang and Jianglin Zhao (Singapore: Springer Nature, 2023), 115–23.

58. Angaindrankumar Gnanasagaran, "Thailand Opens Its Eastern Doors to Investors," *The ASEAN Post*, April 3, 2018.

59. Zen Soo, "Alibaba to Set Up Thai Logistics Centre, Extend Deepening Investment in Southeast Asia," *South China Morning Post*, March 26, 2018.

60. Yukako Ono, "Central Group, JD.com to Pour $500m into JVs in Thailand," *Nikkei Asia*, September 15, 2017.

61. Randy Thanthong-Knight, "Thailand Lays Out Bold EV Plan, Wants ALL Electronic Cars by 2035," *Bloomberg*, April 22, 2021.

62. "BYD to Produce NEVs in Thailand from 2024," *The China Daily*, September 9, 2022.

63. Patpicha Tanakasempipat, "China's BYD Signs Deal to Build First EV Plant in Thailand," *Bloomberg*, September 8, 2022.

64. "Chinese EV Makers Eye Southeast Asia as Competition Escalates," *Bangkok Post*, November 16, 2022.

65. Li Fusheng, "China's Auto Manufacturers Focus on Wider Asian Market," Asian News Network, December 7, 2022.

66. Ma Jingjing, "Chinese EV Makers Eye Southeast Asia to Seize Opportunities against Weakened Japanese Rivals," *Global Times*, July 11, 2022.

67. River Davis, "Developing Nations Aren't Ready for EVs—Unless They Are Made in China," *Mint*, January 8, 2023.

68. Data are extracted from Comtrade, which includes non-public transport passenger vehicles only propelled by electricity, excluding vehicles propelled partly by electricity and partly by other means such as gas.

69. "Indonesia's Nickel Export Ban: Impacts on Supply Chains and the Energy Transition," *The National Bureau of Asian Research*, November 19, 2022.

70. "Chinese Carmaker Launches Electric Car in Indonesia," *Xinhuanet*, August 8, 2022.

71. "Electric Vehicles: On the Road to Sustainable Mobility in Cambodia and Beyond," *UNDP*, May 6, 2022.

72. Sok Sithika, "China Company Plans EV Assembly in Cambodia," *Khmer Times*, October 25, 2022.

73. "Laos Gives Green Light for Investment in EVs," *Xinhuanet*, June 17, 2022.

Chapter 4

1. Joseph Nye, *Soft Power: The Means to Success in World Politics* (New York: PublicAffairs, 2004).

2. Ethan Epstein, "How China Infiltrated U.S. Classrooms," *Politico*, January 17, 2018.

3. Ian Rowen, "The Geopolitics of Tourism: Mobilities, Territory, and Protest in China, Taiwan, and Hong Kong," *Annals of the American Association of Geographers* 106, no. 2 (March 3, 2016): 390.

4. Helena Wu and Andrea Riemenschnitter, "Introduction," *Interventions* 20, no. 8 (November 17, 2018): 1073–84.

5. Tungkeunkunt Kornphanat, "Culture and Commerce: China's Soft Power in Thailand," *International Journal of China Studies* 7, no. 2 (August 2016): 158.

6. Siripetch Trisanawadee, "Chinese Cultural Diplomacy towards ASEAN Countries: Case Study of Confucius Institutes in Thailand," *Manutsayasat Wichakan Journal, Kasetsart University* 27, no. 2 (December 24, 2020): 416–50.

7. Hong Liu, "Opportunities and Anxieties for the Chinese Diaspora in Southeast Asia," *Current History* 115 (2016): 316.

8. An Yalun, "International Promotion of Chinese Language in the New Era," *International Education Studies* 12, no. 7 (June 29, 2019): 67.

9. Shujian Guo, Hyunjung Shin, and Qi Shen, "The Commodification of Chinese in Thailand's Linguistic Market: A Case Study of How Language Education Promotes Social Sustainability," *Sustainability* 12, no. 18 (January 2020): 1.

10. Kornphanat, "Culture and Commerce," 159.

11. The poll can be accessed online at https://yougov.co.uk/topics/international/articles-reports/2019/06/25/mandarin-more-important-learn-french-or-spanish.

12. Budsaba Kanoksilapatham, "National Survey of Teaching Chinese as a Foreign Language in Thailand," Working Paper (Silpakorn University, 2011).

13. http://en.chinaculture.org/focus/2009-11/23/content_447281.htm.

14. "The Strategies Engagement of the Confucius Institutes in Thailand under Thailand 4.0 Policy," Mae Fah Luang University, March 8, 2018, https://en.mfu.ac.th/en-news/en-news-detail/detail/News/1577.html.

15. There are several reasons why they stayed in Thailand. Some claim they stayed at the borderland because of a secret order of Chiang Kai-shek while others claim there was factional fighting between the generals and those in Taiwan, and there are still others who speculate that the troops were benefiting handsomely from the opium trade across the Thai-Burmese border, so there was no economic reason for them to go to Taiwan. Personal interviews, Taipei, September 2014, and Chiang Mai, June 2016.

16. Wen-Chin Chang, *Beyond Borders: Stories of Yunnanese Chinese Migrants of Burma* (Ithaca, New York: Cornell University Press, 2014); Shu-min Huang, *Reproducing Chinese Culture in Diaspora: Sustainable Agriculture and Petrified Culture in Northern Thailand* (Lanham: Lexington Books, 2010); Yihui Qin, *History of Blood and Tears of the Nationalist Army in the Golden Triangle (Jinsanjiao guojun xueleishi)* (Taipei: Academic Sinica and Lianjing Press, 2009).

17. Ann Maxwell Hill, *Merchants and Migrants: Ethnicity and Trade among Yunnanese Chinese in Southeast Asia* (New Haven: Yale University Southeast Asia Studies, 1998).

18. Po-Yi Hung and Ian G. Baird, "From Soldiers to Farmers: The Political Geography of Chinese Kuomintang Territorialization in Northern Thailand," *Political Geography* 58 (May 1, 2017): 1–13.

19. Aranya Siriphon, "The Qiaoban, The PRC Influence and Nationalist Chinese in Northern Thai Borderland," *International Journal of Asian Studies* 13, no. 1 (January 1, 2016): 1–17.

20. Weng-Jeng Chen, *Tangle [Taibei Zhongguo Jie]*, YouTube video, 2010, https://www.youtube.com/watch?v=zFe31GVP6fA.

21. "Chairman Liang Donated One Million Thai Baht for Chiang Mai Jiaolian Normal College," *Thai-Chinese Net*, July 9, 2020, https://thaizhonghua.com/2020/07/09/86894.html.

22. http://chiangmai.china-consulate.org/chn/gdxw/201901/t20190106_5339194.htm.

23. Personal interview in Chiang Mai, 2016.

24. https://www.mfa.gov.cn/ce/cgchiangmai/chn/xwdt/t1859502.htm.

25. Enze Han, "Bifurcated Homeland and Diaspora Politics in China and Taiwan toward the Overseas Chinese in Southeast Asia," *Journal of Ethnic and Migration Studies* 45, no. 4 (March 12, 2019): 577–94.

26. Enze Han, "Re-Encountering the Familiar Other: Contesting 'Re-Sinicization'in Thailand," *Singapore Journal of Tropical Geography* 43, no. 3 (2022): 270–86.

27. Caroline Hau, "Becoming 'Chinese' in Southeast Asia," in *Sinicization and the Rise of China: Civilizational Processes beyond East and West*, ed. Peter J. Katzenstein (London and New York: Routledge, 2012), 176.

28. Hau, "Becoming 'Chinese' in Southeast Asia," 176.

29. Wasana Wongsurawat, "The Social Capital of Being Chinese in Thai Politics," in *The Sociology of Chinese Capitalism in Southeast Asia: Challenges and Prospects*, ed. Yos Santasombat (Singapore: Springer, 2019), 75–92.

30. Hau, "Becoming 'Chinese' in Southeast Asia," 176.

31. Allen Chun, "Fuck Chineseness: On the Ambiguities of Ethnicity as Culture as Identity," *Boundary 2* 23, no. 2 (1996): 111–38.

32. Rowen, "The Geopolitics of Tourism," 386.

33. Walwipha Burusratanaphand, "Chinese Identity in Thailand," *Southeast Asian Journal of Social Science* 23, no. 1 (1995): 43–56.

34. Wasana Wongsurawat, "Successfully Misunderstood: The Untold Realities of the Thai-Chinese Assimilation 'Success Story,'" in *Multicultural Challenges and Redefining Identity in East Asia*, ed. Nam-Hook Kim (London: Routledge, 2016), 123–42.

35. Wasana Wongsurawat, "The Social Capital of Being Chinese in Thai Politics"; Kasian Tejapira, "The Sino-Thais' Right Turn towards China," *Critical Asian Studies* 49, no. 4 (October 2, 2017): 606–18.

36. Liu, "Opportunities and Anxieties," 316.

37. Liu, "Opportunities and Anxieties," 316.

38. Caroline Hau, "Becoming 'Chinese'—But What 'Chinese'?—In Southeast Asia," *The Asia Pacific Journal / Japan Focus* 10, no. 26 (2012): 1–37.

39. "K-Pop? How about T-Pop? Thai Artists Shoot for Global Audience," *Reuters*, December 19, 2020.

40. Rachel Harrison, "Amazing Thai Film: The Rise and Rise of Contemporary Thai Cinema on the International Screen," *Asian Affairs* 36, no. 3 (November 1, 2005): 321–38.

41. Amporn Jirattikorn, "Between Ironic Pleasure and Exotic Nostalgia: Audience Reception of Thai Television Dramas among Youth in China," *Asian Journal of Communication* 31, no. 2 (March 4, 2021): 124–43; Thomas Baudinette, "Lovesick, The Series: Adapting Japanese 'Boys Love' to Thailand and the Creation of a New Genre of Queer Media," *South East Asia Research* 27, no. 2 (April 3, 2019): 115–32.

42. The show's Thai name is แปลรักฉันด้วยใจเธอ, and its Chinese translation is 以你的心诠释我的爱.

43. Aihwa Ong, *Flexible Citizenship: The Cultural Logics of Transnationality* (Durham, North Carolina: Duke University Press Books, 1999); Aihwa Ong and Donald Nonini, eds., *Ungrounded Empires: The Cultural Politics of Modern Chinese Transnationalism* (London: Routledge, 2003).

44. Yiu-Wai Chu and Eve Leung, "Remapping Hong Kong Popular Music: Covers, Localisation and the Waning Hybridity of Cantopop," *Popular Music* 32, no. 1 (2013): 65–78.

45. Hau, "Becoming 'Chinese' in Southeast Asia," 192.

46. Hau, "Becoming 'Chinese' in Southeast Asia," 193.

47. Allen Chun, *Forget Chineseness: On the Geopolitics of Cultural Identification* (Albany, New York: SUNY Press, 2017).

48. Syaru Shirley Lin, *Taiwan's China Dilemma: Contested Identities and Multiple Interests in Taiwan's Cross-Strait Economic Policy* (Stanford: Stanford University Press, 2016).

49. Hui-Ching Chang and Richard Holt, *Language, Politics and Identity in Taiwan: Naming China* (London: Routledge, 2014).

50. Chien-Heui Wu, "The U.S.-China Trade War and Options for Taiwan" (Washington, D.C.: Wilson Center Asia Program, 2019).

51. Malte Philipp Kaeding, "The Rise of 'Localism' in Hong Kong," *Journal of Democracy* 28, no. 1 (2017): 157–71.

52. Tin-yuet Ting, "From 'Be Water' to 'Be Fire': Nascent Smart Mob and Networked Protests in Hong Kong," *Social Movement Studies* 19, no. 3 (May 3, 2020): 362–68; Agnes S. Ku, "New Forms of Youth Activism—Hong Kong's Anti-Extradition Bill Movement in the Local-National-Global Nexus," *Space and Polity* 24, no. 1 (January 2, 2020): 111–17.

53. Han, "Bifurcated Homeland and Diaspora Politics"; Wasana Wongsurawat, *The Crown and the Capitalists: The Ethnic Chinese and the Founding of the Thai Nation* (Seattle: University of Washington Press, 2019).

54. Suzanne Sng, "Malaysian Singer Namewee Says He Is not Anti-China," *The Straits Times*, October 27, 2021, available at https://www.straitstimes.com/life/entertainm ent/malaysian-singer-namewee-says-he-is-not-anti-china.

55. "China Denounces Thai Politicians for Show of Support to Hong Kong Activists," *Reuters*, October 11, 2019.

56. Duncan McCargo and Anyarat Chattharakul, *Future Forward: The Rise and Fall of a Thai Political Party: 150* (Copenhagen: NIAS Press, 2020).

57. "Can Legal Troubles Save Thanathorn from Political Ones?" *Thai PBS World*, January 27, 2021.

58. "Chinese Embassy in Thailand Condemns Politicians for Siding with Hong Kong Pro-Independence Group," *Channel News Asia*, October 11, 2019.

59. "Thanathorn Welcomes China's Bigger Role, Denies Supporting HK Protests," *Khaosod English*, October 28, 2019.

60. "Chinese Netizens Boycott Thai Boys' Love Drama '2gether: The Series' due to Inappropriate Comment about COVID-19 by Leading Actor's Girlfriend," *Global Times*, April 12, 2020.

61. Veronica Sau-Wa Mak, "The Heritagization of Milk Tea: Cultural Governance and Placemaking in Hong Kong," *Asian Anthropology* 20, no. 1 (January 2, 2021): 30–46.

62. "Opinion: Today Hong Kong, Tomorrow Thailand," *Thai Enquirer*, July 2, 2020.

63. "Thais Promptly Reject 'Both Countries are a Family' Statement by Chinese Embassy in Thailand," *Mothership*, April 16, 2020.

64. Michael R. Chambers, "'The Chinese and the Thais Are Brothers': The Evolution of the Sino–Thai Friendship," *Journal of Contemporary China* 14, no. 45 (November 1, 2005): 599–629.

Chapter 5

1. Christine Ornetsmüller, Jean-Christophe Castella, and Peter H. Verburg, "A Multiscale Gaming Approach to Understand Farmer's Decision Making in the Boom of Maize Cultivation in Laos," *Ecology and Society* 23, no. 2 (2018).

2. Yu Sheng and Ligang Song, "Agricultural Production and Food Consumption in China: A Long-Term Projection," *China Economic Review* 53 (February 1, 2019): 15–29.

3. Yuchi Nitta and Apornrath Phoonphongphiphat, "Coronavirus Leaves Tropical Fruits Rotting at China Border Crossings," *Nikkei Asia*, February 6, 2020.

4. Nicholas Thomas, "Going out: China's Food Security from Southeast Asia," *The Pacific Review* 26, no. 5 (December 1, 2013): 531–62.

5. Lila Buckley, "Chinese Agriculture Goes Global: Food Security for All?" (International Institute for Environment and Development, 2012).

6. Deborah Brautigam, *Will Africa Feed China?* (Oxford and New York: Oxford University Press, 2016).

7. Mark Grimsditch, "Chinese Agriculture in Southeast Asia: Investment, Aid and Trade in Cambodia, Laos and Myanmar" (Heinrich-Böll Stiftung Southeast Asia, June 2017).

8. Troy Sternberg, "Chinese Drought, Bread and the Arab Spring," *Applied Geography* 34 (May 1, 2012): 519–24.

9. "Food Price Volatility and Insecurity," *Council on Foreign Relations*, January 16, 2013, https://www.cfr.org/backgrounder/food-price-volatility-and-insecurity.

10. Shaohua Zhan, "The Political Economy of Food Import and Self-Reliance in China: 1949–2019," *Global Food History* 0, no. 0 (December 13, 2021): 1–19.

11. Enze Han and Qiongyu Huang, "Global Commodity Markets, Chinese Demand for Maize, and Deforestation in Northern Myanmar," *Land* 10, no. 11 (November 2021): 1232.

12. Ming Feng et al., "Myanmar Forest Change Product 1979–2019," (The Smithsonian Institution, January 12, 2021).

13. Kevin Woods, "CP Maize Contract Farming in Shan State, Myanmar: A Regional Case of a Place-Based Corporate Agro-Feed System," BICAS Working Paper 14, May 18, 2015.

14. https://www.ndrc.gov.cn/xxgk/zcfb/gg/201909/W020191024490541207787.pdf.

15. Interview in Dehong, Yunnan Province of China, December 2019.

16. Xiaobo Su, "Smuggling and the Exercise of Effective Sovereignty at the China-Myanmar Border," *Review of International Political Economy* 29, no. 4 (2022): 1135–58.

17. "Myanmar, China signs SPS Protocol Agreement for Maize Export," *The Global New Light of Myanmar*, February 2, 2022.

18. Scott Waldron et al., "China's Cross-Border Economic Integration: Formalising Cattle Imports from Myanmar," *China: An International Journal* 20, no. 2 (2022): 101–33.

19. Darrell Peel, "Global Beef Update: Imports," *Beef Magazine*, April 20, 2022, https://www.beefmagazine.com/beef/global-beef-update-imports.

20. Kyaw Lin Htoon, "'At Least the Illegal Routes Are Safe': Cattle Smuggling Makes a Comeback," *Frontier Myanmar*, August 11, 2020.

21. Bertil Lintner and Hseng Noung Lintner, *Land of Jade: A Journey Through Insurgent Burma* (Edinburgh, Ohio: Kiscadale, 1990); Enze Han, *Asymmetrical Neighbors: Borderland State Building between China and Southeast Asia* (New York and London: Oxford University Press, 2019).

22. Kevin Woods, "Ceasefire Capitalism: Military–Private Partnerships, Resource Concessions and Military–State Building in the Burma–China Borderlands," *The Journal of Peasant Studies* 38, no. 4 (October 1, 2011): 747–70.

23. Personal interview, Lashio, summer 2019.

24. Waldron et al., "China's Cross-Border Economic Integration," 119.

25. "Taikang Plans to Invest 1.6 Billion Yuan for Beef Project, Currently Still No Plan for Man-Made Meat Yet," *Sohu*, May 19, 2020, https://www.sohu.com/a/396306148_114988.

26. Enze Han, "Overconfidence, Missteps, and Tragedy: Dynamics of Myanmar's International Relations and the Genocide of the Rohingya," *The Pacific Review*, October 28, 2021, 1–22.

27. Waldron et al., "China's Cross-Border Economic Integration," 122.

28. Patrick Meehan, "Fortifying or Fragmenting the State? The Political Economy of the Opium/Heroin Trade in Shan State, Myanmar, 1988–2013," *Critical Asian Studies* 47, no. 2 (April 3, 2015): 253–82.

29. Kyaw Lin Htoon, "'At Least the Illegal Routes Are Safe.'"

30. Enze Han, "Geopolitics, Ethnic Conflicts along the Border, and Chinese Foreign Policy Changes toward Myanmar," *Asian Security* 13, no. 1 (January 2, 2017): 59–73.

31. Han, "Geopolitics, Ethnic Conflicts along the Border, and Chinese Foreign Policy Changes toward Myanmar."

32. Bill Pritchard, "Fresh Fruit Exports from Mainland Southeast Asian Countries to China: Background Context and Key Questions for Research and Policy," in *Global Production Networks and Rural Development: Southeast Asia as a Fruit Supplier to China*, ed. Bill Pritchard (Cheltenham, UK and Northampton, Massachusetts: Edward Elgar Publishing Ltd, 2021), 1–26.

33. Pritchard, "Fresh Fruit Exports," 20.

34. Nattapon Tantrakoonsab and Wannarat Tantrakoonsab, "Thai Exports of Durian to China: The Expanding Role of Chinese Entrepreneurs," in *Global Production Networks and Rural Development: Southeast Asia as a Fruit Supplier to China*, ed. Bill Pritchard

(Cheltenham, UK and Northampton, Massachusetts: Edward Elgar Publishing Ltd, 2021), 87.

35. Tantrakoonsab and Tantrakoonsab, "Thai Exports of Durian to China," 87.
36. "Thai Durian in Rude Health as Exports Grow," *Bangkok Post*, May 9, 2022.
37. Tan Tam Mei, "Thai Durian Operators in a Prickly Spot as the Authorities Urge Industry to Grow," *Strait Times*, June 12, 2022.
38. "Durian Prices Surge as Demand Increases in China," *Durian Harvests*, September 16, 2018.
39. Pritchard, "Fresh Fruit Exports," 14.
40. Tantrakoonsab and Tantrakoonsab, "Thai Exports of Durian to China," 97.
41. Xiaobo Hua, Yasuyuki Kono, and Le Zhang, "Excavating Agrarian Transformation under 'Secure' Crop Booms: Insights from the China-Myanmar Borderland," *The Journal of Peasant Studies* 50, no. 1 (2023): 339–68.
42. Koji Kubo, "Myanmar's Watermelon Exports to China: Impacts of Unofficial Investment by Chinese on the Diffusion of a Horticultural Crop," in *Global Production Networks and Rural Development: Southeast Asia as a Fruit Supplier to China*, ed. Bill Pritchard (Cheltenham, UK and Northampton, Massachusetts: Edward Elgar Publishing Ltd, 2021), 66.
43. Kubo, "Myanmar's Watermelon Exports to China," 69.
44. Kubo, "Myanmar's Watermelon Exports to China," 72–73.
45. Chun Yang, "Cross-border Expansion of Digital Platforms and Transformation of the Trade and Distribution Networks of Imported Fresh Fruits from Southeast Asia to China," *Global Networks* 22, no. 4 (October 2022): 716–34.
46. Xiaobo Hua, Le Zhang, and Yasuyuki Kono, "Fruit Booms and Investor Mobility along the China-Myanmar and China-Laos Borders," *Ecology and Society* 27, no. 3 (September 26, 2022).
47. Tom Krammer and Kevin Woods, "Financing Dispossession: China's Opium Substitution Programme in Northern Burma" (Amsterdam: Transnational Institute (TNI), 2012).
48. Ko-Lin Chin, *The Golden Triangle: Inside Southeast Asia's Drug Trade* (Ithaca, New York: Cornell University Press, 2009).
49. Bertil Lintner, *Burma in Revolt: Opium and Insurgency since 1948*, 2nd edition (Chiang Mai, Thailand: Silkworm Books, 1999).
50. Xiaobo Su, "Nontraditional Security and China's Transnational Narcotics Control in Northern Laos and Myanmar," *Political Geography* 48 (September 2015): 72–82.
51. Transnational Institute, "Alternative Development or Business as Usual? China's Opium Substitution Policy in Burma and Laos," Drug Policy Briefing No. 33 (Amsterdam: Transnational Institute (TNI), 2010).
52. Stuart Ling and Mai Yer Xiong, "Labour Rights, Child Rights and Gender Justice for Lao Workers in Chinese Banana Plantations in Bokeo" (Plan International, January 2017).
53. "China-Driven Banana Boom in Laos Faces an Uncertain Future," *Produce Report*, March 11, 2018.

54. Xiangming Chen, "'Corridor-Ising' Impact along the Belt and Road: Is the Newly Operational China-Laos Railway a Game-Changer?," *European Financial Review*, February–March (2022): 10.

55. Phayboune Thanabouasy, "Laos Banana Remain Pick of the Bunch for Export to China," *The Laotian Times*, January 10, 2022.

56. Juliet Lu, "Grounding Chinese Investment: Encounters between Chinese Capital and Local Land Politics in Laos," *Globalizations* 18, no. 3 (April 3, 2021): 422–40.

57. Yos Santasombat, "Rent Capitalism and Shifting Plantations in the Mekong Borderlands," *Southeast Asian Affairs*, 2019, 178.

58. Santasombat, "Rent Capitalism and Shifting Plantations," 181.

59. Santasombat, "Rent Capitalism and Shifting Plantations," 178.

60. Cecilie Friis and Jonas Østergaard Nielsen, "Small-Scale Land Acquisitions, Large-Scale Implications: Exploring the Case of Chinese Banana Investments in Northern Laos," *Land Use Policy* 57 (November 30, 2016): 117–29.

61. Mark Inkey, "Chinese Banana Plantations Bring Work and Pollution to Laos," *China Dialogue*, October 14, 2019.

62. "More Chinese-Owned Banana Plantations to Close in Laos," *Radio Free Asia*, April 12, 2017.

63. Prashanth Parameswaran, "What's behind Laos' China Banana Ban?" *The Diplomat*, April 14, 2017.

64. Oliver Ward, "Chinese-owned Banana Plantations Expand in Laos despite Lingering Environmental and Health Concerns," *ASEAN Today*, October 16, 2019.

65. Ward, "Chinese-owned Banana Plantations."

66. "Worker Deaths Show Toxic Chemical Use Continues on Lao Banana Farms," *ASEAN Today*, March 26, 2021.

67. Ling and Xiong, "Labour Rights, Child Rights and Gender Justice," 4.

68. Yuchi Nitta and Apornrath Phoonphongphiphat, "Coronavirus Leaves Tropical Fruit Rotting at China Border Crossings," *Nikkei Asia*, February 6, 2020.

69. Kristin Huang, "Chinese Authorities Take a Leaf from the Trump Playbook and 'Build the Wall' as Part of Covid-19 Curbs," *South China Morning Post*, July 15, 2021.

70. Zhang Fangliang, "China's 'Zero-COVID' Policy: A View from the Border," *Sixth Tone*, June 13, 2022.

71. "Border City Ruili Ramps up Efforts against Imported COVID-19 Cases by Rewarding Tip-offs about Stowaways, Smugglers and Drug Traffickers," *Global Times*, September 21, 2021.

72. "Fear of a Banana Republic," *Bangkok Post*, June 5, 2016.

Chapter 6

1. Nathan Paul Southern and Lindsey Kennedy, "Lao's Criminal Casino Empire: Chinese Gangsters Suspected of Running Brothels and Online Scams, and Trafficking Humans, Animal Parts and Drugs," *South China Morning Post*, October 15, 2022.

2. Pinkaew Laungaramsri, "China in Laos: Enclave Spaces and the Transformation of Borders in the Mekong Region," *The Australian Journal of Anthropology* 30, no. 2 (2019): 195–211.

3. Aidan Jones, "Cambodia's Chinese Scam Gangs are Forcing Desperate Young Asians into Crime—and the Pandemic only Made Things Worse," *South China Morning Post*, August 27, 2022.

4. "Malaysian Job Scam Victim Tells of 'Prison' Beatings in Myanmar," *The Straits Times*, May 18, 2022.

5. Rebecca Ratcliffe, Nhung Nguyen, and Navaon Siradapuvadol, "Sold to Gangs, Forced to Run Online Scams: Inside Cambodia's Cybercrime Crisis," *The Guardian*, October 10, 2022.

6. Huang Yan, "Under Foreign Pressure, Cambodia Dismantles Some "Scam" Compounds," *Nikkei Asia*, October 13, 2022.

7. Chris Lau and Harvey Kong, "Hong Kong Authorities Vow Rescue Bid with Foreign Ministry, Interpol as New WhatsApp Hotline Set up for Victims of Human Trafficking," *South China Morning Post*, August 20, 2022.

8. Lau Fong Mak, *Sociology of Secret Societies: Study of Chinese Secret Societies in Singapore and Peninsular Malaysia* (Kuala Lumpur and New York: Oxford University Press, 1981).

9. Richard Basham, "The Roots of Asian Organized Crime," *IPA Review* 48, no. 4 (1996): 11.

10. Lau Fong Mak, "The Kongsis and the Triad," *Southeast Asian Journal of Social Science* 3, no. 2 (1975): 47–58.

11. Jean Chesneaux, ed., *Popular Movements and Secret Societies in China, 1840–1950* (Stanford: Stanford University Press, 1986).

12. Alan Dupont, "Transnational Crime, Drugs, and Security in East Asia," *Asian Survey* 39, no. 3 (1999): 446; Ko-lin Chin and Sheldon X. Zhang, *The Chinese Heroin Trade: Cross-Border Drug Trafficking in Southeast Asia and Beyond* (New York and London: NYU Press, 2015).

13. Ming Xia, "Organizational Formations of Organized Crime in China: Perspectives from the State, Markets, and Networks," *Journal of Contemporary China* 17, no. 54 (February 1, 2008): 9.

14. John S. Van Oudenaren, "Enduring Menace: The Triad Societies of Southeast China," *Asian Affairs* 41, no. 3 (2014): 127–53.

15. Xia, "Organizational Formations of Organized Crime in China," 11.

16. Daniel Silverstone and Joe Whittle, "'Forget It, Jake. It's Chinatown': The Policing of Chinese Organised Crime in the UK," *The Police Journal* 89, no. 1 (March 1, 2016): 70–84.

17. Matt Ferchen, "The Two Faces of the China Model: The BRI in Southeast Asia," in *Global Perspectives on China's Belt and Road Initiative*, ed. Florian Schneider, Asserting Agency through Regional Connectivity (Amsterdam University Press, 2021), 245–64.

18. Peng Wang and Georgios A. Antonopoulos, "Organized Crime and Illegal Gambling: How Do Illegal Gambling Enterprises Respond to the Challenges Posed

by Their Illegality in China?," *Australian & New Zealand Journal of Criminology* 49, no. 2 (June 1, 2016): 258–80; Peng Wang, "Politics of Crime Control: How Campaign-Style Law Enforcement Sustains Authoritarian Rule in China," *The British Journal of Criminology* 60, no. 2 (March 14, 2020): 422–43.

19. Kerry Brown, "The Anti-Corruption Struggle in Xi Jinping's China: An Alternative Political Narrative," *Asian Affairs* 49, no. 1 (January 2, 2018): 1–10.

20. Pál Nyíri, "Enclaves of Improvement: Sovereignty and Developmentalism in the Special Zones of the China-Lao Borderlands," *Comparative Studies in Society and History* 54, no. 3 (July 2012): 533–62.

21. Daan P. van Uhm and Rebecca W. Y. Wong, "Chinese Organized Crime and the Illegal Wildlife Trade: Diversification and Outsourcing in the Golden Triangle," *Trends in Organized Crime* 24, no. 4 (December 1, 2021): 486–505.

22. Danielle Tan, "'Small Is Beautiful': Lessons from Laos for the Study of Chinese Overseas," *Journal of Current Chinese Affairs* 41, no. 2 (June 1, 2012): 61–94.

23. Alvin Camba, "Between Economic and Social Exclusions: Chinese Online Gambling Capital in the Philippines," *Made in China Journal* (blog), October 19, 2020, 211, https://madeinchinajournal.com/2020/10/19/between-economic-and-social-exclusi ons-chinese-online-gambling-philippines/.

24. "China has a New Casino: the Philippines," *South China Morning Post*, July 7, 2019.

25. "PAGCOR and Four other Agencies Intensify Drive vs. Illegal Online Gambling," Philippine Amusement and Gaming Corporation, March 21, 2019.

26. Alvin Camba and Hangwei Li, "Chinese Workers and Their 'Linguistic Labour': Philippine Online Gambling and Zambian Onsite Casinos," *China Perspectives* 2020, no. 4 (December 1, 2020): 39–47.

27. "China Urges Philippines to Ban Online Gambling," *Reuters*, August 21, 2019.

28. Deqian Kong, "'Eating Spinach': The Taiwanese Working in Philippines Gambling Industry," *The Reporter*, July 17, 2019.

29. Camba, "Between Economic and Social Exclusions," 213.

30. Kong, "'Eating Spinach.'"

31. Camba, "Between Economic and Social Exclusions," 217.

32. Camba, "Between Economic and Social Exclusions," 216.

33. Mong Palatino, "China's Clandestine Gamble in the Philippines," *The Diplomat*, June 1, 2020.

34. Martin Petty, "China Tells Philippines to Tackle Abuses in Online Gaming 'Slavery,'" *Reuters*, August 8, 2019.

35. "Rodrigo Duterte Unwilling to Ban Online Gaming despite China's Requests, Citing Damage to Economy," *South China Morning Post*, September 5, 2019.

36. Sebastian Strangio, "Philippines Readies Crackdown on Chinese Online Gambling Operations," *The Diplomat*, September 28, 2022.

37. Strangio, "Philippines Readies Crackdown on Chinese Online Gambling Operations."

38. Sovinda Po and Kimkong Heng, "Assessing the Impact of Chinese Investments in Cambodia: The Case of Preah Sihanoukville Province," Working Paper on China-Cambodia Relations, Issues & Insights Working Paper (Honolulu: Pacific Forum, May 2019).

39. M. Bo and N. Loughlin, "Overlapping Agendas on the Belt and Road: The Case of the Sihanoukville Special Economic Zone," *Global China Pulse* 1, no. 1 (July 1, 2022): 85.

40. Teri Shaffer Yamada, "Phnom Penh's NagaWorld Resort and Casino," *Pacific Affairs* 90, no. 4 (December 1, 2017): 743–65.

41. Michael Zhu, "Cambodia Conundrum," *Global Gaming Business Magazine*, August 24, 2020.

42. Shaun Turton, "In Cambodia's Boomtown, A Gamble on Chinese Money Goes Sour," *Nikkei Asia*, January 10, 2020.

43. Len Ang, "Online Gambling: The Trap of Cambodian Dependency on Chinese Investment in Sihanoukville," *Cambodianess*, September 21, 2020.

44. Po and Heng, "Assessing the Impact of Chinese Investments in Cambodia."

45. Sebastian Strangio, "China Shows Signs of Cracking Down on 'Sil Road' Crime," *The Diplomat*, October 29, 2020.

46. Andrew Nachemson and Kong Meta, "Chinese Gang Threatens Chaos in Cambodian Province as Rift Deepens between Locals and New Arrivals," *South China Morning Post*, May 14, 2019.

47. Khy Sovuthy, "Ambassador Addresses Worry over Chinese Crime," Khmer Times, February 8, 2018.

48. Jason Tower and Priscilla A. Clapp, "Myanmar's Casino Cities: The Role of China and Transnational Criminal Networks" (Washington, D.C.: United States Institute of Peace, 2020), 8.

49. "Cambodia to Ban Online Gambling, Cites Threat to Social Order," *Bangkok Post*, August 18, 2019.

50. Khuon Narim, "China Supports Cambodia Gambling Ban," *Khmer Times*, August 22, 2019.

51. Ang, "Online Gambling."

52. "'Ghost Buildings' Show Boom Times are Over for Cambodian Resort Town," *Radio Free Asia*, August 16, 2022.

53. David Brenner, *Rebel Politics: A Political Sociology of Armed Struggle in Myanmar's Borderlands* (Ithaca, New York: Cornell University Press, 2019).

54. William W. Davis et al., "Health and Human Rights in Karen State, Eastern Myanmar," *PLOS ONE* 10, no. 8 (August 26, 2015): 1–13.

55. Tower and Clapp, "Myanmar's Casino Cities," 8–13.

56. Andrew Nachemson, "The Mystery Man behind the Shwe Kokko Project," *Frontier Myanmar*, July 7, 2020.

57. Nachemson, "The Mystery Man."

58. Nachemson, "The Mystery Man."

59. "Scam City: How the Coup Brought Shwe Kokko back to Life," *Frontier Myanmar*, June 23, 2022.

60. Nachemson, "The Mystery Man."

61. Embassy of the People's Republic of China in Myanmar, "China Supports Myanmar in Handling the Shwe Kokko New City Issue in Accordance with Laws and Regulations," August 25, 2020.

62. Priscilla A. Clapp and Jason Tower, "Myanmar's Criminal Zones: A Growing Threat to Global Security," *United States Institute of Peace*, November 9, 2022.

63. "Thai Police Arrested China's She Zhijiang, Suspected Gambling Kingpin, 'On the Run for a Decade,'" *South China Morning Post*, August 15, 2022.

64. Nan Lwin, "US Sanctions Chinese Gangster Behind 'Industrial Zone' in Myanmar's Karen State," *The Irrawaddy*, December 10, 2020.

65. Aung Zaw, "In Myanmar's Karen State, Ex-Insurgents Create a Haven for Chinese Casino Bosses," *The Irrawaddy*, August 28, 2020.

66. "东南亚为何成诈骗犯天堂？警察毫无办法" ("Why Southeast Asia Has Become a Haven for Criminals? Police Has No Solution"), *Zhimengcaijing*, July 15, 2022.

67. "柬埔寨的诈骗集团，有多狠？" ("How Cruel Are Criminal Networks in Cambodia?") *163*, May 12, 2022.

68. Clifford Lo, "90-Year-Old Woman Living in Mansion on The Peak Conned out of US$32 Million in Hong Kong's Biggest Phone Scam," *South China Morning Post*, April 19, 2021.

69. Mandy Zuo, "Online 'Pig Butchering' Love Scams Have Gone Global after Getting Their Start in China," *South China Morning Post*, September 30, 2021.

70. "Human Trafficking in Cambodia: Fattening the Victims for the Kill," *Khmer Times*, September 28, 2022.

71. "一男子参与缅北跨境电信诈骗7月四日受审当庭认罪" ("One Man Pleads Guilty on July 4th for Participating in Transnational Scam Operations in Myanmar"), *Beijing Youth Daily*, July 4, 2022.

72. "揭露缅北'杀猪盘'：诈骗集团把业务员当货物一样卖" ("Scam Operations in Northern Myanmar Exposed: Scam Syndicates Sell Their Workers as Slaves"), *China Youth Daily*, November 30, 2021.

73. "重庆警方破获特大跨国电信网络诈骗案涉及东南亚多国" ("Police in Chongqing Exposed Large Transnational Scam Operations That Are Related with Several Countries in Southeast Asia"), *China News Network*, February 18, 2022.

74. "Will the Chinese Government's Crackdown on Cross-Border Crime in Myanmar Work?" *ThinkChina*, September 17, 2021.

75. "中缅边境：大批中国非法移民逃离缅甸回国'自首'但因疫情滞留边境" ("Sino-Myanmar Border: Large Number of Illegal Chinese Migrants Returned to China but Got Stuck at Border Due to COVID"), *BBC Chinese*, July 14, 2021.

76. "拯救非法出境搞电诈的年轻人，劝返只是'上半篇'" ("Save the Youth Who Have Gone Abroad for Online Scams"), *Legal Daily*, March 31, 2022.

77. "'I was a Slave': Up to 100,000 Held Captive by Chinese Cybercriminals in Cambodia," *Los Angeles Times*, November 1, 2022.

78. "柬埔寨诈骗 马来西亚男误信广告遭卖猪仔" ("Scam in Cambodia: Malaysian Guy Got Sold as Slave"), *HK01*, September 4, 2022.

79. "超过百名新加坡人被'卖猪仔'受困柬埔寨诈骗集团基地" ("More Than One Hundred Singaporeans Got Sold as Slaves, Who Are Stuck in Cambodia"), *Oriental Daily*, August 23, 2022.

80. "Hong Konger 'Kidnapped' by SE Asia Scam Ring Pleads for Help," *France 24*, August 24, 2022.

81. "IN FOCUS: When Lucrative Overseas Job Offer Turn into Nightmare Scams for These Malaysians," *Channel News Asia*, September 17, 2022.

82. Laura Dev et al., "Ambiguous Spaces, Empirical Traces: Accounting for Ignorance When Researching around the Illicit," *Progress in Human Geography* 46, no. 2 (April 1, 2022): 652–71; Ray Hudson, "Thinking through the Relationships between Legal and Illegal Activities and Economies: Spaces, Flows and Pathways," *Journal of Economic Geography* 14, no. 4 (2014): 775–95.

83. Peter Andreas, "Illicit International Political Economy: The Clandestine Side of Globalization," *Review of International Political Economy* 11, no. 3 (June 2004): 641–52.

84. Peter Andreas, "International Politics and the Illicit Global Economy," *Perspectives on Politics* 13, no. 3 (September 2015): 782.

85. Bradford Dillman, "Introduction: Shining Light on the Shadows: The Political Economy of Illicit Transactions in the Mediterranean," *Mediterranean Politics* 12, no. 2 (July 1, 2007): 123–39.

86. Aihwa Ong and Donald Nonini, eds., *Ungrounded Empires: The Cultural Politics of Modern Chinese Transnationalism* (London: Routledge, 2003).

Chapter 7

1. Daniel Chirot and Anthony Reid, eds., *Essential Outsiders: Chinese and Jews in the Modern Transformation of Southeast Asia and Central Europe* (Seattle: University of Washington Press, 2011).

2. Mary Mostafanezhad and Tanya Promburom, "'Lost in Thailand': The Popular Geopolitics of Film-Induced Tourism in Northern Thailand," *Social & Cultural Geography* 19, no. 1 (January 2, 2018): 81–101.

3. Aranya Siriphon, "Xinyimin, New Chinese Migrants, and the Influence of the PRC and Taiwan on the Northern Thai Border," in *Impact of China's Rise on the Mekong Region*, ed. Yos Santasombat (New York: Palgrave Macmillan, 2015), 117–46; Pál Nyíri and Danielle Tan, eds., *Chinese Encounters in Southeast Asia: How People, Money, and Ideas from China Are Changing a Region* (Seattle: University of Washington Press, 2016).

4. Hong Liu, "New Migrants and the Revival of Overseas Chinese Nationalism," *Journal of Contemporary China* 14, no. 43 (May 1, 2005): 291–316.

5. Gungwu Wang, *The Chinese Overseas: From Earthbound China to the Quest for Autonomy* (Cambridge, Massachusetts: Harvard University Press, 2002).

6. Taomo Zhou, *Migration in the Time of Revolution: China, Indonesia, and the Cold War* (Ithaca, New York: Cornell University Press, 2019).

7. Leo Suryadinata, *The Making of Southeast Asian Nations: State, Ethnicity, Indigenism and Citizenship* (Singapore: World Scientific, 2015, 2015).

8. Paul J. Bolt, "Looking to the Diaspora: The Overseas Chinese and China's Economic Development, 1978-1994," *Diaspora: A Journal of Transnational Studies* 5, no. 3 (1996): 467–96.

9. Wolfgang Georg Arlt, "The Second Wave of Chinese Outbound Tourism," *Tourism Planning & Development* 10, no. 2 (May 2013): 126–33.
10. Compiled based on statistics provided by the World Tourism Organization (UNWTO).
11. ASEAN-China Centre, "2018 Tourism Facts & Figures in China and between ASEAN & China," February 2, 2020, http://www.asean-china-center.org/english/2020-02/4251.html.
12. Mostafanezhad and Promburom, " 'Lost in Thailand.' "
13. Alice D. Ba, "Is China Leading? China, Southeast Asia and East Asian Integration," *Political Science* 66, no. 2 (December 1, 2014): 143–65.
14. Mostafanezhad and Promburom, " 'Lost in Thailand,' " 94.
15. Aranya Siriphon, "Developing Entrepreneurship Under the Rise of China: Chinese Migrant Entrepreneurs in Tourism-Related Businesses in Chiang Mai," in *The Sociology of Chinese Capitalism in Southeast Asia: Challenges and Prospects*, ed. Yos Santasombat (Singapore: Springer, 2019), 271–89.
16. Personal interviews in Bangkok, November 2019.
17. "Thai Minister Blames Chinese Tour Operators for Boat Disaster," *Reuters*, July 8, 2018.
18. "Prawit Sorry for Offending China Netizens over Boat Tragedy, but Law Offenders to be Punished," *The Nation Thailand*, July 10, 2018.
19. "Thailand to Grant Visa-on-Arrival Fee Waiver for Some Visitors in Bid to Lift Tourism Slump," *The Straits Times*, November 7, 2018.
20. Pál Nyíri and Igor Saveliev, eds., *Globalizing Chinese Migration: Trends in Europe and Asia* (Burlington: Ashgate, 2003).
21. Siriphon, "Commodifying Sovereignty."
22. Romyen Kosaikanont, "Chinese Capital Going Global: Thai-Chinese Industrial Zone and Labor Conditions in Thailand," in *The Sociology of Chinese Capitalism in Southeast Asia: Challenges and Prospects*, ed. Yos Santasombat (Singapore: Springer, 2019), 169–94.
23. "New Wave of Chinese Coming to Live in Thailand," *Bangkok Post*, September 23, 2016.
24. "Chinese Expat Community Swells in Thailand," *The Nation Thailand*, January 9, 2017. Obviously this statistic excludes large numbers of migrant laborers from Myanmar or Cambodia, many in Thailand illegally, from the category of "expats."
25. James Rush, *Opium to Java: Revenue Farming and Chinese Enterprise in Colonial Indonesia, 1860–1910* (Ithaca, New York: Cornell University Press, 1990).
26. Pál Nyíri, "Chinese Entrepreneurs in Poor Countries: A Transnational 'Middleman Minority' and Its Futures," *Inter-Asia Cultural Studies* 12, no. 1 (March 1, 2011): 147.
27. William H. Leggett, "Institutionalising the Colonial Imagination: Chinese Middlemen and the Transnational Corporate Office in Jakarta, Indonesia," *Journal of Ethnic and Migration Studies* 36, no. 8 (September 1, 2010): 1272.
28. Diana S. Kim, *Empires of Vice: The Rise of Opium Prohibition across Southeast Asia* (Princeton: Princeton University Press, 2020).

29. George William Skinner, *Chinese Society in Thailand: An Analytical History* (Ithaca, New York: Cornell University Press, 1957), 102.

30. Han and Khemanitthathai, "Through the Prism of Migration."

31. Information on such legal regulations can be obtained at: http://library.siam-legal.com/thailand-foreign-business-law-q-and-a/.

32. Hongzhi Yin, Athapol Ruangkanjanases, and Chenin Chen, "Factors Affecting Chinese Students' Decision Making toward Thai Universities," *International Journal of Information and Education Technology* 5, no. 3 (2015): 189.

33. Panu Wongcha-um, "Thai Universities Tap into Rising Chinese Demand," *Reuters*, January 17, 2019.

34. Wongcha-um, "Thai Universities Tap into Rising Chinese Demand."

35. Jitsiree Tongnoi, "As Chinese Students Flock to Thai Universities, Some Are in for a Hard Lesson," *South China Morning Post*, October 20, 2019.

36. Shirlena Huang and Brenda S. A. Yeoh, "Transnational Families and Their Children's Education: China's 'Study Mothers' in Singapore," *Global Networks* 5, no. 4 (2005): 379–400.

37. For example, there are many topics on Zhihu that provide information about how to manage life in Thailand for people who are pursuing the international school option; see https://zhuanlan.zhihu.com/p/429369051.

38. The PEW survey can be accessed at http://www.pewglobal.org/2014/07/14/chapter-2-chinas-image/.

39. The Asian Barometer can be accessed at https://www.asianbarometer.org/survey.jsp?page=s10.

40. Tungkeunkunt Kornphanat, "Culture and Commerce: China's Soft Power in Thailand," *International Journal of China Studies* 7, no. 2 (August 2016): 167.

41. There are many posts on social media that talk about why Thailand should fear China, for example in the following webpage on Pantip: https://pantip.com/topic/38898744.

42. Nidhi Eoseewong, for example, traced the historical pattern of Chinese migration to Siam and how different groups of Chinese left different cultural legacies on Thai society; see Nidhi Eoseewong, *Pen and Sail: Literature and History in Early Bangkok* (Chiang Mai: Silkworm Books, 2005).

43. Walter F. Vella, *Chaiyo!: King Vajiravadh and the Development of Thai Nationalism* (Manoa: University of Hawai'i Press, 1986), 194.

44. Skinner, *Chinese Society in Thailand*, 91.

45. Juliette Koning and Michiel Verver, "Historicizing the 'Ethnic' in Ethnic Entrepreneurship: The Case of the Ethnic Chinese in Bangkok," *Entrepreneurship & Regional Development* 25, no. 5–6 (June 1, 2013): 325–48.

46. This self-perception of the Thai being lazy is not unique to the Chinese. The Thais express similar sentiments towards Vietnamese and Burmese migrant laborers who have come to Thailand at different periods and were also perceived as harder-working. I thank Wasana Wongsurawat for raising this excellent point.

47. Jian Gong, Pornpen Detchkhajornjaroensri, and David W. Knight, "Responsible Tourism in Bangkok, Thailand: Resident Perceptions of Chinese Tourist Behaviour," *International Journal of Tourism Research* 21, no. 2 (2019): 227.

48. Teerati Banterng, "China's Image Repair: The Case of Chinese Tourists on Social Media in Thailand," *Global Media Journal* 15, no. 29 (October 21, 2017): 1–11.

49. He Huifeng, "Feeding Frenzy: Internet Users Aghast at Video of Chinese Tourists Shovelling Shrimp at Buffet in Thailand," *South China Morning Post*, March 20, 2016.

50. The "Civilized Tourism Travel Guide" can be accessed online at http://www.yyx.gov.cn/uploadfiles/201711/fab6713d-2044-4573-838d-186d391894ba.pdf.

51. "China to Document Its Tourists Behaving Badly," *Reuters*, April 7, 2015.

52. Mary Mostafanezhad, Joseph M Cheer, and Harng Luh Sin, "Geopolitical Anxieties of Tourism: (Im)Mobilities of the COVID-19 Pandemic," *Dialogues in Human Geography* 10, no. 2 (July 2020): 182–86.

53. Ian Rowen, "The Geopolitics of Tourism: Mobilities, Territory, and Protest in China, Taiwan, and Hong Kong," *Annals of the American Association of Geographers* 106, no. 2 (March 3, 2016): 385–93.

Chapter 8

1. James Jiann Hua To, *Qiaowu: Extra-Territorial Policies for the Overseas Chinese* (Leiden: Brill Academic Publishers, 2014).

2. Gungwu Wang, *China and the Chinese Overseas* (Singapore: Times Academic Press, 1991).

3. Min Zhou, ed., *Contemporary Chinese Diasporas* (New York: Palgrave Macmillan, 2017).

4. Yu-Jie Chen, "'One China' Contention in China–Taiwan Relations: Law, Politics and Identity," *The China Quarterly* 252 (December 2022): 1025–44.

5. Dudley L Poston and Juyin Helen Wong, "The Chinese Diaspora: The Current Distribution of the Overseas Chinese Population," *Chinese Journal of Sociology* 2, no. 3 (July 1, 2016): 348–73

6. Jiaqi M. Liu, "When Diaspora Politics Meet Global Ambitions: Diaspora Institutions Amid China's Geopolitical Transformations," *International Migration Review* 56, no. 4 (2022): 1255–79.

7. Rogers Brubaker, *Nationalism Reframed: Nationhood and the National Question in the New Europe* (New York: Cambridge University Press, 1996). In this chapter, I use diaspora and ethnic minority group interchangeably. Also, in terms of terminology, I opt to use "home state" instead of "host state," and "kin state" instead of "homeland state," which have previously been used in the literature. This is to avoid the political connotation that the diaspora group are mere guests in the current country where they reside. Particularly for the overseas Chinese in Southeast Asia, the vast majority of them have local citizenship and have lived in these countries for multiple generations. Thus, it is more appropriate to use "home state" to refer to the country where they reside, and "kin state" for China.

8. David C. Kang, *China Rising: Peace, Power, and Order in East Asia* (New York: Columbia University Press, 2009).

9. Enze Han, "Modes of Securitization and De-securitization of Transnational Kinship Ties: Overseas Chinese in Southeast Asia amidst Rising Chinese Power," *Journal of Global Security Studies* (forthcoming).

10. Joseph Nye, *Soft Power: The Means to Success in World Politics* (New York: PublicAffairs, 2004).

11. However, we need to note that the origin of such threat perception is exogenous and is not necessarily dependent upon power dynamics. Sometimes, such threat perception is rooted in history, while other times it can be dependent upon contemporary regimes and domestic politics.

12. Brubaker, *Nationalism Reframed*, 6.

13. Harris Mylonas, *The Politics of Nation Building: Making Co-Nationals, Refugees, and Minorities* (New York: Cambridge University Press, 2013).

14. Yossi Shain, *Kinship and Diasporas in International Affairs* (Ann Arbor: University of Michigan Press, 2008).

15. Enze Han and Harris Mylonas, "Interstate Relations, Perceptions, and Power Balance: Explaining China's Policies Toward Ethnic Groups, 1949–1965," *Security Studies* 23, no. 1 (January 1, 2014): 148–81.

16. Enze Han, *Contestation and Adaptation: The Politics of National Identity in China* (New York and London: Oxford University Press, 2013).

17. Ayumi Takenaka, "The Paradox of Diaspora Engagement: A Historical Analysis of Japanese State-Diaspora Relations," *Journal of Ethnic and Migration Studies* 46, no. 6 (April 25, 2020): 1129–45.

18. Gungwu Wang, *The Chinese Overseas: From Earthbound China to the Quest for Autonomy* (Cambridge, Massachusetts: Harvard University Press, 2002).

19. Adam McKeown, "Chinese Emigration in Global Context, 1850–1940," *Journal of Global History* 5, no. 1 (March 2010): 95–124.

20. Enze Han, "Bifurcated Homeland and Diaspora Politics in China and Taiwan towards the Overseas Chinese in Southeast Asia," *Journal of Ethnic and Migration Studies* 45, no. 4 (March 12, 2019): 577–94.

21. Leo Suryadinata, "Government Policies towards the Ethnic Chinese: A Comparison between Indonesia and Malaysia," *Southeast Asian Journal of Social Science* 13, no. 2 (1985): 15–28.

22. George William Skinner, *Chinese Society in Thailand: An Analytical History* (Ithaca, New York: Cornell University Press, 1957), 181.

23. To, *Qiaowu*, 51.

24. Jeffery Sng and Pimpraphai Bisalputra, *A History of the Thai-Chinese* (Singapore: Editions Didier Millet, 2015), 270.

25. Skinner, *Chinese Society in Thailand*, 262–67.

26. Disaphol Chansiri, *The Chinese Émigrés of Thailand in the Twentieth Century* (Youngstown, New York: Cambria Press, 2008), 71.

27. Eiji Murashima, "The Thai-Japanese Alliance and The Overseas Chinese in Thailand," in *Southeast Asian Minorities in the Wartime Japanese Empire*, ed. Paul H. Kratoska (Oxford: RoutledgeCurzon, 2005), 192–223.

28. Skinner, *Chinese Society in Thailand*, 276.

29. Skinner, *Chinese Society in Thailand*, 381.

30. Kanniga Sachakul, "Education as a Means for National Integration: Historical and Comparative Study of Chinese and Muslim Assimilation in Thailand" (PhD diss., Ann Arbor, University of Michigan, 1984), 188.

31. Sittithep Eaksittipong, "From Chinese 'in' to Chinese 'of' Thailand: The Politics of Knowledge Production during the Cold War," *Rian Thai: International Journal of Thai Studies* 10, no. 1 (January 1, 2017).

32. Yi Li, *Chinese in Colonial Burma: A Migrant Community in A Multiethnic State* (New York: Palgrave Macmillan, 2017).

33. Diana S. Kim, *Empires of Vice: The Rise of Opium Prohibition across Southeast Asia* (Princeton: Princeton University Press, 2020), 230.

34. Matthew J. Bowser, "Partners in Empire? Co-Colonialism and the Rise of Anti-Indian Nationalism in Burma, 1930–1938," *The Journal of Imperial and Commonwealth History* 49, no. 1 (January 2, 2021): 118–47.

35. Robert H. Taylor, *The State in Myanmar* (London: C Hurst & Co., 2008); David I. Steinberg, *Burma: The State of Myanmar* (Washington, D.C: Georgetown University Press, 2001).

36. Matthew J. Walton, "The 'Wages of Burman-Ness:' Ethnicity and Burman Privilege in Contemporary Myanmar," *Journal of Contemporary Asia* 43, no. 1 (February 1, 2013): 1–27.

37. Kei Nemoto, "The Concepts of Dobama ('Our Burma') and Thudo-Bama ('Their Burma') in Burmese Nationalism, 1930–1948," *Journal of Burma Studies* 5, no. 1 (March 30, 2011): 3.

38. Mikael Gravers, *Nationalism as Political Paranoia in Burma: An Essay on the Historical Practice of Power* (London: Routledge, 1999), 31; Alicia Turner, *Saving Buddhism: The Impermanence of Religion in Colonial Burma* (Honolulu: University of Hawai'i Press, 2017).

39. Renaud Egreteau, "Burmese Indians in Contemporary Burma: Heritage, Influence, and Perceptions since 1988," *Asian Ethnicity* 12, no. 1 (February 1, 2011): 40.

40. Robert A. Holmes, "Burmese Domestic Policy: The Politics of Burmanization," *Asian Survey* 7, no. 3 (1967): 188–97.

41. Elaine Lynn-Ee Ho and Lynette J. Chua, "Law and 'Race' in the Citizenship Spaces of Myanmar: Spatial Strategies and the Political Subjectivity of the Burmese Chinese," *Ethnic and Racial Studies* 39, no. 5 (April 8, 2016): 896–916.

42. Riza Afita Surya, "VOC and Chinese in Java: Identifying the Migration Motives in the Seventeenth Century," *European Journal of Humanities and Social Sciences* 2, no. 6 (December 11, 2022): 109–17.

43. Oiyan Liu, "Countering 'Chinese Imperialism': Sinophobia and Border Protection in the Dutch East Indies," *Indonesia*, no. 97 (2014): 87–110.

44. A.R.T. Kemasang, "The 1740 Massacre of Chinese in Java: Curtain Raiser for the Dutch Plantation Economy," *Bulletin of Concerned Asian Scholars* 14, no. 1 (March 1, 1982): 61–71.

45. Taomo Zhou, *Migration in the Time of Revolution: China, Indonesia, and the Cold War* (Ithaca, New York: Cornell University Press, 2019), 6.

46. Leo Suryadinata, ed., *Ethnic Chinese in Contemporary Indonesia* (Singapore: ISEAS-Yusof Ishak Institute, 2008).

47. Jemma Purdey, *Anti-Chinese Violence in Indonesia, 1996–1999* (Honolulu: University of Hawaii Press, 2006).

48. Taomo Zhou, "China and the Thirtieth of September Movement," *Indonesia*, no. 98 (2014): 29–58.

49. Samsu Rizal Panggabean and Benjamin Smith, "Explaining Anti-Chinese Riots in Late 20th Century Indonesia," *World Development: Ethnicity and Ethnic Strife* 39, no. 2 (February 1, 2011): 231–42.

50. Evelyn Goh, ed., *Rising China's Influence in Developing Asia* (New York and London: Oxford University Press, 2016).

51. Benedict Anderson, "Riddles of Yellow and Red," *New Left Review* 97, Jan–Feb (2016): 19.

52. Wasana Wongsurawat, "The Social Capital of Being Chinese in Thai Politics," in *The Sociology of Chinese Capitalism in Southeast Asia: Challenges and Prospects*, ed. Yos Santasombat (Singapore: Springer, 2019), 75–92.

53. Kasian Tejapira, "The Misbehaving Jeks: The Evolving Regime of Thainess and Sino-Thai Challenges," *Asian Ethnicity* 10, no. 3 (October 1, 2009): 276.

54. Enze Han, "Entrenching Authoritarian Rule and Thailand's Foreign Policy Dilemma as a Middle Power," *Asia Policy* 17, no. 4 (2022): 181–98.

55. Jiemin Bao, "Lukchin: Chinese Thai Transnational Bridge Builders," in *Chinese Transnational Networks* (London and New York: Routledge, 2006), 92–106.

56. "China Cools and HIS Retreats as Ma Intrigues," *The Standard*, January 31, 2023.

57. "Jack Ma's Movements Send Hong Kong Penny Stock Soaring," *Nikkei Asia*, February 1, 2023.

58. "China's Sinovac Attracts $515m to Help Double COVID Vaccine Output," *Nikkei Asia*, December 7, 2020.

59. Enze Han, "Borderland Ethnic Politics and Changing Sino-Myanmar Relations," in *War and Peace in the Borderlands of Myanmar: The Kachin Ceasefire, 1994–2011*, ed. Mandy Sadan (Copenhagen: NIAS Press, 2016); Enze Han, "Under the Shadow of Sino-US Great Power Competition: Myanmar and Thailand's Alignment Choices," *Chinese Journal of International Politics* 11, no. 1 (2018): 81–104.

60. Enze Han, "Overconfidence, Missteps, and Tragedy: Dynamics of Myanmar's International Relations and the Genocide of the Rohingya," *The Pacific Review*, October 28, 2021, 1–22.

61. Nick Cheesman, "How in Myanmar 'National Races' Came to Surpass Citizenship and Exclude Rohingya," *Journal of Contemporary Asia* 47, no. 3 (May 27, 2017): 461–83.

62. Enze Han, *Asymmetrical Neighbors: Borderland State-Building between China and Southeast Asia* (New York and London: Oxford University Press, 2019).

63. Min Zin, "Burmese Attitude toward Chinese: Portrayal of the Chinese in Contemporary Cultural and Media Works," *Journal of Current Southeast Asian Affairs* 31, no. 1 (January 1, 2012): 115–31.

64. Yun Sun, "China and the Changing Myanmar," *Journal of Current Southeast Asian Affairs* 31, no. 4 (2012): 51.

65. Debby Sze Wan Chan, "Asymmetric Bargaining between Myanmar and China in the Myitsone Dam Controversy: Social Opposition Akin to David's Stone against Goliath," *The Pacific Review* 30, no. 5 (September 3, 2017): 674–91.

66. Han, "Borderland Ethnic Politics and Changing Sino-Myanmar Relations."

67. "After Attacks on Chinese Businesses, Myanmar Imposes 'Full Martial Law' in Yangon," *South China Morning Post*, March 15, 2021.

68. Personal communication.

69. Dewi Fortuna Anwar, "Indonesia-China Relations: To Be Handled with Care," Perspective (Singapore: ISEAS Yusof Ishak Institute, March 28, 2019), 3.

70. Harryanto Aryodiguno, "Changes in Chinese-Indonesian Identity: Indonesianization or Re- Sinicization?," *AEGIS: Journal of International Relations* 3, no. 1 (August 2, 2019).

71. Charlotte Setijadi, "Chinese Indonesians in the Eyes of the Pribumi Public," Perspective (Singapore: ISEAS Yusof Ishak Institute, 2017), 8.

72. Mohamed Nawab Mohamed Osman and Prashant Waikar, "Fear and Loathing: Uncivil Islamism and Indonesia's Anti-Ahok Movement," *Indonesia* 106 (October 2018): 89–109.

73. Evan A. Laksmana, "Variations on a Theme: Dimensions of Ambivalence in Indonesia-China Relations," *Harvard Asia Quarterly* 13, no. 1 (May 1, 2011): 24–31.

74. Prashanth Parameswaran, "Between Aspiration and Reality: Indonesian Foreign Policy after the 2014 Elections," *The Washington Quarterly* 37, no. 3 (July 3, 2014): 153–65.

75. Truston Jianheng Yu and Enze Han, "Indonesia's Relations with China in the Age of COVID-19," *Journal of Current Southeast Asian Affairs*, February 1, 2023.

76. Ardhitya Eduard Yeremia, "Indonesian Diplomats' and Foreign Policy Scholars' Perceptions and Their Implications on Indonesian Foreign Ministry Bureaucratic Responses to a Rising China," *The Pacific Review* 35, no. 3 (2022): 529–56.

77. Nicholas R. Lardy, *China in the World Economy* (Peterson Institute for International Economics, 1994).

78. Min Zhou and Xiangyi Li, "Remittances for Collective Consumption and Social Status Compensation: Variations on Transnational Practices among Chinese International Migrants," *International Migration Review* 52, no. 1 (March 1, 2018): 4–42.

79. Audrye Wong, "The Diaspora and China's Foreign Influence Activities" (Washington, D.C.: Wilson Center, 2021–2022).

80. Biao Xiang, "Promoting Knowledge Exchange through Diaspora Networks (The Case of the People's Republic of China)," in *Converting Migration Drains into Gains: Harnessing the Resources of Overseas Professionals*, ed. C. Wescott and J. Brinkerhoff (Manila: Asian Development Bank, 2006).

81. Wanjing (Kelly) Chen, "Harden the Hardline, Soften the Softline: Unravelling China's Qiaoling-Centred Diaspora Governance in Laos," *The China Quarterly* 250 (June 2022): 397–416.

82. Elaine Lynn-Ee Ho and Fiona McConnell, "Conceptualizing 'Diaspora Diplomacy': Territory and Populations Betwixt the Domestic and Foreign," *Progress in Human Geography* 43, no. 2 (April 1, 2019): 235–55.

Chapter 9

1. Interview in Bangkok, October 2022.
2. "'Family': Thailand Ministers Welcome Chinese Tourists with Flowers after Beijing Relaxes Covid Travel Restrictions," *South China Morning Post*, January 9, 2023.
3. Sebastian Strangio, *In the Dragon's Shadow: Southeast Asia in the Chinese Century* (New Haven: Yale University Press, 2020), 279.
4. Simone McCarthy, "Asia Must Not Become Arena for 'Big Power Contest,' Says China's Xi as APEC Summit Gets Underway," *CNN*, November 18, 2022.
5. Shannon Tiezzi, "In Xi's 'New Era,' China's Foreign Policy Centers on 'Struggle,'" *The Diplomat*, March 8, 2023.
6. ASEAN Studies Centre, "The State of Southeast Asia: 2023 Survey Report" (Singapore: ISEAS Yusof Ishak Institute, 2023), 25.
7. ASEAN Studies Centre, 37.

Bibliography

Ambrosio, Thomas. "Constructing a Framework of Authoritarian Diffusion: Concepts, Dynamics, and Future Research." *International Studies Perspectives* 11, no. 4 (November 1, 2010): 375–92.

Anderson, Benedict. "Riddles of Yellow and Red." *New Left Review* 97, Jan–Feb (2016): 7–20.

Andreas, Peter. "Illicit International Political Economy: The Clandestine Side of Globalization." *Review of International Political Economy* 11, no. 3 (June 2004): 641–52.

Andreas, Peter. "International Politics and the Illicit Global Economy." *Perspectives on Politics* 13, no. 3 (September 2015): 782–88.

Antwi-Boateng, Osman, and Mamudu Abunga Akudugu. "Golden Migrants: The Rise and Impact of Illegal Chinese Small-Scale Mining in Ghana." *Politics & Policy* 48, no. 1 (2020): 135–67.

Anwar, Dewi Fortuna. "Indonesia-China Relations: To Be Handled with Care." *Perspective*. Singapore: ISEAS Yusof Ishak Institute, March 28, 2019.

Arlt, Wolfgang Georg. "The Second Wave of Chinese Outbound Tourism." *Tourism Planning & Development* 10, no. 2 (May 2013): 126–33.

Aryodiguno, Harryanto. "Changes in Chinese-Indonesian Identity: Indonesianization or Re- Sinicization?" *AEGIS: Journal of International Relations* 3, no. 1 (August 2, 2019).

ASEAN Studies Centre. "The State of Southeast Asia: 2021 Survey Report." Singapore: ISEAS Yusof Ishak Institute, 2021.

ASEAN Studies Centre. "The State of Southeast Asia: 2023 Survey Report." Singapore: ISEAS Yusof Ishak Institute, 2023.

Ba, Alice D. "China and ASEAN: Renavigating Relations for a 21st-Century Asia." *Asian Survey* 43, no. 4 (August 1, 2003): 622–47.

Ba, Alice D. "Is China Leading? China, Southeast Asia and East Asian Integration." *Political Science* 66, no. 2 (December 1, 2014): 143–65.

Bader, Julia. "China, Autocratic Patron? An Empirical Investigation of China as a Factor in Autocratic Survival." *International Studies Quarterly* 59, no. 1 (March 1, 2015): 23–33.

Bader, Julia. "Propping up Dictators? Economic Cooperation from China and Its Impact on Authoritarian Persistence in Party and Non-Party Regimes." *European Journal of Political Research* 54, no. 4 (2015): 655–72.

Banterng, Teerati. "China's Image Repair: The Case of Chinese Tourists on Social Media in Thailand." *Global Media Journal* 15, no. 29 (October 21, 2017): 1–11.

Bao, Jiemin. "Lukchin: Chinese Thai Transnational Bridge Builders." In *Chinese Transnational Networks*, edited by Tan Chee-Beng, 92–106. London & New York: Routledge, 2006.

Basham, Richard. "The Roots of Asian Organized Crime." *IPA Review* 48, no. 4 (1996): 11.

Baudinette, Thomas. "Lovesick, The Series: Adapting Japanese 'Boys Love' to Thailand and the Creation of a New Genre of Queer Media." *South East Asia Research* 27, no. 2 (April 3, 2019): 115–32.

Beckley, Michael. "China's Century? Why America's Edge Will Endure." *International Security* 36, no. 3 (December 28, 2011): 41–78.

Blanchard, Jean-Marc F. "Probing China's Twenty-First-Century Maritime Silk Road Initiative (MSRI): An Examination of MSRI Narratives." *Geopolitics* 22, no. 2 (April 3, 2017): 246–68.

Bo, M., and N. Loughlin. "Overlapping Agendas on the Belt and Road: The Case of the Sihanoukville Special Economic Zone." *Global China Pulse* 1, no. 1 (July 1, 2022): 85–98.

Bolt, Paul J. "Looking to the Diaspora: The Overseas Chinese and China's Economic Development, 1978–1994." *Diaspora: A Journal of Transnational Studies* 5, no. 3 (1996): 467–96.

Bowser, Matthew J. "Partners in Empire? Co-Colonialism and the Rise of Anti-Indian Nationalism in Burma, 1930–1938." *The Journal of Imperial and Commonwealth History* 49, no. 1 (January 2, 2021): 118–47.

Brautigam, Deborah. *Will Africa Feed China?* Oxford and New York: Oxford University Press, 2016.

Brautigam, Deborah, and Xiaoyang Tang. "China's Investment in Special Economic Zones in Africa." In *Special Economic Zones: Progress, Emerging Challenges, and Future Directions*, edited by Thomas Farole and Gokhan Akinci, 69–100. Washington, D.C.: World Bank, 2011.

Brenner, David. *Rebel Politics: A Political Sociology of Armed Struggle in Myanmar's Borderlands*. Ithaca: Cornell University Press, 2019.

Brenner, David, and Enze Han. "Forgotten Conflicts: Producing Knowledge and Ignorance in Security Studies." *Journal of Global Security Studies* 7, no. 1 (March 1, 2022): 1–17.

Breslin, Shaun. "China and the South: Objectives, Actors and Interactions." *Development and Change* 44, no. 6 (2013): 1273–94.

Brooks, Stephen G., and William C. Wohlforth. "The Rise and Fall of the Great Powers in the Twenty-First Century: China's Rise and the Fate of America's Global Position." *International Security* 40, no. 3 (January 1, 2016): 7–53.

Brown, Kerry. "The Anti-Corruption Struggle in Xi Jinping's China: An Alternative Political Narrative." *Asian Affairs* 49, no. 1 (January 2, 2018): 1–10.

Brownlee, Jason. "The Limited Reach of Authoritarian Powers." *Democratization* 24, no. 7 (November 10, 2017): 1326–44.

Brubaker, Rogers. *Nationalism Reframed: Nationhood and the National Question in the New Europe*. New York: Cambridge University Press, 1996.

Buchan, Patrick, and Brian Harding. "Power, Norms, and Institutions: The Future of the Indo-Pacific from a Southeast Asia Perspective." Washington, D.C: Center for Strategic & International Studies, June 2020.

Buckley, Lila. "Chinese Agriculture Goes Global: Food Security for All?" International Institute for Environment and Development, 2012.

Bui, Nhung T. "Managing Anti-China Nationalism in Vietnam: Evidence from the Media during the 2014 Oil Rig Crisis." *The Pacific Review* 30, no. 2 (March 4, 2017): 169–87.

Burusratanaphand, Walwipha. "Chinese Identity in Thailand." *Southeast Asian Journal of Social Science* 23, no. 1 (1995): 43–56.

Busbarat, Pongphisoot. "'Bamboo Swirling in the Wind': Thailand's Foreign Policy Imbalance between China and the United States." *Contemporary Southeast Asia; Singapore* 38, no. 2 (August 2016): 233–57.

Busbarat, Pongphisoot. Thailand in 2017: Stability without Certainties." In *Southeast Asian Affairs 2018*, edited by D. Singh and M. Cook, 343–62. Singapore: ISEAS–Yusof Ishak Institute, 2018.

Camba, Alvin. "Between Economic and Social Exclusions: Chinese Online Gambling Capital in the Philippines." *Made in China Journal* (blog), October 19, 2020. https://madeinchinajournal.com/2020/10/19/between-economic-and-social-exclusions-chinese-online-gambling-philippines/

Camba, Alvin. "Derailing Development: China's Railway Projects and Financing Coalitions in Indonesia, Malaysia, and the Philippines." Global China Initiative Working Paper 008. Boston: Boston University Global Development Policy Center, 2020.

Camba, Alvin, and Hangwei Li. "Chinese Workers and Their 'Linguistic Labour': Philippine Online Gambling and Zambian Onsite Casinos." *China Perspectives* 2020, no. 4 (December 1, 2020): 39–47.

Centre for Strategic and International Studies. "Seeking Strategic Options for Myanmar: Reviewing Five-Point Consensus and Anticipating the Future of Democracy in Myanmar A Policy Paper Compendium." Jakarta, Indonesia: Centre for Strategic and International Studies (CSIS) Pakarti Centre, 2022.

Chachavalpongpun, Pavin, ed. *Good Coup Gone Bad: Thailand's Political Development Since Thaksin's Downfall*. Singapore: Institute of Southeast Asian Studies, 2014.

Chachavalpongpun, Pavin. "The Necessity of Enemies in Thailand's Troubled Politics." *Asian Survey* 51, no. 6 (2011): 1019–41.

Chambers, Michael R. "'The Chinese and the Thais Are Brothers': The Evolution of the Sino-Thai Friendship." *Journal of Contemporary China* 14, no. 45 (November 1, 2005): 599–629.

Chan, Debby Sze Wan. "Asymmetric Bargaining between Myanmar and China in the Myitsone Dam Controversy: Social Opposition Akin to David's Stone against Goliath." *The Pacific Review* 30, no. 5 (September 3, 2017): 674–91.

Chan, Sarah. "Singapore–China Connectivity and Its Role in the Belt and Road Initiative." *China: An International Journal* 17, no. 4 (2019): 34–49.

Chang, Hui-Ching, and Richard Holt. *Language, Politics and Identity in Taiwan: Naming China*. London: Routledge, 2014.

Chang, Wen-Chin. *Beyond Borders: Stories of Yunnanese Chinese Migrants of Burma*. Ithaca: Cornell University Press, 2014.

Chansiri, Disaphol. *The Chinese Émigrés of Thailand in the Twentieth Century*. Youngstown, N.Y.: Cambria Press, 2008.

Cheesman, Nick. "How in Myanmar 'National Races' Came to Surpass Citizenship and Exclude Rohingya." *Journal of Contemporary Asia* 47, no. 3 (May 27, 2017): 461–83.

Chen, Wanjing (Kelly). "Harden the Hardline, Soften the Softline: Unravelling China's Qiaoling-Centred Diaspora Governance in Laos." *The China Quarterly* 250 (June 2022): 397–416.

Chen, Xiangming. "'Corridor-Ising' Impact along the Belt and Road: Is the Newly Operational China-Laos Railway a Game-Changer?" *European Financial Review* February–March (2022): 4–14.

Chen, Yu-Jie. "'One China' Contention in China–Taiwan Relations: Law, Politics and Identity." *The China Quarterly* 252 (December 2022): 1025–44.

Chesneaux, Jean, ed. *Popular Movements and Secret Societies in China, 1840–1950*. Stanford: Stanford University Press, 1986.

Chin, Ko-Lin. *The Golden Triangle: Inside Southeast Asia's Drug Trade.* Ithaca: Cornell University Press, 2009.

Chin, Ko-lin, and Sheldon X. Zhang. *The Chinese Heroin Trade: Cross-Border Drug Trafficking in Southeast Asia and Beyond.* New York and London: NYU Press, 2015.

Chirot, Daniel, and Anthony Reid, eds. *Essential Outsiders: Chinese and Jews in the Modern Transformation of Southeast Asia and Central Europe.* Seattle: University of Washington Press, 2011.

Chou, Mark, Chengxin Pan, and Avery Poole. "The Threat of Autocracy Diffusion in Consolidated Democracies? The Case of China, Singapore and Australia." *Contemporary Politics* 23, no. 2 (April 3, 2017): 175–94.

Christensen, Thomas. *The China Challenge: Shaping the Choices of a Rising Power.* New York: W. W. Norton & Company, 2015.

Chu, Yiu-Wai, and Eve Leung. "Remapping Hong Kong Popular Music: Covers, Localisation and the Waning Hybridity of Cantopop." *Popular Music* 32, no. 1 (2013): 65–78.

Chun, Allen. *Forget Chineseness: On the Geopolitics of Cultural Identification.* Albany, New York: SUNY Press, 2017.

Chun, Allen. "Fuck Chineseness: On the Ambiguities of Ethnicity as Culture as Identity." *Boundary 2* 23, no. 2 (1996): 111–38.

Davis, William W., Luke C. Mullany, Eh Kalu Shwe Oo, Adam K. Richards, Vincent Iacopino, and Chris Beyrer. "Health and Human Rights in Karen State, Eastern Myanmar." *PLOS ONE* 10, no. 8 (August 26, 2015): 1–13.

Dev, Laura, Karly Marie Miller, Juliet Lu, Lauren S Withey, and Tracy Hruska. "Ambiguous Spaces, Empirical Traces: Accounting for Ignorance When Researching around the Illicit." *Progress in Human Geography* 46, no. 2 (April 1, 2022): 652–71.

Dillman, Bradford. "Introduction: Shining Light on the Shadows: The Political Economy of Illicit Transactions in the Mediterranean." *Mediterranean Politics* 12, no. 2 (July 1, 2007): 123–39.

Dupont, Alan. "Transnational Crime, Drugs, and Security in East Asia." *Asian Survey* 39, no. 3 (1999): 433–55.

Eaksittipong, Sittithep. "From Chinese 'in' to Chinese 'of' Thailand: The Politics of Knowledge Production during the Cold War." *Rian Thai: International Journal of Thai Studies* 10, no. 1 (January 1, 2017): 99–116.

Egreteau, Renaud. "Burmese Indians in Contemporary Burma: Heritage, Influence, and Perceptions since 1988." *Asian Ethnicity* 12, no. 1 (February 1, 2011): 33–54.

Eoseewong, Nidhi. *Pen and Sail: Literature and History in Early Bangkok.* Chiang Mai: Silkworm Books, 2005.

Felbermayr, Gabriel, Hendrik Mahlkow, and Alexander Sandkamp. "Cutting through the Value Chain: The Long-Run Effects of Decoupling the East from the West." *Empirica* 50, no. 1 (February 1, 2023): 75–108.

Feng, Ming, Joseph O. Sexton, Panshi Wang, Huang Qiongyu, Sumalika Biswas, and Peter Leimgruber. "Myanmar Forest Change Product 1979–2019." The Smithsonian Institution, January 12, 2021.

Ferchen, Matt. "The Two Faces of the China Model: The BRI in Southeast Asia." In *Global Perspectives on China's Belt and Road Initiative*, edited by Florian Schneider, 245–64. Asserting Agency through Regional Connectivity. Amsterdam University Press, 2021.

Fleisher, Belton, Haizheng Li, and Min Qiang Zhao. "Human Capital, Economic Growth, and Regional Inequality in China." *Journal of Development Economics* 92, no. 2 (July 1, 2010): 215–31.

Friis, Cecilie, and Jonas Østergaard Nielsen. "Small-Scale Land Acquisitions, Large-Scale Implications: Exploring the Case of Chinese Banana Investments in Northern Laos." *Land Use Policy* 57 (November 30, 2016): 117–29.

Fung, Courtney J. "Separating Intervention from Regime Change: China's Diplomatic Innovations at the UN Security Council Regarding the Syria Crisis." *The China Quarterly* 235 (September 2018): 693–712.

Fung, Courtney J., Enze Han, Kai Quek, and Austin Strange. "Conditioning China's Influence: Intentionality, Intermediaries, and Institutions." *Journal of Contemporary China* 32, no. 139 (April 15, 2022): 1–16.

Gadavanij, Savitri. "Contentious Polities and Political Polarization in Thailand: Post-Thaksin Reflections." *Discourse & Society* 31, no. 1 (January 1, 2020): 44–63.

Goh, Evelyn. "Great Powers and Hierarchical Order in Southeast Asia: Analyzing Regional Security Strategies." *International Security* 32, no. 3 (2007): 113–57.

Goh, Evelyn, ed. *Rising China's Influence in Developing Asia*. New York and London: Oxford University Press, 2016.

Goh, Evelyn. "The Modes of China's Influence: Cases from Southeast Asia." *Asian Survey* 54, no. 5 (2014): 825–48.

Goh, Evelyn. *The Struggle for Order: Hegemony, Hierarchy, and Transition in Post-Cold War East Asia*. Oxford: Oxford University Press, 2015.

Gong, Jian, Pornpen Detchkhajornjaroensri, and David W. Knight. "Responsible Tourism in Bangkok, Thailand: Resident Perceptions of Chinese Tourist Behaviour." *International Journal of Tourism Research* 21, no. 2 (2019): 221–33.

Gravers, Mikael. *Nationalism as Political Paranoia in Burma: An Essay on the Historical Practice of Power*. London: Routledge, 1999.

Grimsditch, Mark. "Chinese Agriculture in Southeast Asia: Investment, Aid and Trade in Cambodia, Laos and Myanmar." Heinrich-Böll Stiftung Southeast Asia, June 2017.

Gu, Jing. "China's Private Enterprises in Africa and the Implications for African Development." *The European Journal of Development Research* 21, no. 4 (September 1, 2009): 570–87.

Guo, Shujian, Hyunjung Shin, and Qi Shen. "The Commodification of Chinese in Thailand's Linguistic Market: A Case Study of How Language Education Promotes Social Sustainability." *Sustainability* 12, no. 18 (January 2020): 7344.

Hackenesch, Christine. "Not as Bad as It Seems: EU and US Democracy Promotion Faces China in Africa." *Democratization* 22, no. 3 (April 16, 2015): 419–37.

Hameiri, Shahar, and Lee Jones. "Rising Powers and State Transformation: The Case of China." *European Journal of International Relations* 22, no. 1 (March 1, 2016): 72–98.

Hamilton, Clive. *Silent Invasion: China's Influence in Australia*. Richmond, Australia: Hardie Grant, 2018.

Han, Enze. *Asymmetrical Neighbors: Borderland State Building between China and Southeast Asia*. New York and London: Oxford University Press, 2019.

Han, Enze. "Bifurcated Homeland and Diaspora Politics in China and Taiwan towards the Overseas Chinese in Southeast Asia." *Journal of Ethnic and Migration Studies* 45, no. 4 (March 12, 2019): 577–94.

Han, Enze. "Borderland Ethnic Politics and Changing Sino-Myanmar Relations." In *War and Peace in the Borderlands of Myanmar: The Kachin Ceasefire, 1994–2011*, edited by Mandy Sadan, 149–68. Copenhagen: NIAS Press, 2016.

Han, Enze. *Contestation and Adaptation: The Politics of National Identity in China*. New York and London: Oxford University Press, 2013.

Han, Enze. "Entrenching Authoritarian Rule and Thailand's Foreign Policy Dilemma as a Middle Power." *Asia Policy* 17, no. 4 (2022): 181–98.

Han, Enze. "Geopolitics, Ethnic Conflicts along the Border, and Chinese Foreign Policy Changes toward Myanmar." *Asian Security* 13, no. 1 (January 2, 2017): 59–73.

Han, Enze. "Mainland Southeast Asia's Environmental Challenges from China." *Perspective*. Singapore: ISEAS Yusof Ishak Institute, 2020.

Han, Enze. "Non-State Chinese Actors and Their Impact on Relations between China and Mainland Southeast Asia." *ISEAS Trends in Southeast Asia*, no. 1 (2021): 1–19.

Han, Enze. "Overconfidence, Missteps, and Tragedy: Dynamics of Myanmar's International Relations and the Genocide of the Rohingya." *The Pacific Review* 36, no. 3 (2023): 581–602.

Han, Enze. "Re-Encountering the Familiar Other: Contesting 'Re-Sinicization'in Thailand."*Singapore Journal of Tropical Geography* 43, no. 3 (2022): 270–86.

Han, Enze. "Under the Shadow of China-US Competition: Myanmar and Thailand's Alignment Choices." *The Chinese Journal of International Politics* 11, no. 1 (2018): 81–104.

Han, Enze, and Qiongyu Huang. "Global Commodity Markets, Chinese Demand for Maize, and Deforestation in Northern Myanmar." *Land* 10, no. 11 (November 2021): 1232.

Han, Enze, and Sirada Khemanitthathai. "Through the Prism of Migration: History of Migration and Contemporary Chinese Engagement with Thailand." *Journal of Contemporary China* 32, no. 142 (2023): 620–34.

Han, Enze, and Harris Mylonas. "Interstate Relations, Perceptions, and Power Balance: Explaining China's Policies Toward Ethnic Groups, 1949–1965." *Security Studies* 23, no. 1 (January 1, 2014): 148–81.

Harrison, Rachel. "Amazing Thai Film: The Rise and Rise of Contemporary Thai Cinema on the International Screen." *Asian Affairs* 36, no. 3 (November 1, 2005): 321–38.

Hau, Caroline. "Becoming 'Chinese' in Southeast Asia." In *Sinicization and the Rise of China: Civilizational Processes beyond East and West*, edited by Peter J. Katzenstein, 175–206. London and New York: Routledge, 2012.

Hau, Caroline. "Becoming 'Chinese'—But What 'Chinese'?—In Southeast Asia." *The Asia Pacific Journal / Japan Focus* 10, no. 26 (2012): 1–37.

Hess, Steve, and Richard Aidoo. "Democratic Backsliding in Sub-Saharan Africa and the Role of China's Development Assistance." *Commonwealth & Comparative Politics* 57, no. 4 (October 2, 2019): 421–44.

Hiebert, Murray. *Under Beijing's Shadow: Southeast Asia's China Challenge*. Washington, D.C: Center for Strategic & International Studies, 2020.

Hill, Ann Maxwell. *Merchants and Migrants: Ethnicity and Trade among Yunnanese Chinese in Southeast Asia*. New Haven: Yale University Southeast Asia Studies, 1998.

Ho, Elaine Lynn-Ee, and Lynette J. Chua. "Law and 'Race' in the Citizenship Spaces of Myanmar: Spatial Strategies and the Political Subjectivity of the Burmese Chinese." *Ethnic and Racial Studies* 39, no. 5 (April 8, 2016): 896–916.

Ho, Elaine Lynn-Ee, and Fiona McConnell. "Conceptualizing 'Diaspora Diplomacy': Territory and Populations Betwixt the Domestic and Foreign." *Progress in Human Geography* 43, no. 2 (April 1, 2019): 235–55.

Ho, Selina. "Infrastructure and Chinese Power." *International Affairs* 96, no. 6 (November 1, 2020): 1461–85.

Holmes, Robert A. "Burmese Domestic Policy: The Politics of Burmanization." *Asian Survey* 7, no. 3 (1967): 188–97.

Holt, John Clifford. *Myanmar's Buddhist-Muslim Crisis: Rohingya, Arakanese, and Burmese Narratives of Siege and Fear*. Honolulu: University of Hawai'i Press, 2019.

Hua, Xiaobo, Yasuyuki Kono, and Le Zhang. "Excavating Agrarian Transformation under 'Secure' Crop Booms: Insights from the China-Myanmar Borderland." *The Journal of Peasant Studies* 50, no. 1 (2023): 339–68.

Hua, Xiaobo, Le Zhang, and Yasuyuki Kono. "Fruit Booms and Investor Mobility along the China-Myanmar and China-Laos Borders." *Ecology and Society* 27, no. 3 (September 26, 2022): 1–17.

Huang, Shirlena, and Brenda S. A. Yeoh. "Transnational Families and Their Children's Education: China's 'Study Mothers' in Singapore." *Global Networks* 5, no. 4 (2005): 379–400.

Huang, Shu-min. *Reproducing Chinese Culture in Diaspora: Sustainable Agriculture and Petrified Culture in Northern Thailand*. Lanham: Lexington Books, 2010.

Huang, Xueli, and Chi Renyong. "Chinese Private Firms' Outward Foreign Direct Investment: Does Firm Ownership and Size Matter?" *Thunderbird International Business Review* 56, no. 5 (2014): 393–406.

Huang, Yanzhong, and Sheng Ding. "Dragon's Underbelly: An Analysis of China's Soft Power." *East Asia* 23, no. 4 (December 1, 2006): 22–44.

Huang, Yukon. *Cracking the China Conundrum: Why Conventional Economic Wisdom Is Wrong*. New York City: Oxford University Press, 2017.

Hudson, Ray. "Thinking through the Relationships between Legal and Illegal Activities and Economies: Spaces, Flows and Pathways." *Journal of Economic Geography* 14, no. 4 (2014): 775–95.

Hudson, Valerie M., and Benjamin S. Day. *Foreign Policy Analysis: Classic and Contemporary Theory*. Lanham: Rowman & Littlefield, 2019.

Hung, Po-Yi, and Ian G. Baird. "From Soldiers to Farmers: The Political Geography of Chinese Kuomintang Territorialization in Northern Thailand." *Political Geography* 58 (May 1, 2017): 1–13.

Ikenberry, G. John. *Liberal Leviathan: The Origins, Crisis, and Transformation of the American World Order: The Rise, Decline and Renewal*. Princeton: Princeton University Press, 2011.

Ikenberry, G. John. "The End of Liberal International Order?" *International Affairs* 94, no. 1 (January 1, 2018): 7–23.

IMF. "Lao People's Democratic Republic: Staff Report for the 2016 Article IV Consultation - Debt Sustainability Analysis." Washington, D.C.: International Monetary Fund, 2017.

Inkey, Mark. "Chinese Banana Plantations Bring Work and Pollution to Laos." *China Dialogue*, October 14, 2019.

Jacques, Martin. *When China Rules the World: The Rise of the Middle Kingdom and the End of the Western World*. London: Penguin, 2012.

Jervis, Robert. *Perception and Misperception in International Politics*. 2nd edition. Princeton: Princeton University Press, 2017.

Jirattikorn, Amporn. "Between Ironic Pleasure and Exotic Nostalgia: Audience Reception of Thai Television Dramas among Youth in China." *Asian Journal of Communication* 31, no. 2 (March 4, 2021): 124–43.

Jones, Lee, and Yizheng Zou. "Rethinking the Role of State-Owned Enterprises in China's Rise." *New Political Economy* 22, no. 6 (November 2, 2017): 743–60.

Kaeding, Malte Philipp. "The Rise of 'Localism' in Hong Kong." *Journal of Democracy* 28, no. 1 (2017): 157–71.

Kang, David C. *China Rising: Peace, Power, and Order in East Asia*. New York: Columbia University Press, 2009.

Kang, David C. *East Asia Before the West*. New York: Columbia University Press, 2010.

Kanoksilapatham, Budsaba. "National Survey of Teaching Chinese as a Foreign Language in Thailand." Working Paper. Silpakorn University, 2011.

Katzenstein, Peter J. *Sinicization and the Rise of China: Civilizational Processes Beyond East and West*. Abingdon: Routledge, 2013.

Kemasang, A.R.T. "The 1740 Massacre of Chinese in Java: Curtain Raiser for the Dutch Plantation Economy." *Bulletin of Concerned Asian Scholars* 14, no. 1 (March 1, 1982): 61–71.

Kim, Diana S. *Empires of Vice: The Rise of Opium Prohibition across Southeast Asia*. Princeton: Princeton University Press, 2020.

Kongkirati, Prajak. "From Illiberal Democracy to Military Authoritarianism: Intra-Elite Struggle and Mass-Based Conflict in Deeply Polarized Thailand." *The ANNALS of the American Academy of Political and Social Science* 681, no. 1 (January 1, 2019): 24–40.

Koning, Juliette, and Michiel Verver. "Historicizing the 'Ethnic' in Ethnic Entrepreneurship: The Case of the Ethnic Chinese in Bangkok." *Entrepreneurship & Regional Development* 25, no. 5–6 (June 1, 2013): 325–48.

Kornphanat, Tungkeunkunt. "Culture and Commerce: China's Soft Power in Thailand." *International Journal of China Studies* 7, no. 2 (August 2016): 151–73.

Kosaikanont, Romyen. "Chinese Capital Going Global: Thai-Chinese Industrial Zone and Labor Conditions in Thailand." In *The Sociology of Chinese Capitalism in Southeast Asia: Challenges and Prospects*, edited by Yos Santasombat, 169–94. Singapore: Springer, 2019.

Krammer, Tom, and Kevin Woods. "Financing Dispossession: China's Opium Substitution Programme in Northern Burma." Amsterdam: Transnational Institute (TNI), 2012.

Ku, Agnes S. "New Forms of Youth Activism: Hong Kong's Anti-Extradition Bill Movement in the Local-National-Global Nexus." *Space and Polity* 24, no. 1 (January 2, 2020): 111–17.

Kubo, Koji. "Myanmar's Watermelon Exports to China: Impacts of Unofficial Investment by Chinese on the Diffusion of a Horticultural Crop." In *Global Production Networks and Rural Development: Southeast Asia as a Fruit Supplier to China*, edited by Bill Pritchard, 63–81. Cheltenham, UK and Northampton, MA: Edward Elgar Publishing Ltd, 2021.

Kuik, Cheng-Chwee. "Host-Country Agency and Hedging in Infrastructure Cooperation: Definitions, Drivers, and Determination." In *The Rise of the Infrastructure State: How US China Rivalry Shapes Politics and Place Worldwide*, edited by Seth Schindler and Jessica DiCarlo, 194–212. Bristol: Bristol University Press, 2022.

Kuik, Cheng-Chwee. "The Essence of Hedging: Malaysia and Singapore's Response to a Rising China." *Contemporary Southeast Asia: A Journal of International and Strategic Affairs* 30, no. 2 (2008): 159–85.

Lai, Karen P. Y., Shaun Lin, and James D. Sidaway. "Financing the Belt and Road Initiative (BRI): Research Agendas beyond the 'Debt-Trap' Discourse." *Eurasian Geography and Economics* 61, no. 2 (March 3, 2020): 109–24.

Lake, David A. "Domination, Authority, and the Forms of Chinese Power." *The Chinese Journal of International Politics* 10, no. 4 (December 1, 2017): 357–82.

Laksmana, Evan A. "Variations on a Theme: Dimensions of Ambivalence in Indonesia-China Relations." *Harvard Asia Quarterly* 13, no. 1 (May 1, 2011): 24–31.

Lampton, David M., Selina Ho, and Cheng-Chwee Kuik. *Rivers of Iron: Railroads and Chinese Power in Southeast Asia*. Oakland: University of California Press, 2020.

Lardy, Nicholas R. *China in The World Economy*. Washington, D.C.: Peterson Institute for International Economics, 1994.

Laungaramsri, Pinkaew. "China in Laos: Enclave Spaces and the Transformation of Borders in the Mekong Region." *The Australian Journal of Anthropology* 30, no. 2 (2019): 195–211.

Laungaramsri, Pinkaew. "Commodifying Sovereignty: Special Economic Zones and the Neoliberalization of the Lao Frontier." In *Impact of China's Rise on the Mekong Region*, edited by Yos Santasombat, 117–46. New York: Palgrave Macmillan, 2015.

Lee, Ching Kwan. *The Specter of Global China: Politics, Labor, and Foreign Investment in Africa*. Chicago and London: University of Chicago Press, 2018.

Leggett, William H. "Institutionalising the Colonial Imagination: Chinese Middlemen and the Transnational Corporate Office in Jakarta, Indonesia." *Journal of Ethnic and Migration Studies* 36, no. 8 (September 1, 2010): 1265–78.

Leng, Thearith. "Underlying Factors of Cambodia's Bandwagoning with China's Belt and Road Initiative." *East Asia* 36, no. 3 (September 1, 2019): 243–53.

Lertchoosakul, Kanokrat. "The White Ribbon Movement: High School Students in the 2020 Thai Youth Protests." *Critical Asian Studies* 53, no. 2 (April 3, 2021): 206–18.

Levy, Jack S. "Misperception and the Causes of War: Theoretical Linkages and Analytical Problems." *World Politics* 36 (1983): 76.

Li, Yi. *Chinese in Colonial Burma: A Migrant Community in a Multiethnic State*. New York: Palgrave Macmillan, 2017.

Lieberthal, Kenneth G., and David M. Lampton, eds. *Bureaucracy, Politics, and Decision Making in Post-Mao China*. Berkeley: University of California Press, 1992.

Liff, Adam P., and G. John Ikenberry. "Racing toward Tragedy?: China's Rise, Military Competition in the Asia Pacific, and the Security Dilemma." *International Security* 39, no. 2 (October 1, 2014): 52–91.

Lin, Syaru Shirley. *Taiwan's China Dilemma: Contested Identities and Multiple Interests in Taiwan's Cross-Strait Economic Policy*. Stanford: Stanford University Press, 2016.

Ling, Stuart, and Mai Yer Xiong. "Labour Rights, Child Rights and Gender Justice for Lao Workers in Chinese Banana Plantations in Bokeo." Plan International, January 2017.

Lintner, Bertil. *Burma in Revolt: Opium and Insurgency since 1948*. 2nd edition. Chiang Mai, Thailand: Silkworm Books, 1999.

Lintner, Bertil, and Hseng Noung Lintner. *Land of Jade: A Journey Through Insurgent Burma*. Edinburgh, Ohio: Kiscadale, 1990.

Liou, Chih-shian. "Rent-Seeking at Home, Capturing Market Share Abroad: The Domestic Determinants of the Transnationalization of China State Construction Engineering Corporation." *World Development* 54 (February 1, 2014): 220–31.

Liu, Hong. "New Migrants and the Revival of Overseas Chinese Nationalism." *Journal of Contemporary China* 14, no. 43 (May 1, 2005): 291–316.

Liu, Hong. "Opportunities and Anxieties for the Chinese Diaspora in Southeast Asia." *Current History* 115 (2016): 312–18.

Liu, Jiaqi M. "When Diaspora Politics Meet Global Ambitions: Diaspora Institutions Amid China's Geopolitical Transformations." *International Migration Review*, January 19, 2022.

Liu, Oiyan. "Countering 'Chinese Imperialism': Sinophobia and Border Protection in the Dutch East Indies." *Indonesia*, no. 97 (2014): 87–110.

Liu, Xuepeng, and Huimin Shi. "Anti-Dumping Duty Circumvention through Trade Rerouting: Evidence from Chinese Exporters." *The World Economy* 42, no. 5 (2019): 1427–66.

Liu-Farrer, Gracia. "Educationally Channeled International Labor Mobility: Contemporary Student Migration from China to Japan." *International Migration Review* 43, no. 1 (March 1, 2009): 178–204.

Loughlin, Neil. "Chinese Linkage, Leverage, and Cambodia's Transition to Hegemonic Authoritarianism." *Democratization* 28, no. 4 (May 19, 2021): 840–57.

Lu, Juliet. "Grounding Chinese Investment: Encounters between Chinese Capital and Local Land Politics in Laos." *Globalizations* 18, no. 3 (April 3, 2021): 422–40.

Mak, Lau Fong. *Sociology of Secret Societies: Study of Chinese Secret Societies in Singapore and Peninsular Malaysia*. Kuala Lumpur and New York: Oxford University Press, 1981.

Mak, Lau Fong. "The Kongsis and the Triad." *Southeast Asian Journal of Social Science* 3, no. 2 (1975): 47–58.

Mak, Veronica Sau-Wa. "The Heritagization of Milk Tea: Cultural Governance and Placemaking in Hong Kong." *Asian Anthropology* 20, no. 1 (January 2, 2021): 30–46.

Marshall, Andrew MacGregor. *A Kingdom in Crisis: Thailand's Struggle for Democracy in the Twenty-First Century*. London: Zed Books, 2014.

Maung Aung Myoe. *In the Name of Pauk-Phaw: Myanmar's China Policy since 1948*. Singapore: Institute of Southeast Asian Studies; London, 2011.

McCargo, Duncan, and Anyarat Chattharakul. *Future Forward: The Rise and Fall of a Thai Political Party*. Copenhagen: NIAS Press, 2020.

McKeown, Adam. "Chinese Emigration in Global Context, 1850–1940." *Journal of Global History* 5, no. 1 (March 2010): 95–124.

Mearsheimer, John J. "The Gathering Storm: China's Challenge to US Power in Asia." *The Chinese Journal of International Politics* 3, no. 4 (December 1, 2010): 381–96.

Mearsheimer, John J. *Why Leaders Lie: The Truth about Lying in International Politics*. London and New York: Oxford University Press, 2013.

Meehan, Patrick. "Fortifying or Fragmenting the State? The Political Economy of the Opium/Heroin Trade in Shan State, Myanmar, 1988–2013." *Critical Asian Studies* 47, no. 2 (April 3, 2015): 253–82.

Melnykovska, Inna, Hedwig Plamper, and Rainer Schweickert. "Do Russia and China Promote Autocracy in Central Asia?" *Asia Europe Journal* 10, no. 1 (May 1, 2012): 75–89.

Merton, Robert K. "The Unanticipated Consequences of Purposive Social Action." *American Sociological Review* 1, no. 6 (1936): 894–904.

Min Zin. "Burmese Attitude toward Chinese: Portrayal of the Chinese in Contemporary Cultural and Media Works." *Journal of Current Southeast Asian Affairs* 31, no. 1 (January 1, 2012): 115–31.

Morgenbesser, Lee. "Cambodia's Transition to Hegemonic Authoritarianism." *Journal of Democracy* 30, no. 1 (2019): 158–71.

Morgenbesser, Lee. "Misclassification on the Mekong: The Origins of Hun Sen's Personalist Dictatorship." *Democratization* 25, no. 2 (February 17, 2018): 191–208.

Mostafanezhad, Mary, Joseph M. Cheer, and Harng Luh Sin. "Geopolitical Anxieties of Tourism: (Im)Mobilities of the COVID-19 Pandemic." *Dialogues in Human Geography* 10, no. 2 (July 2020): 182–86.

Mostafanezhad, Mary, and Tanya Promburom. "'Lost in Thailand': The Popular Geopolitics of Film-Induced Tourism in Northern Thailand." *Social & Cultural Geography* 19, no. 1 (January 2, 2018): 81–101.

Murashima, Eiji. "The Thai-Japanese Alliance and The Overseas Chinese in Thailand." In *Southeast Asian Minorities in the Wartime Japanese Empire*, edited by Paul H. Kratoska, 192–223. Oxford: RoutledgeCurzon, 2005.

Murphy, Ann Marie. "Beyond Balancing and Bandwagoning: Thailand's Response to China's Rise." *Asian Security* 6, no. 1 (January 22, 2010): 1–27.

Mylonas, Harris. *The Politics of Nation Building: Making Co-Nationals, Refugees, and Minorities*. New York: Cambridge University Press, 2013.

Nakanishi, Yoshihiro. *Strong Soldiers, Failed Revolution: The State and Military in Burma, 1962–88*. Singapore: NUS Press, 2013.

Nathan, Andrew J. "China's Challenge." *Journal of Democracy* 26, no. 1 (2015): 156–70.

National Economic and Social Development Board. "Thailand's Special Economic Zones." Bangkok, 2016.

Nemoto, Kei. "The Concepts of Dobama ('Our Burma') and Thudo-Bama ('Their Burma') in Burmese Nationalism, 1930–1948." *Journal of Burma Studies* 5, no. 1 (March 30, 2011): 1–16.

Ngin, Chanrith. "The Undetermined Costs and Benefits of Cambodia's Engagement with China's Belt and Road Initiative." *Perspective*. Singapore: ISEAS Yusof Ishak Institute, 2022.

Norris, William J. *Chinese Economic Statecraft: Commercial Actors, Grand Strategy, and State Control*. Ithaca, New York and London: Cornell University Press, 2016.

Nye, Joseph. *Soft Power: The Means to Success in World Politics*. New York: PublicAffairs, 2004.

Nyíri, Pál. "Chinese Entrepreneurs in Poor Countries: A Transnational 'Middleman Minority' and Its Futures." *Inter-Asia Cultural Studies* 12, no. 1 (March 1, 2011): 145–53.

Nyíri, Pál. "Enclaves of Improvement: Sovereignty and Developmentalism in the Special Zones of the China-Lao Borderlands." *Comparative Studies in Society and History* 54, no. 3 (July 2012): 533–62.

Nyíri, Pál. "The Yellow Man's Burden: Chinese Migrants on a Civilizing Mission." *The China Journal*, no. 56 (2006): 83–106.

Nyíri, Pál, and Igor Saveliev, eds. *Globalizing Chinese Migration: Trends in Europe and Asia*. Burlington: Ashgate, 2003.

Nyíri, Pál, and Danielle Tan, eds. *Chinese Encounters in Southeast Asia: How People, Money, and Ideas from China Are Changing a Region*. Seattle: University of Washington Press, 2016.

Oh, Yoon Ah. "Power Asymmetry and Threat Points: Negotiating China's Infrastructure Development in Southeast Asia." *Review of International Political Economy* 25, no. 4 (July 4, 2018): 530–52.

Oliveira, Gustavo de L. T., Galen Murton, Alessandro Rippa, Tyler Harlan, and Yang Yang. "China's Belt and Road Initiative: Views from the Ground." *Political Geography*, August 3, 2020, online first.

Ong, Aihwa. *Flexible Citizenship: The Cultural Logics of Transnationality*. Durham, North Carolina: Duke University Press Books, 1999.

Ong, Aihwa, and Donald Nonini, eds. *Ungrounded Empires: The Cultural Politics of Modern Chinese Transnationalism*. London: Routledge, 2003.

Ornetsmüller, Christine, Jean-Christophe Castella, and Peter H. Verburg. "A Multiscale Gaming Approach to Understand Farmer's Decision Making in the Boom of Maize Cultivation in Laos." *Ecology and Society* 23, no. 2 (2018): 1–25.

Osman, Mohamed Nawab Mohamed, and Prashant Waikar. "Fear and Loathing: Uncivil Islamism and Indonesia's Anti-Ahok Movement." *Indonesia* 106 (October 2018): 89–109.

Panggabean, Samsu Rizal, and Benjamin Smith. "Explaining Anti-Chinese Riots in Late 20th Century Indonesia." *World Development: Ethnicity and Ethnic Strife*, 39, no. 2 (February 1, 2011): 231–42.

Parameswaran, Prashanth. "Between Aspiration and Reality: Indonesian Foreign Policy After the 2014 Elections." *The Washington Quarterly* 37, no. 3 (July 3, 2014): 153–65.

Phanishsarn, Aksornsri. "The Link Between the EEC of Thailand 4.0 Model and China's BRI: A New Chapter of Thailand-China Economic Relations." In *Exchanges and Mutual Learning Among Asian Civilizations*, edited by Linggui Wang and Jianglin Zhao, 115–23. Singapore: Springer Nature, 2023.

Po, Sovinda, and Kimkong Heng. "Assessing the Impact of Chinese Investments in Cambodia: The Case of Preah Sihanoukville Province." A Working Paper on China-Cambodia Relations. Issues & Insights Working Paper. Honolulu: Pacific Forum, May 2019.

Po, Sovinda, and Christopher B. Primiano. "An 'Ironclad Friend': Explaining Cambodia's Bandwagoning Policy towards China." *Journal of Current Southeast Asian Affairs* 39, no. 3 (December 2020): 444–64.

Po, Sovinda, and Kearrin Sims. "The Myth of Non-Interference: Chinese Foreign Policy in Cambodia." *Asian Studies Review* 46, no. 1 (January 2, 2022): 36–54.

Polyakova, Alina, and Chris Meserole. *Exporting Digital Authoritarianism: The Russian and Chinese Models*. Washington, D.C.: Brookings, 2019.

Portes, Alejandro. "The Hidden Abode: Sociology as Analysis of the Unexpected: 1999 Presidential Address." *American Sociological Review* 65, no. 1 (2000): 1–18.

Pritchard, Bill. "Fresh Fruit Exports from Mainland Southeast Asian Countries to China: Background Context and Key Questions for Research and Policy." In *Global Production Networks and Rural Development: Southeast Asia as a Fruit Supplier to China*, edited by Bill Pritchard, 1–26. Cheltenham, UK and Northampton, Massachusetts: Edward Elgar Publishing Ltd, 2021.

Purdey, Jemma. *Anti-Chinese Violence in Indonesia, 1996–1999*. Honolulu: University of Hawaii Press, 2006.

Qin, Yihui. *History of Blood and Tears of the Nationalist Army in the Golden Triangle [Jinsanjiao guojun xueleishi]*. Taipei: Academic Sinica and Lianjing Press, 2009.

Reilly, Benjamin. "Southeast Asia: In The Shadow of China." *Journal of Democracy* 24, no. 1 (2013): 156–64.

Rowedder, Simon. "Railroading Land-Linked Laos: China's Regional Profits, Laos' Domestic Costs?" *Eurasian Geography and Economics* 61, no. 2 (March 3, 2020): 152–61.

Rowen, Ian. "The Geopolitics of Tourism: Mobilities, Territory, and Protest in China, Taiwan, and Hong Kong." *Annals of the American Association of Geographers* 106, no. 2 (March 3, 2016): 385–93.

Roy, Denny. "Assertive China: Irredentism or Expansionism?" *Survival* 61, no. 1 (January 2, 2019): 51–74.

Rush, James. *Opium to Java: Revenue Farming and Chinese Enterprise in Colonial Indonesia, 1860–1910*. Ithaca, New York: Cornell University Press, 1990.

Sachakul, Kanniga. "Education as a Means for National Integration: Historical and Comparative Study of Chinese and Muslim Assimilation in Thailand." PhD diss., University of Michigan, 1984.

Santasombat, Yos. "Rent Capitalism and Shifting Plantations in the Mekong Borderlands." *Southeast Asian Affairs*, (2019): 177–91. https://www.jstor.org/stable/26939694.

Santasombat, Yos, ed. *The Sociology of Chinese Capitalism in Southeast Asia: Challenges and Prospects*. Singapore: Springer Singapore, 2019.

Sauvant, Karl P., and Victor Zitian Chen. "China's Regulatory Framework for Outward Foreign Direct Investment." *China Economic Journal* 7, no. 1 (January 2, 2014): 141–63.

Setijadi, Charlotte. "Chinese Indonesians in the Eyes of the Pribumi Public." *Perspective*. Singapore: ISEAS Yusof Ishak Institute, 2017.

Shain, Yossi. *Kinship and Diasporas in International Affairs*. Ann Arbor: University of Michigan Press, 2008.

Shambaugh, David. *China Goes Global*. New York and London: Oxford University Press, 2013.

Shambaugh, David. "U.S.-China Rivalry in Southeast Asia: Power Shift or Competitive Coexistence?" *International Security* 42, no. 4 (May 1, 2018): 85–127.

Shambaugh, David. *Where Great Powers Meet: America and China in Southeast Asia*. New York: Oxford University Press, 2020.

Sheng, Yu, and Ligang Song. "Agricultural Production and Food Consumption in China: A Long-Term Projection." *China Economic Review* 53 (February 1, 2019): 15–29.

Shirk, Susan L. *China: The Fragile Superpower*. New York and London: Oxford University Press, 2007.

Shuang Geng, "Foreign Ministry Spokesperson Geng Shuang's Regular Press Conference," September 12, 2017. Press meeting of the Chinese Ministry of Foreign Affairs.

Sidaway, James D, Simon C Rowedder, Chih Yuan Woon, Weiqiang Lin, and Vatthana Pholsena. "Introduction: Research Agendas Raised by the Belt and Road Initiative." *Environment and Planning C: Politics and Space* 38, no. 5 (August 1, 2020): 795–802.

Silverstone, Daniel, and Joe Whittle. "'Forget It, Jake. It's Chinatown': The Policing of Chinese Organised Crime in the UK." *The Police Journal* 89, no. 1 (March 1, 2016): 70–84.

Siriphon, Aranya. "Developing Entrepreneurship Under the Rise of China: Chinese Migrant Entrepreneurs in Tourism-Related Businesses in Chiang Mai." In *The Sociology of Chinese Capitalism in Southeast Asia: Challenges and Prospects*, edited by Yos Santasombat, 271–89. Singapore: Springer, 2019.

Siriphon, Aranya. "The Qiaoban, The PRC Influence and Nationalist Chinese in Northern Thai Borderland." *International Journal of Asian Studies* 13, no. 1 (January 1, 2016): 1–17.

Siriphon, Aranya. "Xinyimin, New Chinese Migrants, and the Influence of the PRC and Taiwan on the Northern Thai Border." In *Impact of China's Rise on the Mekong Region*, edited by Yos Santasombat, 117–46. New York: Palgrave Macmillan, 2015.

Skinner, George William. *Chinese Society in Thailand an Analytical History*. Ithaca, New York: Cornell University Press, 1957.

Slater, Dan. "The Elements of Surprise: Assessing Burma's Double-Edged Détente." *South East Asia Research* 22, no. 2 (June 1, 2014): 171–82.

Sng, Jeffery, and Pimpraphai Bisalputra. *A History of the Thai-Chinese*. Singapore: Editions Didier Millet, 2015.

Soest, Christian von. "Democracy Prevention: The International Collaboration of Authoritarian Regimes." *European Journal of Political Research* 54, no. 4 (2015): 623–38.

Steinberg, David I. *Burma: The State of Myanmar*. Washington, D.C: Georgetown University Press, 2001.

Sternberg, Troy. "Chinese Drought, Bread and the Arab Spring." *Applied Geography* 34 (May 1, 2012): 519–24.

Storey, Ian. "China's Bilateral Defense Diplomacy in Southeast Asia." *Asian Security* 8, no. 3 (September 1, 2012): 287–310.

Strangio, Sebastian. *In the Dragon's Shadow: Southeast Asia in the Chinese Century*. New Haven, Connecticut: Yale University Press, 2020.

Su, Xiaobo. "Nontraditional Security and China's Transnational Narcotics Control in Northern Laos and Myanmar." *Political Geography* 48 (September 2015): 72–82.

Su, Xiaobo. "Smuggling and the Exercise of Effective Sovereignty at the China-Myanmar Border." *Review of International Political Economy* 29, no. 4 (2022): 1135–58.

Sun, Yun. "China and the Changing Myanmar." *Journal of Current Southeast Asian Affairs* 31, no. 4 (2012): 51.

Surya, Riza Afita. "VOC and Chinese in Java: Identifying the Migration Motives in the Seventeenth Century." *European Journal of Humanities and Social Sciences* 2, no. 6 (December 11, 2022): 109–17.

Suryadinata, Leo, ed. *Ethnic Chinese in Contemporary Indonesia*. Singapore: ISEAS-Yusof Ishak Institute, 2008.

Suryadinata, Leo. "Government Policies towards the Ethnic Chinese: A Comparison between Indonesia and Malaysia." *Southeast Asian Journal of Social Science* 13, no. 2 (1985): 15–28.

Suryadinata, Leo. *The Making of Southeast Asian Nations: State, Ethnicity, Indigenism and Citizenship*. Singapore: World Scientific, 2015.

Suryadinata, Leo. *Understanding the Ethnic Chinese in Southeast Asia*. Singapore: Institute of Southeast Asian Studies, 2007.

Sutherland, Dylan, and Lutao Ning. "Exploring 'Onward-Journey' ODI Strategies in China's Private Sector Businesses." *Journal of Chinese Economic and Business Studies* 9, no. 1 (February 1, 2011): 43–65.

Tagliacozzo, Eric, and Wen-chin Chang, eds. *Chinese Circulations: Capital, Commodities, and Networks in Southeast Asia*. Durham, North Carolina: Duke University Press Books, 2011.

Takenaka, Ayumi. "The Paradox of Diaspora Engagement: A Historical Analysis of Japanese State-Diaspora Relations." *Journal of Ethnic and Migration Studies* 46, no. 6 (April 25, 2020): 1129–45.

Tan, Danielle. "Chinese Enclaves in the Golden Triangle Borderlands: An Alternative Account of State Formation in Laos." In *Chinese Encounters in Southeast Asia: How People, Money, and Ideas from China Are Changing a Region*, edited by Pál Nyíri and Danielle Tan, 151–71. Seattle: University of Washington Press, 2016.

Tan, Danielle. "'Small Is Beautiful': Lessons from Laos for the Study of Chinese Overseas." *Journal of Current Chinese Affairs* 41, no. 2 (June 1, 2012): 61–94.

Tantrakoonsab, Nattapon, and Wannarat Tantrakoonsab. "Thai Exports of Durian to China: The Expanding Role of Chinese Entrepreneurs." In *Global Production Networks and Rural Development: Southeast Asia as a Fruit Supplier to China*, edited by Bill Pritchard, 82–105. Cheltenham, UK and Northampton, Massachussets: Edward Elgar Publishing Ltd, 2021.

Taylor, Robert. *General Ne Win: A Political Biography*. Singapore: Institute of Southeast Asian Studies, 2015.

Taylor, Robert H. *The State in Myanmar*. London: C Hurst & Co, 2008.

Tejapira, Kasian. "The Misbehaving Jeks: The Evolving Regime of Thainess and Sino-Thai Challenges." *Asian Ethnicity* 10, no. 3 (October 1, 2009): 263–83.

Tejapira, Kasian. "The Sino-Thais' Right Turn towards China." *Critical Asian Studies* 49, no. 4 (October 2, 2017): 606–18.

Thomas, Nicholas. "Going out: China's Food Security from Southeast Asia." *The Pacific Review* 26, no. 5 (December 1, 2013): 531–62.

Thunø, Mette, and Frank N. Pieke. "Institutionalizing Recent Rural Emigration from China to Europe: New Transnational Villages in Fujian." *International Migration Review* 39, no. 2 (June 1, 2005): 485–514.

Tian, Lihui, and Xin Li. "Global Expansion with Takeovers and Value Creation with Integration in China: A Case Study of Alibaba and Lazada." *Asia Pacific Business Review* 29, no. 2 (2023): 372–91.

Ting, Tin-yuet. "From 'Be Water' to 'Be Fire': Nascent Smart Mob and Networked Protests in Hong Kong." *Social Movement Studies* 19, no. 3 (May 3, 2020): 362–68.

To, James Jiann Hua. *Qiaowu: Extra-Territorial Policies for the Overseas Chinese.* Leiden: Brill Academic Publishers, 2014.

Tower, Jason, and Priscilla A. Clapp. *Myanmar's Casino Cities: The Role of China and Transnational Criminal Networks.* Washington, D.C.: United States Institute of Peace, 2020.

Transnational Institute. "Alternative Development or Business as Usual? China's Opium Substitution Policy in Burma and Laos." Drug Policy Briefing No. 33. Amsterdam: Transnational Institute (TNI), 2010.

Trisanawadee, Siripetch. "Chinese Cultural Diplomacy towards ASEAN Countries: Case Study of Confucius Institutes in Thailand." *Manutsayasat Wichakan Journal, Kasetsart University* 27, no. 2 (December 24, 2020): 416–50.

Turner, Alicia. *Saving Buddhism: The Impermanence of Religion in Colonial Burma.* Honolulu: University of Hawai'i Press, 2017.

Uhm, Daan P. van, and Rebecca W. Y. Wong. "Chinese Organized Crime and the Illegal Wildlife Trade: Diversification and Outsourcing in the Golden Triangle." *Trends in Organized Crime* 24, no. 4 (December 1, 2021): 486–505.

Van Oudenaren, John S. "Enduring Menace: The Triad Societies of Southeast China." *Asian Affairs* 41, no. 3 (2014): 127–53.

Vella, Walter F. *Chaiyo!: King Vajiravadh and the Development of Thai Nationalism.* Manoa: University of Hawai'i Press, 1986.

Waldron, Scott, Zhizhi Si, Theingi Myint, and Dominic Smith. "China's Cross-Border Economic Integration: Formalising Cattle Imports from Myanmar." *China: An International Journal* 20, no. 2 (2022): 101–33.

Walton, Matthew J. "The 'Wages of Burman-Ness:' Ethnicity and Burman Privilege in Contemporary Myanmar." *Journal of Contemporary Asia* 43, no. 1 (February 1, 2013): 1–27.

Wang, Gungwu. *China and the Chinese Overseas.* Singapore: Times Academic Press, 1991.

Wang, Gungwu. *The Chinese Overseas: From Earthbound China to the Quest for Autonomy.* Cambridge: Harvard University Press, 2002.

Wang, Peng. "Politics of Crime Control: How Campaign-Style Law Enforcement Sustains Authoritarian Rule in China." *The British Journal of Criminology* 60, no. 2 (March 14, 2020): 422–43.

Wang, Peng, and Georgios A Antonopoulos. "Organized Crime and Illegal Gambling: How Do Illegal Gambling Enterprises Respond to the Challenges Posed by Their Illegality in China?" *Australian & New Zealand Journal of Criminology* 49, no. 2 (June 1, 2016): 258–80.

Wei, Yehua Dennis. "Regional Inequality in China." *Progress in Human Geography* 23, no. 1 (March 1, 1999): 49–59.

Weiss, Jessica Chen. "A World Safe for Autocracy? China's Rise and the Future of Global Politics." *Foreign Affairs* 98, no. 4 (2019): 92–102.

Weng-Jeng Chen, *Tangle [Taibei Zhongguo Jie]*. YouTube video, 2010. https://www.yout ube.com/watch?v=zFe31GVP6fA.

Womack, Brantly. *China and Vietnam: The Politics of Asymmetry*. Cambridge and New York: Cambridge University Press, 2006.

Wong, Audrye. "The Diaspora and China's Foreign Influence Activities." Washington, D.C.: Wilson Center, 2021–2022.

Wong, Mathew Y. H. "Chinese Influence, U.S. Linkages, or Neither? Comparing Regime Changes in Myanmar and Thailand." *Democratization* 26, no. 3 (April 3, 2019): 359–81.

Wongsurawat, Wasana. "Successfully Misunderstood: The Untold Realities of the Thai-Chinese Assimilation 'Success Story.'" In *Multicultural Challenges and Redefining Identity in East Asia*, edited by Nam-Hook Kim, 123–42. London: Routledge, 2016.

Wongsurawat, Wasana. *The Crown and the Capitalists: The Ethnic Chinese and the Founding of the Thai Nation*. Seattle: University of Washington Press, 2019.

Wongsurawat, Wasana. "The Social Capital of Being Chinese in Thai Politics." In *The Sociology of Chinese Capitalism in Southeast Asia: Challenges and Prospects*, edited by Yos Santasombat, 75–92. Singapore: Springer, 2019.

Woods, Kevin. "Ceasefire Capitalism: Military–Private Partnerships, Resource Concessions and Military–State Building in the Burma–China Borderlands." *The Journal of Peasant Studies* 38, no. 4 (October 1, 2011): 747–70.

Woods, Kevin. "CP Maize Contract Farming in Shan State, Myanmar: A Regional Case of a Place-Based Corporate Agro-Feed System." BICAS Working Paper 14, May 18, 2015.

Wu, Chien-Heui. *The U.S.-China Trade War and Options for Taiwan*. Washington, D.C: Wilson Center Asia Program, 2019.

Wu, Helena, and Andrea Riemenschnitter. "Introduction." *Interventions* 20, no. 8 (November 17, 2018): 1073–84.

Xia, Ming. "Organizational Formations of Organized Crime in China: Perspectives from the State, Markets, and Networks." *Journal of Contemporary China* 17, no. 54 (February 1, 2008): 1–23.

Xiang, Biao. "Promoting Knowledge Exchange through Diaspora Networks (The Case of the People's Republic of China)." In *Converting Migration Drains into Gains: Harnessing the Resources of Overseas Professionals*, edited by C. Wescott and J. Brinkerhoff, 33–72. Manila, Philippines: Asian Development Bank, 2006.

Xu, Yi-Chong. "Chinese State-Owned Enterprises in Africa: Ambassadors or Freebooters?" *Journal of Contemporary China* 23, no. 89 (September 3, 2014): 822–40.

Yalun, An. "International Promotion of Chinese Language in the New Era." *International Education Studies* 12, no. 7 (June 29, 2019): 67.

Yamada, Teri Shaffer. "Phnom Penh's NagaWorld Resort and Casino." *Pacific Affairs* 90, no. 4 (December 1, 2017): 743–65.

Yang, Chun. "Cross-border Expansion of Digital Platforms and Transformation of the Trade and Distribution Networks of Imported Fresh Fruits from Southeast Asia to China." *Global Networks* 22, no. 4 (October 2022): 716–34.

Yeremia, Ardhitya Eduard. "Indonesian Diplomats' and Foreign Policy Scholars' Perceptions and Their Implications on Indonesian Foreign Ministry Bureaucratic Responses to a Rising China." *The Pacific Review* 35, no. 3 (2022): 529–56.

Yeung, Yue-man, Joanna Lee, and Gordon Kee. "China's Special Economic Zones at 30." *Eurasian Geography and Economics* 50, no. 2 (March 1, 2009): 222–40.

Yin, Hongzhi, Athapol Ruangkanjanases, and Chenin Chen. "Factors Affecting Chinese Students' Decision Making toward Thai Universities." *International Journal of Information and Education Technology* 5, no. 3 (2015): 189–95.

Yu, Truston Jianheng, and Enze Han. "Indonesia's Relations with China in the Age of COVID-19." *Journal of Current Southeast Asian Affairs*, February 1, 2023.

Zhan, Shaohua. "The Political Economy of Food Import and Self-Reliance in China: 1949–2019." *Global Food History* 8, no. 3 (2022): 194–212.

Zhang, Ketian. "Cautious Bully: Reputation, Resolve, and Beijing's Use of Coercion in the South China Sea." *International Security* 44, no. 1 (July 1, 2019): 117–59.

Zhang, Yongjin, and Barry Buzan. "The Tributary System as International Society in Theory and Practice." *The Chinese Journal of International Politics* 5, no. 1 (March 1, 2012): 3–36.

Zhao, Suisheng. "Rethinking the Chinese World Order: The Imperial Cycle and the Rise of China." *Journal of Contemporary China* 24, no. 96 (November 2, 2015): 961–82.

Zhou, Min, ed. *Contemporary Chinese Diasporas*. New York: Palgrave Macmillan, 2017.

Zhou, Min, and Xiangyi Li. "Remittances for Collective Consumption and Social Status Compensation: Variations on Transnational Practices among Chinese International Migrants1." *International Migration Review* 52, no. 1 (March 1, 2018): 4–42.

Zhou, Taomo. "China and the Thirtieth of September Movement." *Indonesia*, no. 98 (2014): 29–58.

Zhou, Taomo. *Migration in the Time of Revolution: China, Indonesia, and the Cold War*. Ithaca, New York: Cornell University Press, 2019.

Zwart, Frank de. "Unintended but Not Unanticipated Consequences." *Theory and Society* 44, no. 3 (2015): 283–97.

Index

For the benefit of digital users, indexed terms that span two pages (e.g., 52–53) may, on occasion, appear on only one of those pages.

Tables and figures are indicated by *t* and *f* following the page number

Printed in the USA/Agawam, MA
August 2, 2024

870361.010